A-10s over Kosovo

The Victory of Airpower over a Fielded Army as Told by the Airmen Who Fought in Operation Allied Force

Edited by

CHRISTOPHER E. HAAVE, Colonel, USAF
and
PHIL M. HAUN, Lieutenant Colonel, USAF

Air University Press
Maxwell Air Force Base, Alabama

December 2003

Air University Library Cataloging Data

A-10s over Kosovo : the victory of airpower over a fielded army as told by the airmen who fought in Operation Allied Force / edited by Christopher E. Haave and Phil M. Haun.

  p. : ill., ports. ; cm.

  Includes bibliographical references and index.

  ISBN 1-58566-122-8

  1. Operation Allied Force, 1999—Aerial operations, American. 2. Operation Allied Force, 1999—Personal narratives, American. 3. A-10 (Jet attack plane) 4. United States. Air Force—History. 5. Air power. 6. North Atlantic Treaty Organization—Yugoslavia—Kosovo (Serbia) 7. Air warfare. I. Title. II. Haave, Christopher E. III. Haun, Phil M.

  949.7103—dc21

First Printing December 2003
Second Printing September 2004
Third Printing March 2006
Fourth Printing September 2006

Disclaimer

Opinions, conclusions, and recommendations expressed or implied within are solely those of the editors and do not necessarily represent the views of Air University, the United States Air Force, the Department of Defense, or any other US government agency. Cleared for public release: distribution unlimited.

Air University Press
131 West Shumacher Avenue
Maxwell AFB AL 36112-6615
http://aupress.maxwell.af.mil

We owe much of our combat success to many outstanding folks who were not present at either Aviano AB or Gioia del Colle AB. Those folks include families and friends who supported us from afar, leaders and commanders who placed faith in our abilities, fellow warriors who shared the danger in the air, dedicated professionals at home bases who provided the logistical lifeblood, and all the past and present members of the A-10 and Air Force communities who trained us right. All these loved ones and colleagues deserve the lion's share of credit for the A-10 achievements during Allied Force.

Contents

Illustrations

TO: Liaisons
RE: Gifts and Bindery Decisions

TITLE *A-10s Over Kosovo: The Victory of Airpower Over A Fielded Army as Told by the Airmen Who Fought in Operation Allied Force*

DISCARD/WITHDRAW?_____

If we already hold a copy of this title, how many copies do you want to keep?_____

Any particular location you want item placed, i.e. ref., stacks, etc.? *circ. collection*

Other_____
Reviewer_____

Tables

Foreword

In the spring of 1999, NATO engaged in a precedent-setting air campaign over Serbia and Kosovo known as Operation Allied Force (OAF). This event marked a milestone for airpower, as it was, arguably, the first time airpower alone was decisive in achieving victory in combat. By the end of the conflict, in June 1999, America and its allies had mounted a monumental effort to achieve the immediate goals of halting ethnic cleansing in Kosovo and providing for the return of hundreds of thousands of refugees. Ground forces, introduced following the end of the air campaign, have subsequently been employed to secure the peace.

Several books have already been written about OAF, though not as many as might have been expected given the implications for NATO and airpower that came out of that conflict. Those that have been written focus primarily on the strategic level, the events, diplomacy, and decisions by senior military and political leaders that led to the conflict and determined its conduct. This is not that kind of book. This is about the other end of the spectrum as told by those that flew and fought at the most basic level during the war—the A-10 pilots of the 40th Expeditionary Operations Group (EOG).

I was privileged to command the 52d Air Expeditionary Wing during OAF. The 40th EOG was one of four such groups in my wing. Its members' job was to find and destroy fielded Serb forces in Kosovo and to provide combat search and rescue for downed allied aircrews. This is their story. They take you into the cockpit where you learn how the strategic policy was ultimately put into action.

After the war, one senior Air Force officer said, "About 80 percent of the airpower effort was magnificent, but the other 20 percent was pretty ugly." Through the eyes of the 40th EOG, you'll see the good, the bad, and the ugly. You will appreciate the enormous pressures placed on our fighter pilots as they strove to find and verify valid military targets, protect the civilian population against collateral damage, destroy fielded Serbian forces, and rescue downed airmen. You'll appreciate how well and how professionally they carried out their mission, and you will experience the frustration that comes from waging war within the inevitable restrictions placed by our leaders.

OAF was an unusual war in many ways. Indeed, due to allied political sensitivities, we didn't even call it a "war" for quite some time. Gen Wesley K. Clark, supreme allied commander in Europe termed it *diplomacy by force* until he retired. While victory was ultimately achieved, it was never declared. Nevertheless, for those who flew in it, OAF was war, and especially for the A-10 pilots it was tough, dangerous, and personal. I'm honored to have led these outstanding warriors, and I support their effort to preserve their experiences in writing. There are important lessons here for all of us. This is their story, in their own words— exciting, unvarnished, and on target.

SCOTT P. VAN CLEEF
Brigadier General, USAF
Commander
52d Air Expeditionary Wing

Prologue

Lt Col Chris "Kimos" Haave

In May 1999, our 81st Expeditionary Fighter Squadron (EFS) was flying out of Gioia del Colle Air Base (AB), Italy, conducting around-the-clock combat operations in support of Operation Allied Force (OAF). In the midst of this, several pilots began talking about writing a book. Those of us who were airpower and military-history buffs noticed that the combat we were experiencing was far different from much of what we had studied. After Slobodan Milosevic capitulated and OAF ended in June, we took stock of what we had done and promised each other to write down our combat experiences and observations. *A-10s over Kosovo* is the fruit of that commitment.

Our initial vision for this book was to let each pilot tell an anecdote or two. Taken collectively, those stories would provide others with an idea of what an A-10 group had, or had not, accomplished. However, as we wrote and exchanged ideas, we decided that the book should focus primarily on the missions. Therefore, in the end, our book includes many personal accounts of our relocation and beddown, aircraft maintenance, and combat experiences; we tried to describe the tactical execution of those missions and the many activities that directly, or indirectly, supported them.

We have limited our focus to the contributions of the 40th Expeditionary Operations Group (EOG) comprised of personnel from the 81st EFS at Spangdahlem AB, Germany, and the 74th EFS from Pope Air Force Base, North Carolina. While we fondly mention some of the combat contributions of our fellow A-10 warriors in the 104th EOG who operated out of Trapani AB, Sicily, we do not tell their complete story.

The scope of *A-10s over Kosovo* is limited to the 40th EOG's participation in OAF. For simplicity's sake we use the Kosovo engagement zone (KEZ) to describe that area of Kosovo and southeastern Serbia where A-10 aircrews flew their portion of the air campaign against fielded Serbian forces. Additionally, "Sandys" (A-10 pilots qualified to lead combat search and rescue [CSAR] missions) were responsible to cover the entire OAF theater of operations. Covering that around-the-clock CSAR alert during the entire 78-day campaign required A-10 crews to spend as many hours on ground alert as actually flying.

This book's objectives are to include firsthand accounts by those who participated and share the observations and conclusions seen from their tactical points of view. We humbly acknowledge that we did not thoroughly research the operational and strategic levels of the air campaign, nor did we investigate the many decisions up and down the chain of command that affected the missions and the rules of engagement (ROE). Also beyond our scope was a rigorous analysis of the international political-military discussions and decisions above the level we could directly observe. For these reasons, we have limited our focus to the expeditionary squadron and group levels. While the reader might occasionally sense some frustration in an author's personal account, we have collectively attempted to refrain from drawing conclusions about why we were ordered to conduct our operations in a particular manner. We do not feel qualified to comment on the appropriateness of particular courses of action (COA) and ROEs. However, since our firsthand tactical experience allowed us to observe the effect that those COAs and ROEs had on our missions, we are comfortable in sharing those observations with our readers and pointing out those areas we consider worthy of further investigation and improvement.

We have presented each contributor's account, editing only for clarity, accuracy, and to avoid repeating each other's stories. We found that letting each participant speak freely was the most legitimate way to tell the A-10 story. We have organized these stories to illustrate each chapter's theme and have tried to retain their you-are-there quality.

One of our purposes is to attract readers at all levels in the Air Force. Thus we discussed an Air Force *tenet of airpower* that—on various days—was followed, could have been better employed, or was ignored. We also hope that our honest attempt to provide an accurate, albeit tactical, perspective on the effects that higher-headquarters direction had on our tactical level of combat will be of interest to that wider audience. We refrained from second-guessing those whose decision-making processes and environments we did not observe. Finally, we did attempt to present our narratives in a storytelling style that students of airpower history (and perhaps the occupants of a fighter-pilot bar) might find interesting.

Even before the end of the air campaign, we felt that documenting our experiences would be valuable. A-10 pilots contributed to several significant and unique Air Force accomplishments during OAF: (1) this operation marked the first time that an airborne forward air controller (AFAC) aircraft led a large-force mission package into combat; (2) it also included the first major air campaign in which no friendly aircrews were killed or taken prisoner—A-10 aircrews led the packages that rescued the only two pilots shot down; (3) although the official battle damage assessment (BDA) is incomplete, A-10s most likely destroyed more field-deployed Serb weaponry than any other allied weapon system; and (4) the two-ship AFAC's first combat test in a 360-degree threat environment was a great success—none of the fighters controlled by A-10 AFACs were lost, only two A-10s received any battle damage, and there were no known collateral civilian casualties.

This book also presents many unique aspects of A-10 operations in the KEZ. A-10 AFACs directed strikes by nearly every type of NATO aircraft. US fighter aircraft were occasionally under the operational control of a foreign officer (an allied officer sometimes filled the position of director of the combined air operations center [CAOC]). Fighter aircraft were also able to loiter with near impunity over a robust radar and infrared-guided air defense network during day and night operations. A drone, for the first time, worked concurrently with an AFAC to successfully locate, attack, and destroy targets. Allied ground units provided counterbattery radar plots through the airborne battlefield command and control center (ABCCC) aircraft to assist A-10s in locating and destroying enemy artillery—coining the phrase "close ground support."

Chapter 1 establishes the overall context of the A-10 involvement in OAF and includes a description of participating units, their aircraft, and their weapons capabilities. It discusses mission types and typical missions, daily operations cycles, and theater geography and force-beddown locations. The appendix adds further political and military context.

Our personal experiences led us to select certain themes around which to organize our book. Those themes, starting with chapter 2, are as follows: mission leadership; beddown, maintenance, and combat support; enemy action; target identification and ROE; the Flat Face–Giraffe hunt; tactical innovation; and "my turn in the barrel." Each chapter begins with a short discussion of the particular theme around which it is structured; the authors then tell their associated stories. In reality, a few of those stories may touch on more than one theme, and some stories may contain ideas that do not specifically fit any theme. However, we believe that all the widely ranging stories, from a new wingman's account of his first combat sortie to a commander's description of relocating his unit while executing combat operations, add value and integrity to the book.

We in the 40th EOG Hog community owe much of our combat success to many outstanding folks who were not present at either Aviano AB or Gioia del Colle AB. They include families and friends who supported us from afar, leaders and commanders who placed faith in our abilities, fellow warriors who shared the danger in the air, dedicated professionals at home bases who provided the logistical lifeblood, and all the past and present members of the A-10 and Air Force communities who trained us right. All these loved ones and colleagues deserve the lion's share of credit for the A-10 achievements during Allied Force.

These stories, then, are our accounts of personal experiences and do not pretend to provide definitive answers to weighty questions of strategy or doctrine. However, we do hope you enjoy reading them as much as we did writing them.

Contributors

Capt Nathan S. Brauner

Capt Nate "Foghorn" Brauner is from Northridge, California, and graduated from the United States Air Force Academy (USAFA) in 1991. He has accumulated more than 1,500 flying hours in the A-10 and has served as an A-10 replacement training unit (RTU) instructor pilot at Davis-Monthan Air Force Base (AFB), Arizona. He has also served at Laughlin AFB, Texas; Wright-Patterson AFB, Ohio; Pope AFB, North Carolina; and Spangdahlem Air Base (AB), Germany.

Capt Joseph S. Brosious

Capt Joe "Joe Bro" Brosious is a graduate of the University of Colorado, and has served tours at Osan AB, South Korea, and Spangdahlem. Following Operation Allied Force (OAF) he served as an A-10 RTU instructor pilot at Davis-Monthan.

Maj Dawn M. Brotherton

Maj Dawn Brotherton is from Champion, Ohio, and graduated from Ohio State University in 1988. She holds a master's degree from Central Missouri State University and is a personnel officer by trade. Major Brotherton has had assignments at Whiteman AFB, Missouri; Osan; Nellis AFB, Nevada; Spangdahlem; and Randolph AFB, Texas. Following OAF, Dawn served as the chief of personnel-officer assignments at Randolph. Dawn is married to Pete, and they have a beautiful daughter Rachel.

Maj Peter R. Brotherton

Maj Pete "Bro" Brotherton is from Wilton, Connecticut, and graduated from Embry-Riddle University in 1985. He has accumulated more than 3,000 flying hours in the A-10, F-4G, and AT-38 with assignments at England AFB, Louisiana; Holloman AFB, New Mexico; Osan; Nellis; and Spangdahlem. Following OAF Bro served in the Air Force Reserve in San Antonio, Texas.

Maj David W. Brown

Maj Dave Brown is from Terre Haute, Indiana, and graduated from Indiana State University in 1986. He has flown the AT-38, F-15, A-10, and F-16 block 40 aircraft with assignments at Holloman; Elmendorf AFB, Alaska; Hickam AFB, Hawaii; Spangdahlem; and Eielson AFB, Alaska. After OAF he commanded the 354th Maintenance Squadron at Eielson. Dave and his wife, Patricia, have three children—David Jr., Christopher, and Megan. Dave enjoys outdoor activities, including camping, fishing, and hunting.

Capt Kevin Bullard

Capt Kevin "Boo" Bullard is from Charleston, South Carolina, and holds a Bachelor of Science degree in civil engineering from the USAFA class of 1989. He has accumulated more than 2,700 total flying hours and is currently serving in the USAF Reserves as a full-time instructor pilot at Columbus AFB, Mississippi. Since departing active-duty service, he has had the opportunity to hunt, fish, and spend time with his wife and two daughters.

1st Lt Scott R. Cerone

1st Lt Scott "Hummer" Cerone is a 1995 graduate of the USAFA where he was a four-year varsity-letter winner in lacrosse. He has 1,200 hours in the A/OA-10 and during OAF was assigned to the 74th Fighter Squadron "Flying Tigers" at Pope. Following OAF, Scott was stationed at Osan and currently is assigned to Davis-Monthan as an A/OA-10 FTU instructor pilot.

1st Lt Michael A. Curley

1st Lt Mike "Scud" Curley is from Pittsfield, Massachusetts, and holds a Bachelor of Science degree in behavioral science from the USAFA, class of 1995. He accumulated more than 700 flying hours in the A-10 at Spangdahlem and Osan.

1st Lt Allen E. Duckworth

1st Lt Allen "JAKS" Duckworth is from Columbus, Indiana, and is a 1996 graduate of the USAFA. He has accumulated more than 570 flying hours in the A-10 at Spangdahlem and Davis-Monthan.

Capt Andrew J. Gebara

Capt Andrew J. "Buffy" Gebara is a 12-year Air Force veteran from Highland, California. He is a 1991 graduate of the United States Naval Academy and holds a master's degree from Syracuse University's Maxwell School of Citizenship and Public Affairs. In addition to his time over Kosovo, Captain Gebara has been assigned to Spangdahlem and Barksdale AFB, Louisiana. He is a senior pilot with more than 2,600 hours of flying time in the A-10, AT-38, B-2, and B-52 aircraft. Buffy is currently serving as an instructor pilot in the B-2 "stealth bomber" at Whiteman.

Maj David E. Gross

Maj Dave "Devo" Gross holds a Bachelor of Science degree from the University of Florida and a master's degree in public administration from Webster University. He has flown more than 2,500 hours in the A-10, T-3A, F-4G Wild Weasel, and F-16 aircraft during his assignments at Plattsburgh AFB, New York; Columbus; England; Randolph; Nellis; and Spangdahlem. Currently he is an F-16 pilot in the Tulsa Oklahoma Air National Guard (ANG) and flies for American Airlines. Dave and his wife, Nadine, have a son, Matthew, and are expecting the birth of another son.

Col Christopher E. Haave

Col Chris "Kimos" Haave was born on 20 July 1960 and graduated from the USAFA in 1982. After pilot training at Laughlin, he flew the A-10 at RAF Woodbridge, United Kingdom, and the AT-38B at Holloman. He studied as an Olmsted Scholar in Lyon, France, and Boston, Massachusetts; attended the French Joint Defense College; and held staff positions at the Pentagon, the US Mission to NATO in Brussels, and the Supreme Headquarters Allied Powers Europe. He commanded the 81st Fighter Squadron "Panthers" at Spangdahlem from July 1998 to April 2000, and is currently the commander of the 612th Air Operations Group at Davis-Monthan.

1st Lt Johnny L. Hamilton

1st Lt Johnny "CBU" Hamilton is from Converse, Texas, and a 1996 graduate of Angelo State University with a Bachelor of Science degree in psychology. He has accumulated almost 800 flying hours in the A-10 at Spangdahlem and Osan. CBU is currently serving a two-year sentence as an air liaison officer at Fort Hood, Texas.

Lt Col Phil M. Haun

Lt Col Phil "Goldie" Haun was born on 7 February 1964 and is from Cecilia, Kentucky. He holds a Bachelor of Science degree in environmental engineering from Harvard University and a Master of Arts in economics from Vanderbilt University. Goldie is a weapons-school graduate with more than 2,000 flying hours in the A-10 with assignments at RAF Bentwaters, England; Osan; Spangdahlem; and Eielson. He attended Air Command and Staff College and the School of Advanced Air and Space Studies (SAASS) at Maxwell AFB, Alabama, following OAF. He is currently serving as the operations officer of the 355th Fighter Squadron (FS) at Eielson. Goldie and his wife, Bonnie, have two children—Clayton and Sadie.

Lt Col Mark E. Koechle

Lt Col Mark "Coke" Koechle is from Kokomo, Indiana, and is a 1983 graduate of Purdue University with Bachelor of Science degree in aeronautical engineering. He has accumulated more than 3,300 flying hours in the A-10 with assignments at RAF Bentwaters; Nellis; Fort Leavenworth, Kansas; Ramstein AB, Germany; and Spangdahlem. He commanded the 81st Fighter Squadron Panthers prior to his recent departure to attend the National War College, Washington, D.C. Coke is one of the few A-10 pilots to have flown in both OAF and Operation Desert Storm.

1st Lt Stuart C. Martin

1st Lt Stu "Co" Martin is a 1995 graduate of the USAFA where he received a Bachelor of Science degree in behavioral science. He accumulated more than 800 hours in the A-10 during his first operational assignment at Spangdahlem. He is continuing to fly the A-10 at Pope while assigned to the 74th FS.

Capt Francis M. McDonough

Capt Marty "JD" McDonough is from Orono, Maine, and graduated from the USAFA in 1989. He has accumulated more than 2,500 flying hours in the A-10 and T-38 aircraft with assignments at Columbus, Osan, Pope, and Spangdahlem. Marty is currently the USAFE chief of A/OA-10 standardization and evaluation at headquarters in Ramstein.

Capt James P. Meger

Capt James "Meegs" Meger from Lancaster, New York, graduated from the USAFA in 1992 with a Bachelor of Science degree in engineering. Meegs has flown more than 500 hours in the AT-38B and more than 1,500 hours in the A-10 during assignments to Osan and Spangdahlem. He is currently assigned to Langley AFB, Virginia, flying the F-15.

Capt Michael J. Shenk

Capt Mike "Hook" Shenk is from Downers Grove, Illinois, and graduated from Southern Illinois University at Carbondale in 1988. He has accumulated more than 2,600 flying hours in the T-38 and A-10 with assignments at Columbus, Spangdahlem, and Willow Grove Joint Reserve Base, Horsham Township, Pennsylvania. Hook is currently the assistant weapons officer for the 103d FS at Willow Grove and a flight officer for United Airlines.

Capt Ronald F. Stuewe

Capt Ron "Stu" Stuewe is from Papillion, Nebraska, and is a 1993 graduate from the USAFA. He has accumulated more than 1,500 flying hours in the A-10 with assignments at Shaw AFB, South Carolina; Pope; and Osan. Stu attended weapon school following OAF and is currently an instructor at the USAF Weapons School at Nellis.

Col Alan E. Thompson

Col Al "Moose" Thompson holds a business degree from the University of Connecticut. He served tours in both the Air and Joint Staff. He served as the 52d FW vice commander and commanded the 40th Expeditionary Operations Group at Gioia del Colle AB, Italy, during OAF. He also has commanded an operational support squadron and the Air Force Warrior Preparation Center at Einsiedlerhof Air Station, Germany. Colonel Thompson is a command pilot and has accumulated more than 3,500 flying hours in single-seat fighter and attack aircraft during his 14 assignments. Those assignments include Columbus; RAF Bentwaters; Davis-Monthan; Kunsan; Spangdahlem; and Misawa AB, Japan. After serving as a professor of air and space studies, and commanding the Air Force Reserve Officer Training Corps (AFROTC) detachment at the University of Pittsburgh, Colonel Thompson was selected to command the AFROTC program nationwide.

Capt Ripley E. Woodard

Capt "Rip" Woodard is from Houston/ Klein, Texas, and is a 1989 graduate of Texas A&M University. He has accumulated more than 2,700 flying hours in the A-10, AT-38, and T-37 aircraft during assignments at Reese AFB, Texas; Spangdahlem; Randolph; and Williams AFB, Texas. Rip is currently an AT-38 instructor pilot in the Introduction to Fighter Fundamentals course at Randolph.

Chronology

1999

7 January   The 81st Fighter Squadron (FS) deploys with six A-10s to Aviano AB, Italy, in support of Joint Forge.*

15 January   The Organization for Security and Cooperation in Europe (OSCE) Kosovo Verification Mission (KVM) reports a serious deterioration of the situation in the area. KVM patrols witness Serb army (VJ) tanks and armored vehicles firing directly into houses near Malopoljce and Petrova, and notes houses burning in Racak.

16 January   Returning to Racak, the KVM confirms that Serb security forces had killed 45 Albanian civilians and stated that it had evidence of arbitrary detentions, extrajudicial killings, and the mutilation of unarmed civilians by the security forces of the Former Republic of Yugoslavia (FRY).

28 January   Secretary General Javier Solana of NATO issues a statement indicating that NATO fully supports the enhanced status for Kosovo, preservation of the territorial integrity of the FRY, and protection of the rights of all ethnic groups. The statement calls for FRY authorities to immediately bring the force levels, posture, and actions of the Yugoslav army and the Special Police into strict compliance with their commitments to NATO on 25 October 1998 and to end the excessive and disproportionate use of force in accordance with these commitments.

30 January	NATO's primacy focus remains on the peace negotiations in Rambouillet, France; all the while, intelligence reports clearly show a significant buildup of FRY forces in Kosovo. The North Atlantic Council (NAC) gives Secretary General Solana the authority to authorize air strikes against targets on FRY territory.
7 February	The 81st FS is extended for 30 days and directed to stand up combat search and rescue (CSAR).*
1 March	The 81st FS is extended indefinitely and is authorized 15 A-10s.*
19 March	After the Kosovar Albanians sign the proposed agreement, negotiations are suspended, and the Serb delegates leave Paris without signing it. They denounce the Western ultimatum as a violation of international law and the UN charter. The KVM withdraws from Kosovo. Almost one-third of the FRY's total armed forces, massed in and around Kosovo, commences the systematic expulsion of Kosovo's ethnic Albanians, code-named Operation Horseshoe. Many were driven out of their homes and villages. Some victims are summarily executed, hundreds of thousands are displaced, and many lose their homes when Serbs set fire to them.
21 March	US Ambassador Richard C. Holbrooke is dispatched to Belgrade to deliver a "final warning" to Slobodan Milosevic.
23 March	Ambassador Holbrooke departs Belgrade, having received no concessions of any kind from Milosevic. Subsequently, Secretary General Solana directs Gen Wesley K. Clark, supreme allied commander Europe (SACEUR) to initiate air operations in the FRY.

24 March	Operation Allied Force (OAF) commences with combat operations against Serbian forces.*
25 March	The Yugoslav government breaks off diplomatic relations with the United States, France, Germany, and the United Kingdom.
27 March	After an F-117 is lost near Belgrade, a successful 81st-led CSAR effort recovers the pilot.*
30 March	Combined Air Interdiction of Fielded Forces (CAIFF) begins operations but is limited to 10 miles penetration of Kosovo.*
1 April	Serbian forces capture three US soldiers in the FRY of Macedonia.
3 April	NATO missiles strike central Belgrade for the first time and destroy the Yugoslav and Serbian interior ministries.
5 April	Maj Devo Gross flies his first combat sortie with Capt Lester Less.*
6 April	The first successful A-10 attack occurs during OAF. Weather finally permits an AFAC to locate and destroy a Serb truck park.* Lt Col Kimos Haave controls an 18-ship package against military vehicles and petroleum, oils, and lubricants (POL) targets.*
7 April	CAIFF operations changes its name to Serb army (VJ)–Serb Interior Ministry police (MUP) Engagement Zone (VMEZ); included all of Kosovo.* Maj Dirt Fluhr transmits on the radio: "Hey, they're shooting at us!"*

8 April	Capt JD McDonough destroys fuel trucks.*
9 April	Capt Rip Woodard successfully recovers his A-10 after experiencing a dual-engine flameout in the weather at flight level (FL) 300.*
10 April	The NAC approves the concept of operations and the operations plan for Allied Harbor, the NATO humanitarian effort in Albania.
11 April	The 81st FS moves to Gioia del Colle.* Col Al Thompson stands up the 40th Expeditionary Operations Group (EOG).*
14 April	Bear 31 (an F-16 AFAC) leads an attack on a column of approximately 100 vehicles. Many are destroyed, and 64 noncombatants are killed before Cub 31 (Capt JD McDonough) identifies the convoy as civilian. Bear 31 then terminates the F-16 and French Jaguar attacks.*
15 April	This is the first day that Macedonian airspace can be used to fly attack missions.* The VMEZ changes to the Kosovo engagement zone (KEZ).* Five 74th FS aircraft, nine pilots, and 65 support personnel arrive from Pope AFB and are integrated into 81st EFS.*
21 April	All European Union countries agree to stop oil-product deliveries by or through member states to the FRY. NATO missiles hit the Belgrade headquarters of Milosevic's Serbian Socialist Party and his private residence; the allies believed that both could command and control VJ/MUP forces.

22 April	Alliance nations reaffirm the conditions that will bring an end to the air campaign and announce an intensification of that campaign.
	Maj Devo Gross and Capt Boo Bullard destroy a group of 20–30 military trucks near U-Town and six tanks in a river bed.*
1 May	Four 40th EOG Sandys lead the rescue of Hammer 34, an F-16 pilot shot down in northern Serbia.*
	Maj Corn Mays, Maj Devo Gross, Capt Meegs Meger, and Lt Scud Curley dodge multiple surface-to-air missiles (SAM) and attack a troop concentration.*
	Col Al Thompson, Lt Col Kimos Haave, and others discuss ROE and Apache helicopter options with Lt Gen Mike Short and Lt Gen John Hendrix, USA, at Tirana, Albania.*
	Three captured US soldiers are released into the custody of US civil rights leader Jesse Jackson.
2 May	Maj Goldie Haun kills a self-propelled artillery piece and strafes two tanks, is hit by an SA-14 missile, and recovers to Skopje, Macedonia.*
4 May	Great Flat Face–Giraffe Hunt begins.*
5 May	The ROEs change. The "within 10 nautical miles (NM) of the border" sanctuary is replaced by three zones: 0–2, 2–5, and 5–10 NM of border, with progressively increasing likelihood of target approval.*
7 May	NATO planes accidentally bomb the Chinese Embassy in Belgrade, killing three and wounding 20. NATO describes the bombing as a "tragic mistake" caused by "faulty information." The United States and NATO say that the intended target was a Yugoslav building with military use, but US maps used in the planning of the operation were old and had the embassy located at a previous address.

11 May	An A-10 AFAC is hit beneath the cockpit by a shoulder-fired missile. The warhead does not detonate, and the pilot is able to recover the aircraft to Gioia.*
	A Predator UAV operator provides Lt Col Coke Koechle's flight with real-time target coordinates of a Serb army command post and hidden armored vehicles. The Serb command post and armor targets are destroyed.*
	Lt Col Surgeon Dahl flies the last flight of his tour (fini-flight) with wingman Lt Hummer Cerone on his first combat sortie; several military vehicles are destroyed with secondary explosions.*
14 May	At least 79 people are killed and 58 wounded when NATO missiles hit Korisa, a village in southern Kosovo.
	Capt Hook Shenk flies a mission check-ride; Capt Scrape Johnson evaluates while flying as Hook's wingman. They attack targets and dodge a SAM.*
19 May	Russia says mediation efforts with the West are deadlocked. A NATO bomb kills 10 inmates in a Pristina jail.
	The 104th EOG arrives at Trapani AB, Sicily.
22 May	A UN humanitarian mission visits Kosovo, as NATO admits its mistake in bombing Kosovo Liberation Army positions at Kosare, near the border with Albania. Sources close to the KLA say seven guerillas were killed and 15 injured.
	Milosevic and four other Serbian leaders are indicted by the UN International Criminal Tribunal for the former Yugoslavia (ICTY) for crimes against humanity. The indictment is amended and expanded on 29 June 2001.

23 May	NATO begins a bombing campaign against the Yugoslav electricity grid, creating a major disruption of power that affects many military-related activities and water supplies.
	The 104th EOG begins to fly missions out of Trapani AB, Sicily.
31 May	1st Lt Hummer Cerone and 1st Lt Co Martin pass their flight-lead check rides and pin on captain bars.
8 June	The West and Russia reach a landmark agreement on a draft UN resolution at the annual meeting of the heads of state of the eight major industrial democracies (G8) in Cologne, France. NATO calls on Milosevic to resume military talks on troop withdrawal at once. Talks between senior NATO and FRY officers on a Serb pullout from Kosovo resume in Macedonia and continue into the night.
9 June	This is the last day authorized for NATO forces to expend ordnance.
	Slobodan Milosevic capitulates and agrees to withdraw forces from Kosovo.*
	Maj James "Jimbo" MacCauley and 1st Lt Scud Curley are shot at by mobile SAMs, return the attack, and score a probable SAM kill.*
	Col Al Thompson attacks armored personnel carriers (APC) near Mount Osljak.*
	Military talks continue with senior NATO and FRY officers. Late in the day, the two parties sign the Military Technical Agreement.
10 June	Secretary General Solana calls for a suspension of NATO air strikes after receiving definite evidence that Serb forces are withdrawing from northern Kosovo. The UN Security Council adopts Resolution 1244 on Kosovo. In Cologne, G8 ministers draft a plan to anchor the Balkans to Western Europe and rebuild Kosovo.

11 June	Col Al Thompson passes command of the 40th EOG to Col Gregg Sanders and returns to Spangdahlem.*
20 June	In accordance with the 9 June Military Technical Agreement, Serb forces completely withdraw from Kosovo, leading Secretary General Solana to officially end NATO's bombing campaign in the Former Republic of Yugoslavia.
30 June	A-10s cease CSAR and close air support (CAS) alert as NATO occupation forces enter the KEZ.*

2000

6 October	Milosevic concedes defeat in the presidential election to Vlajislav Kostunica. Milosevic gives up power after widespread protests and Russian urging.

2001

29 June	Prime Minister Zoran Djindjic of Serbia invokes Yugoslavia's obligations under international law to support the transfer of Milosevic to the UN war crimes tribunal at The Hague. Milosevic is charged with committing crimes against humanity in Kosovo and Croatia. In November 2001, the charge of genocide is added, stemming from his alleged activity during the 1992–95 Bosnian war.

2002

12 February	Milosevic's trial begins in The Hague with Milosevic acting as his own defense lawyer. He is the first head of state to face an international war-crimes court.

The A-10, Its Missions, and the Hog Units That Flew in Operation Allied Force

Lt Col Chris "Kimos" Haave

Introduction

The A-10 Thunderbolt II is the last in a long line of fighter and attack aircraft named "Thunder," which were built by the Fairchild Republic Aircraft Company of Farmingdale, New York. Its notable ascendants include its namesake the P-47 Thunderbolt, the F-84 Thunderjet, the F-84F Thunderstreak, and the storied F-105 Thunderchief, whose name was familiarly abbreviated to "Thud." The Thunderbolt II was developed to provide close air support (CAS) and improve on the Air Force's experience with the reliable Vietnam War–era Douglas A-1E "Skyraiders." The A-1E was a rugged and versatile ground-attack fighter that could loiter for extended periods in the target area and effectively employ a wide variety of air-to-ground weaponry. These attributes well served the CAS and combat search and rescue (CSAR) mission needs; pilots flying the A-1E on CSAR missions were first to use the "Sandy" call sign. To provide similar capabilities, the A-10 was designed as a straight-wing, subsonic attack aircraft uniquely equipped with an internal seven-barrel GAU-8 30 millimeter (mm) Gatling gun. It can also employ a large variety of weapons—including AGM-65 Maverick missiles—and can defend itself with air intercept missiles (AIM). Early in its history, the A-10's appearance earned it the beloved nickname "Warthog," which is often shortened to "Hog." Many A-10 units have unofficial patches or coffee mugs with the motto "Go Ugly Early"—a

1

testimony to its unique allure and the affection felt by those associated with it.

A-10 Thunderbolt II, . . . Warthog, . . . Hog

The nomenclature of the A-10 is often confusing because the designations "A-10," "OA-10," and "A/OA-10" have been used to identify essentially identical aircraft. In reality, the aircraft designation reflects its assigned mission and the qualification of its pilot. "A-10" normally identifies an aircraft dedicated to the CAS mission, while "OA-10" refers to one used in the airborne forward air controller (AFAC) role. Each unit's aircraft is then designated either A-10 or OA-10 as a reflection of the weighting of that unit's CAS and AFAC tasking. Fighter squadrons (FS) must maintain an appropriate number of pilots qualified in each of those missions in addition to those qualified for CSAR, which is not directly related to either aircraft designation. During Operation Allied Force (OAF), Warthog squadrons were tasked for all three missions; and in accordance with standard Air Force nomenclature, they were identified as flying the "A/OA-10." In this book, however, we use the convention "A-10" for all Hogs, regardless of squadron, tail number, or mission.

Current A-10 Roles and Missions

The number and complexity of A-10 missions have increased dramatically since the end of the Cold War. Until Operation Desert Storm, Hog squadrons trained almost exclusively for high-intensity combat against Warsaw Pact–style integrated air defense systems (IADS) and massed armor formations. As a result, A-10 pilot training and weapons loads were optimized for daytime, low-altitude CAS missions in joint operations with Army units. In addition, A-10 pilots practiced some daytime, low-altitude air interdiction (AI). Night flying focused on in-flight refueling and instrument flying to facilitate deployments. Only those highly qualified pilots who had attended weapons school (the United States Air Force [USAF] Fighter Weapons Instructor Course) were qualified for CSAR missions. The remaining unit pilots, even the very experienced ones, had no CSAR training.

The A-10 picked up the AFAC mission in the late 1980s as the Air Force retired the OV-10 and OA-37 from its active inventory. The Hogs were designated as OA-10s, formed into tactical air support squadrons, and flew the AFAC mission exclusively, as had the OV-10 and OA-37 units before them. Pilots in OA-10 units were not qualified in ground-attack missions and generally did not carry offensive air-to-ground weapons. In Operation Desert Storm separate A-10 and OA-10 squadrons were tasked and employed in attack and AFAC roles. That changed in 1995, and from that point forward all A-10 squadrons became responsible for all A-10 missions.

During Operations Desert Shield and Desert Storm, A-10 squadrons developed tactics for medium altitude and night employment in response to post–Cold War changes in threats, targets, and geography specific to the Southwest Asian theater and its particular circumstances. Since then, the emphasis in A-10 tasking and tactics development has continued to steadily move from only daytime, low-altitude missions towards daytime and nighttime, medium-altitude missions.

The missions flown by A-10 units in Operation Allied Force and the way they developed and evolved over time are described in more detail in the beginning of chapter 2. Lt Col

Goldie Haun also provides a detailed look at the history of attacking fielded forces during the period that followed Vietnam through the operations in Kosovo (see appendix). Air Force Doctrine Document 2-1.3, *Counterland,* provides definitive, up-to-date descriptions of these missions.

Close Air Support

The CAS mission is principally characterized by the aircrew's detailed coordination and integration with the "supported" ground units, and the attack of targets in "close" proximity to those friendly troops. CAS is the classic mission celebrated in movies when threatened troops "call for air." Soon after the call, aircraft attack the menacing enemy while under the firm control of an airborne or ground forward air controller (FAC) and within view of the friendly soldiers. CAS is high-intensity combat operations made difficult by the unacceptable possibility of fratricide, and all A-10 units regularly practice it. Air Warrior I exercises at Nellis Air Force Base (AFB), Nevada, focus on supporting large ground-unit maneuvers, while Air Warrior II exercises at Barksdale AFB, Louisiana, concentrate on low-intensity combat and are often conducted in urban settings.

CAS can be flown during the day or at night and at low or medium altitudes. Since CAS is a direct fire-support mission for ground maneuver, supporting those ground forces in what they are attempting to accomplish becomes the key factor in determining how to employ the A-10.

During Operation Allied Force there was no CAS tasking since there were no friendly ground troops engaged in hostilities. At the end of the conflict and as a precaution, A-10s were assigned airborne and ground-alert CAS missions for several weeks as the North Atlantic Treaty Organization (NATO) deployed ground forces into Kosovo.

Air Interdiction

Air interdiction, according to Department of Defense (DOD) and NATO documents, is the use of air operations to destroy, neutralize, or delay the enemy's military potential (enemy forces, combat support, logistics, and infrastructure) before it can engage friendly forces; the airpower is employed at such distance from friendly forces that detailed integration of each air mission sortie with the fire and movement of friendly forces is not required. During the Cold War, NATO doctrine clearly distinguished between *deep interdiction* against fixed targets such as bridges and fuel depots, and *battlefield air interdiction* (BAI) against second-echelon mobile forces. These definitions and the Cold War environment led to broad corporate agreement on which aircraft would be appropriate to use in various roles and on specific types of targets. Even today, long after the end of the Cold War and the significant changes in the nature of potential enemy threats, many military and civilian observers hold outdated, stereotypical views on interdiction. For example, many analysts still argue that F-15Es should only be used to attack bridges and radar sites deep in enemy territory and that A-10s should be limited to attacking tanks close to friendly forces. Current Air Force doctrine recognizes that many factors (e.g., threats, targets, terrain, weather, and political considerations) must be considered when deciding how to best employ airpower in the interdiction mission. The selection of the right asset to achieve specific interdiction objectives cannot be preordained but must be the result of careful analysis.

Almost all OAF missions in Kosovo were AI, or in support of AI, since enemy ground forces were never engaged against friendly ground forces. As we will see, a wide range of aircraft—A-10s, AV-8Bs, F-15Es, B-52s, and numerous other NATO aircraft—successfully attacked mobile and fixed Serb targets in and around Kosovo.

Airborne Forward Air Control

Forward air control is the generic term for the direction of offensive-air-support missions in close proximity to friendly ground troops. The term *forward control* is opposed to *rear control*, which refers to the coordination of air strikes by either a ground-based air support operations center or an EC-130E airborne battlefield command and control center (ABCCC). The person directing the air strikes, the FAC, can be deployed with the ground forces or in an aircraft as an AFAC or FAC[A].

5

Joint documents have adopted the acronym FAC(A), although many Air Force unit instruction manuals have used and still use AFAC. No matter what they are called or where they are located, the FAC is the final clearance authority for an attacking pilot to expend weapons near friendly forces.

Controlling OAF air strikes in the absence of friendly ground forces did not meet the current definition of CAS by either joint or Air Force (AF) doctrine. The latter defines *killer scouts* as attack aircraft used for AI in an armed reconnaissance role to validate and mark targets for dedicated attack missions against lucrative targets in a specified geographic zone—pretty much the role we had in OAF. The A-10 community, however, has for years used *air strike control* (ASC) to describe directing aircraft strikes under any circumstance. I will avoid any further discussion of these definitions because I believe that what we did in OAF was FACing in the classical sense. An inaccurate bomb dropped on targets in Kosovo would have had such a severe, negative impact on the coalition's unity and commitment that FACs in the classical role were required to ensure positive target identification, control attacking aircraft, and prevent inadvertent attacks on innocent civilians. In Kosovo, innocent civilians were in close proximity to the enemy, and for all practical considerations, these missions took on the same urgency and significance as CAS. The airmen who directed and flew these sorties kept their doctrinal terms simple and consistently referred to the control of any air strike as FACing and the pilots as FACs or AFACs. The authors will follow that convention throughout this book.

Traditionally, flying an AFAC mission is like being a traffic cop in the sky. The first duty of the AFAC is to know the ground situation in detail, including the ground commander's intended scheme of maneuver and objectives throughout the day's battle. Prior to takeoff, AFACs study the target areas, the types of fighter aircraft they will control on those targets, and the munitions those aircraft will bring to the fight. Once airborne, the AFAC checks in with E-3 airborne warning and control system (AWACS) and ABCCC controllers to get updates on the air and ground situation and starts adjusting the game plan. Nearing the target area—if appropriate—he contacts the ground FAC and organizes the list of targets with the strike aircraft on the way. If armed with appropriate ordnance, the AFAC can begin attacking targets while waiting for the strikers. The AFAC authenticates the strikers when they arrive, using a challenge-and-response code to confirm their identity and preclude the enemy's use of tactical deception. He then updates the strikers on the target area and passes a standardized target-attack briefing. That briefing includes target type, coordinates, timing factors, weapons to employ, threats relative to the target location, and restrictions on the attack heading (to ensure that no friendly forces, noncombatants, sensitive areas, or structures are damaged by the fighter's ordnance).

After all this preparation and coordination, the attack finally begins with the AFAC getting the strikers' "eyes on target" by using visual descriptions, "marking" the target with ordnance, or both. The AFAC usually fires rockets with a white phosphorous charge, known as a "Willy Pete," that blooms on impact to mark the target. However, he can use anything, such as an exploding bomb or a burning vehicle that had been previously attacked, that will help focus the fight lead's eyes on the target. After the flight lead confirms the target location, the AFAC clears the flight to expend ordnance on the target, repeating any heading or other attack restrictions. The AFAC watches the fighters and the target area throughout the attack to provide visual warning for enemy surface-to-air fire and to ensure that the fighters really are following the attack heading required and are aiming at the right target. If in doubt, the AFAC can terminate the fighters' attack by using the abort code passed in the formatted brief.

After the leader drops on the target, the AFAC adjusts the aim point for each of the successive wingman's deliveries, based on the results of the previous attacks. The AFAC continues to control the formation's attack until the strikers run out of weapons, fuel, or time on station—whichever comes first. The AFAC then directs the fighters' egress direction and altitude to deconflict with inbound fighters.

In addition to the A-10s, two F-16CG squadrons from Aviano Air Base (AB), Italy, and the F-14s from the USS *Theodore Roosevelt,* in the Adriatic, also flew as AFACs. Naturally, these three very different aircraft performed the AFAC mission quite differently. For target acquisition, F-16s and F-14s used targeting pods that provided a magnified in-the-cockpit picture of the target area while A-10 pilots flew with gyrostabilized 12- or 15-power binoculars, which they often called "binos." In much of the weather conditions during OAF, binos had much better visual resolution than targeting pods.

A-10s flew more than 1,000 AFAC missions during the 78 days of the OAF air campaign. Thousands of allied aircraft, representing practically every attack aircraft in the NATO inventory, were controlled by A-10s. The specifics of how A-10s performed the OAF AFAC mission are discussed in chapter 2.

Combat Search and Rescue

CSAR—possibly the most audacious Air Force mission—is made possible by airmen who dare to penetrate bad-guy land and recover recently shot down aviators from under the very nose of the enemy—an enemy who has many reasons for wanting to capture hapless aviators and is all too eager to do so. Those aviators are usually downed in combat and in the course of expending ordnance on the enemy's troops. The enemy knows that the potential prize can be exploited for intelligence (intel), propaganda, and other political ends—not to mention the pleasure of retribution. For example, during the Gulf War, Saddam Hussein tried to use photos and videos of captured aviators to negatively affect allied public support for the air campaign.

With the increased use of airpower as the first instrument for coercion and peacemaking, the capture of an airman becomes more likely and could provide an enemy with a method of influencing public opinions, especially within allied democracies. An enemy may try to force "confessions" and intel disclosures from captured aviators. Dictators have demonstrated a willingness to subject helpless and, perhaps, wounded air warriors to public ridicule for political advantage without regard to the prisoner-of-war protections afforded by the Geneva convention. With the desire to support and maintain the high morale of allied airmen—and deny the enemy any opportunity for a propaganda advantage—the United States and its NATO allies place CSAR at the top of their "must have" capabilities in their combat planning.

During the preparations for OAF, NATO commanders ensured the availability of adequate CSAR forces. The size and nature of those forces reflected the specific combat circumstances. There are two crucial elements to CSAR success: a recovery vehicle to pick up the survivors and an on-scene commander (OSC) who locates the survivor, protects him or her if necessary, and directs the recovery vehicle to come forward when the area is safe. The recovery vehicle is usually a rescue or special forces helicopter, and the OSC is usually a specially trained A-10 pilot. However, other vehicles and pilots are capable of performing these functions, and there may be many other CSAR actors when the enemy threat is medium to high. These other elements could include the air-refueling tankers; a C-130 ABCCC to provide overall mission coordination and tracking of airborne assets; air-to-air fighters to provide air defense; F-16CJs and other similarly equipped aircraft to provide suppression of enemy air defenses (SEAD) and protection against enemy radar-guided surface-to-air missile (SAM) systems; jamming aircraft such as EA-6Bs; and any type of strike aircraft to provide air-to-ground firepower against enemy ground forces attempting to capture the survivors. These aircraft are often already in the target area performing their primary combat missions when the need arises, and they are then retasked to support the CSAR effort.

Another important element of the CSAR forces is the NATO airborne early warning (NAEW) aircraft, which provides radar coverage and directions to the tankers. The NAEW uses the E-3A aircraft, but its communications equipment is more limited than that of the USAF AWACS, and its aircrews are trained differently than US aircrews. These differences result in a lesser overall capability.

The specially trained and designated CSAR on-scene commanders have carried the Sandy call sign since the Vietnam War. Due to the difficulty and complexity of the mission, only the most experienced and capable A-10 pilots are selected to train as Sandys. They must stay cool and use exceptional judgment to find and talk to the survivor without giving away information to the enemy, who may also be listening or watching. The Sandy must have an extraordinary situational awareness to keep track of the survivor, numerous support aircraft, rescue helicopters, and enemy activity on the ground. An accurate synthesis of this information is absolutely critical to the success of the Sandy's decision to commit to a helo pickup. Additionally, all CSAR participants must have unshakeable courage because their mission often means going deep into bad-guy land and exposure to significant ground and air threats.

In the Balkan theater the dedicated CSAR assets included MH-53J Pave Low helicopters from the 20th and 21st Special Operations Squadrons at Royal Air Force (RAF) Mildenhall, England. They had deployed regularly to Brindisi AB, Italy, since the mid-1990s. The A-10 Sandy aircraft were usually from the 81st FS/EFS (expeditionary fighter squadrons) from Spangdahlem AB, Germany, flying out of Aviano AB, and Gioia del Colle AB, Italy. During the years of routine deployments (from 1993 to 1999), these units flew CSAR exercises together in Bosnia with support from the NAEW and ABCCC but with little involvement with SEAD, air-to-air, or other attack aircraft. During this time, A-10 Sandys occasionally exercised with Italian and French forces using their Puma helicopters as recovery vehicles.

The first Kosovo crisis in October and November of 1998 led to the Spangdahlem Hogs being sent to Aviano to "stand up" a CSAR alert. At that time, the 81st pilots initiated the development of standardized CSAR procedures for the Balkan area by coordinating with personnel assigned to the CSAR cell at the combined air operations center (CAOC) in Vicenza, Italy, and representatives (rep) from the theater's NAEW, ABCCC, and Pave Low communities. They renewed that process of coordination and cooperation during their return to Aviano in January, February, and March 1999. With the beginning of hostilities on 24 March, the 81st "stood up" a ground and airborne CSAR alert capability. With only a single two-hour exception on 11 April (during the 81st's move from Aviano to Gioia del Colle), the 81st—along with the 74th FS and the 131st FS—maintained a continuous ground and/or airborne alert throughout the campaign. During the course of the air campaign, CSAR was 100 percent effective, successfully rescuing one F-117 pilot and one F-16CG pilot. Seven Hog drivers from the 81st and two from the 74th participated in those rescues—making crucial decisions at critical junctures, as well as ensuring that the pilots were picked up and that the helos made it in and out safely. Their personal accounts appear in subsequent chapters.

A-10 Weapons

The Hog can carry a wide variety of weapons—and a bunch of them. On the in-flight mission cards Aviano planners listed the standard munitions load in a column labeled for each aircraft so the AFAC could quickly match the right weapon to the right target. These cards were distributed to all units involved in the Kosovo Engagement Zone (KEZ) and showed most aircraft as having one or two types of weapons available. Under the A-10 label, however, the column just reads, "Lots."

Because the Hog has 11 suspension points for hanging weapons, missile rails, and electronic countermeasures, A-10 units in OAF could easily mix and match weapons based on day or night, AFAC, strike, or CSAR missions. The standard items for all A-10 missions included an AN/ALQ-131 electronic countermeasures pod; two AIM-9M Sidewinder heat-seeking air-to-air missiles on a single dual-rail launcher; a Pave Penny laser-spot-tracker pod; a GAU-8 Avenger cannon (a 30 mm, seven-barrel Gatling gun) loaded with a combat mix of 1,150 depleted-uranium armor-piercing and high-explosive shells; and two AGM-65D Maverick missiles with imaging infrared (IIR) guidance and a large 125-pound (lb) cone-shaped-charge warhead. For day AFAC and CSAR alert sorties, the 81st loaded two pods of seven Willy Pete rockets for marking targets and two versatile Mk-82 "slick" 500 lb bombs with air-burst radar fuses set to explode at about five meters above ground.

These bombs did a great job of marking targets—even from 20,000 feet, any pilot could see a 500 lb bomb exploding, especially an airburst that made even more smoke than a ground-

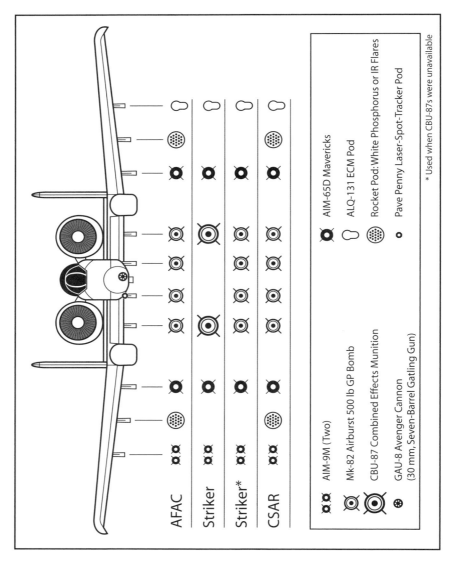

A-10 mission loads during OAF

AFAC	AIM-9M (Two)
Striker	Mk-82 Airburst 500 lb GP Bomb
Striker*	CBU-87 Combined Effects Munition
CSAR	GAU-8 Avenger Cannon (30 mm, Seven-Barrel Gatling Gun)
	AIM-65D Mavericks
	ALQ-131 ECM Pod
	Rocket Pod: White Phosphorus or IR Flares
	Pave Penny Laser-Spot-Tracker Pod

* Used when CBU-87s were unavailable

burst. Airburst bombs were also more tactically viable against dug-in or soft, mobile targets. While slick, unguided bombs dropped by a Hog with no radar are fairly accurate, they are not precision weapons by any stretch of the imagination. An airburst gives the weapon a good chance of inflicting blast and shrapnel damage on the softer parts of an artillery piece inside an open revetment. A 500 lb bomb with a contact fuse that hits just one meter outside the target's revetment is good only for making a lot of noise. After the first week of AFAC missions, the 81st decided to carry two additional airburst Mk-82 bombs. With only 1,000 lbs of extra weight and very little extra drag, they provided additional capability to attack targets when other fighters were not available.

USAF Photo

Loading Mk-82 slicks on an A-10

For night AFAC and CSAR missions, A-10 units replaced Willy Pete rockets with flare rockets that illuminated the target area for pilots wearing night vision goggles (NVG)—standard for all A-10 night operations. These rockets contained a canister that opened after launch and deployed a ground-illumination flare which then slowly descended by parachute and provided the Hog driver with up to three minutes of infrared (IR) illumination of ground targets and enemy activities.

On A-10s tasked for strike sorties, but without AFAC duties, we swapped out our two rocket pods for two cluster bomb units (CBU). We selected the CBU-87 combined effects munition (CEM) because of its effectiveness against many target types. Since both the rocket pods and CEM create significant drag on an already slow Hog, we never carried both at the same time. These CEM cluster bombs opened up and dispensed bomblets over a significant area, with warheads that had fragmentation, incendiary, and antiarmor kill mechanisms. CBU-87s gave the Hog pilots the ability to damage targets without using precision-guided ordnance.

USAF Photo

Loading a combined effects munition (CBU-87) on an A-10

Given the missions A-10s fly, particularly CAS, and the lethality of the weapons they employ, one can understand why A-10 pilots learned to "speak Army," read maps, and become familiar with the little unit symbols and phase lines Army officers are so fond of putting on maps. These capabilities are why Hog drivers and maintainers tend to be the liaison of understanding between the fast-mover Air Force and the guys who pound sand and eat snakes for a living. Having already mentioned a few of the A-10 units involved in OAF, the chapter now introduces the rest of the Hog units and their commanders.

14

A-10 Units in Operation Allied Force

During OAF, pilots assigned to eight fighter squadrons flew A-10s from five of those squadrons to form three EFSs at two deployed locations (Aviano AB/Gioia del Colle AB and Trapani AB, Sicily). The 81st FS became the 81st EFS, began OAF while deployed to Aviano AB, and then moved to Gioia del Colle AB on 11 April 1999. Pilots from the 70th FS, 74th FS, and 75th FS flew five 74th FS aircraft and formed the 74th EFS. They joined the 81st EFS at Gioia del Colle under the operational control (OPCON) of the 40th Expeditionary Operations Group (EOG). Pilots and aircraft from three Air National Guard A-10 units (103d, 172d, and 190th FSs) formed the 131st EFS, organized under the 104th EOG, at Trapani AB. The 40th EOG and the 104th EOG were organized with the 52d EOG (F-16/F-117) at Spangdahlem AB, Germany, to make up the 52d Air Expeditionary Wing (AEW).

USAF Photo by SMSgt Rose Reynolds

A-10 leads fellow 52d AEW aircraft past a German castle. The wing also included a deployed F-117 FS.

81st Fighter Squadron "Panthers"

During the 1993 Air Force restructuring, the 81st FS, known as the "Panthers," stood up as part of the 52d Fighter Wing at

Spangdahlem AB, Germany, with some personnel and aircraft from the deactivated 81st Fighter Wing at RAF Bentwaters, England. Subsequently, the 81st FS deployed many times to the Balkan theater, and, until the spring of 1997, a portion of the squadron maintained a near-continuous presence at Aviano AB, Italy, in support of AFAC operations over Bosnia. At that time the 31st AEW, based at Aviano AB and flying F-16CGs, relieved the 81st by assuming the Bosnia AFAC tasking. Afterward, the 81st FS Panthers only were required to operate out of Aviano when the situation in the former Yugoslavia called for additional capability, or when the F-16s were deployed and unable to fulfill the AFAC mission. As a consequence of this arrangement, the Panthers began a one-month deployment to Aviano AB in January 1999 with six aircraft and 100 personnel to backfill their F-16 AFAC counterparts—the 510th FS, nicknamed "Buzzards." In response to the growing Kosovo crisis, the 81st increased its presence to 15 A-10s and 170 personnel before the outbreak of hostilities on 24 March. During this time, the Panthers flew CAS and AFAC sorties in Bosnia supporting Operation Deliberate Force. With timely approval, the Panthers also were able to practice CSAR operations with US, Italian, and French air force and navy rescue helicopters.

USAF Photo

A-10s of the 81st EFS at Gioia del Colle AB, Italy

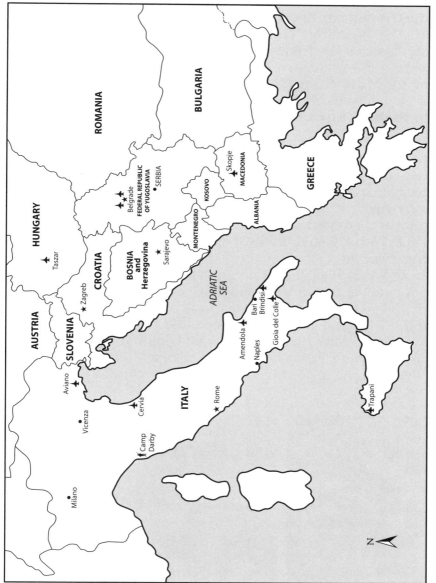

OAF theater of operations

The 81st repositioned all of its personnel and aircraft on 11 April from Aviano to Gioia del Colle. With three additional Spangdahlem aircraft, the 81st was then equipped with 18 A-10s and conducted combat operations until the end of hostilities on 9 June. The squadron continued to maintain CSAR and CAS ground alert for the following two weeks. Most Panther A-10s returned to Spangdahlem on 28 June, with the last six flying home on 11 July. Lt Col Chris "Kimos" Haave commanded the 81st EFS.

74th Fighter Squadron "Flying Tigers"

The 74th EFS was formed initially with personnel and aircraft of the 74th FS Flying Tigers, Pope AFB, North Carolina, in response to a US European Command (EUCOM) request for four additional aircraft. After the success of the 81st's AFAC missions in early April, EUCOM decided to increase the A-10 presence over Kosovo. To ensure the availability of four operationally ready jets, the 74th FS answered the call with five "Hogs with teeth" (Flying Tiger aircraft maintained the shark's teeth nose-art tradition of World War II) and nine pilots with a good mix of abilities, including the invaluable AFAC and CSAR qualifications. Later, the 74th EFS at Gioia del Colle received six more pilots from the 74th and 75th FSs at Pope and the 70th FS at Moody AFB, Georgia. After Serb president Slobodan Milosevic's capitulation, the Flying Tigers began their return to Pope on 24 June. Maj John "Scratch" Regan commanded the 74th EFS.

USAF Photo

74th EFS patch and Flying Tiger nose art

40th Expeditionary Operations Group

United States Air Forces in Europe (USAFE) stood up the 40th EOG on 11 April when the 81st EFS redeployed to Gioia del Colle. The 40th initially included the 81st EFS, the 40th Expeditionary Logistics Squadron (ELS), and the 40th Expeditionary Support Squadron (ESS). When the 74th EFS arrived in-theater, it became part of the 40th EOG and integrated completely in the

USAF Photo

Col Al Thompson after flying a mission in the KEZ

day-to-day operations of the group. Throughout this book, the 40th EOG will be synonymous with "A-10s at Gioia." Col Alan E. Thompson commanded the 40th EOG.

104th Expeditionary Operations Group

The 103d FS, Barnes Air National Guard (ANG) Base, Massachusetts; 172d FS, Battle Creek ANG Base, Michigan; and 190th FS, Boise ANG Base, Idaho, contributed six aircraft each to form the 131st EFS under the OPCON of the 104th EOG. With only a few days' warning, members of these three units organized an 18-aircraft EFS, deployed, and, by 19 May, established operations at Trapani AB, on the western coast of Sicily. Since the commonly used names of these three units all started with the same letter (Barnes, Battle Creek, and Boise), they collectively called themselves the "Killer Bees." Their two weapons-instructor pilots arrived at Gioia del Colle several days ahead of the rest of the advance team and flew their first combat missions with the Panthers and the Flying Tigers. They were able to get a first look at the target areas and gain experience working with numerous NATO aircraft. Because the 104th EOG included many veteran instructor pilots and maintainers with lots of years of deployed operational experience, the Killer Bees were able to quickly commence operations in the unfamiliar, Spartan-like facilities. Staying true to the expeditionary Hog mind-set, the 131st EFS launched their first combat sorties on 21 May, within days of their arrival at Trapani. They participated in all A-10 missions for the remainder of the hostilities and returned to their bases in late June. Col Daniel Swift, from Barnes ANG Base, commanded the 104th EOG.

31st Air Expeditionary Wing and 31st Expeditionary Operations Group

The 31st AEW was the host unit at Aviano AB and had OPCON of the 81st EFS from January 1999 until the Panthers' departure for Gioia del Colle on 11 April 1999. As such, the 31st AEW provided invaluable direction as well as operational and logistical support as the 81st flew its first combat missions over Serbia. Brig Gen Daniel P. Leaf commanded the 31st AEW, and Col Jeffrey Eberhart commanded the 31st EOG.

52d Air Expeditionary Wing

The 52d AEW at Spangdahlem was one of three fighter wings in USAFE and the home unit for the 81st FS. After the 81st EFS moved from Aviano to Gioia del Colle, the 52d stood up the 40th EOG at Gioia del Colle. Through the 40th EOG, the 52d AEW reestablished OPCON over the 81st EFS and the

74th EFS. It later stood up the 104th EOG at Trapani to provide OPCON and support for the 131st EFS. The 52d AEW had OPCON over three EOGs—the two A-10 EOGs in Italy and the

USAF Photo

Col Al Thompson, 40th EOG/CC; Brig Gen Scott Van Cleef, 52d AEW/CC; and Lt Col Chris Haave, 81st EFS/ CC, at Gioia del Colle AB, Italy

52d EOG at Spangdahlem AB, the group responsible for two squadrons of F-16CJs and one squadron of F-117 Nighthawks. Brig Gen Scott P. Van Cleef commanded the 52d AEW, and Col Jan-Marc Jouas commanded the 52d EOG.

Allied Air Forces Southern Europe and Sixteenth Air Force

Lt Gen Michael C. Short was a dual-hatted US/NATO commander, directing both USAFE's Sixteenth Air Force, headquartered at Aviano AB, and NATO's Allied Air Forces Southern Europe (AIRSOUTH), headquartered at Naples, Italy. As a NATO commander, his subordinate units included Interim

Combined Air Operations Center 5 (ICAOC-5, hereafter CAOC) at Vicenza. During combat operations, General Short spent most of his time at Vicenza.

The following chapters describe particular aspects of A-10 missions that helped defeat the Serbian army on the ground—an accomplishment made possible by the efforts of Hog drivers and their control of allied high-tech airpower over Kosovo.

USAF Photo

Lt Gen Mike Short, Sixteenth Air Force commander, speaking to troops as Lt Col Chris Haave observes

Mission Leadership
at the Tactical Level

Introduction

Lt Col Chris "Kimos" Haave

The car almost drove itself as it twisted down the mountain road from Mister C's Antares Hotel in Piancavallo to Aviano AB, Italy. Capt John A. "Buster" Cherry and I had been up and down this road often enough to unconsciously negotiate the sharp turns in the darkness in our mighty Fiat Punto. What interested us most, at 0130 on that morning of 30 March, was the clearing sky visible for 10s of miles to the south. From the switchbacks on the south side of the Dolomite Mountains, we could look down the Adriatic Sea in the direction of Kosovo and then, looking up, could see bright stars through the thin layers of stratus clouds.

As we pulled up to the 510th FS (F-16CG) building, we saw many other cars in the parking lots and noticed a hubbub of activity in the cramped quarters of our generous hosts, the Buzzards. Our squadron, the 81st FS Panthers, had shared its small operations building since 7 January, and it had come to feel like home. In the main briefing room that morning, we would brief the first-ever large, multinational force package to participate in an AFAC mission. It was also the first time in combat history that A-10s would lead such a large mission package. The package would include the following aircraft types: NAEW, E-8 joint surveillance, joint surveillance target attack radar system (JSTARS), ABCCC, Dutch F-16AM air defender, F-16CJ SEAD, EA-6B electronic jammer, F-15Es, French Super Etendard, and British GR-7 Harrier striker.

USAF Photo by SrA Stan Parker

Combat-loaded A-10 taking off from Aviano with the Dolomite Mountains in the background

Leading a Large, Multinational Force Package

It was not obvious that A-10s would, or even should, lead this highly visible and complex mission. While we had deployed to Aviano on 7 January to backfill the Buzzard's AFAC tasking, we had focused on preparing for the CSAR mission from the time of our arrival to the first OAF air strikes on 24 March. We had flown AFAC sorties in Bosnia and participated in practice interdiction packages, but we spent most of our time training for CSAR, with our own pilots and our likely collaborators—US Special Forces and Italian and French helicopter crews. We had also coordinated extensively with the ABCCC and NAEW crews and provided them with standardized CSAR checklists and procedures.

The A-10s initially had a low priority for mission resources. We knew that the CAOC was serious about ensuring a ready CSAR capability, but since CSAR was a foggy notion for most fast-mover aviators, we had to fight long and hard to ensure we had what we needed to accomplish that mission. For example, the plan for the 24 March start of the OAF air campaign called for our A-10s to be on CSAR ground alert at

Aviano AB. Tankers were in short supply, and all noncritical refueling had been eliminated. Since our A-10s cruise at only 300 knots, it was obvious to us that it would take more than two hours to reach and help recover an airman who might be shot down striking targets 600 miles away in Serbia. We convinced the planners that our response time was too long, and they agreed to let us fly an airborne CSAR alert over the Adriatic, without scheduled air-to-air refueling support. We would take fuel from an unscheduled tanker (aka bootleg a tanker) only if a shoot down occurred. After the successful 27 March rescue of the F-117 pilot (Vega 31), our priority for resources increased, and a dedicated tanker was routinely scheduled to support the Sandys on airborne alert.

Before March and except for us, few people thought about using A-10s to attack ground targets. During the weeks between the end of our planned 30-day Operation Deliberate Force rotation and the start of OAF on 24 March, we had quietly increased the number of our A-10s deployed to Aviano from six to 15. Part of the buildup was consciously approved through all channels. We had convinced the CAOC that CSAR alert for both northern and southern Serbia would require a minimum of eight combat-ready A-10s with at least two spares. Some of the other forward-deployed Hogs were the consequence of the 31st AEW's approving our requests to park more jets in its allotted area and the dynamics of moving crews and aircraft in and out of Aviano. For example, after six weeks at Aviano, I had returned to Spangdahlem on 7 March and left Lt Col Mark "Coke" Koechle, the 81st operations officer, in charge of our detachment of 12 A-10s. Two weeks later we received the warning order to be ready to go on 24 March. I returned with a two-ship of A-10s to Aviano, increasing our force to 14. A couple of days later, another Hog pilot transported some critically needed parts to Aviano, and, voilà, we had 15 A-10s—our force structure at the beginning of OAF.

How would these Hogs be used? Our recent Bosnia experience (1994 and 1995) convinced us that our bosses would ask for A-10 expertise when we began to engage fielded forces. Maj Goldie Haun, our squadron's weapons and tactics officer, had already given this question much thought and had prepared a concept on how to conduct AFAC-led NATO force packages against fielded forces. On 12 March Colonel Johnson and Colonel Carpenter (CAOC division chiefs for operations [C3] and plans [C5]) came to Aviano to discuss employment concepts with Col Jeffrey Eberhart (our 31st EOG commander). Coke and Goldie were invited to their meeting, and Goldie quickly briefed them on his AFAC concept. During the next two days, FS weapons officers and leadership representatives (rep) from the 81st (A-10s), 510th and 555th (F-16CGs), 23d (F-16CJ), and 492d and 494th (F-15Es) hashed out the plan's details. The result was Goldie's plan, which had A-10s leading the day missions and F-16CGs leading the night missions.

The plan was briefed to Brig Gen Dan Leaf, commander of the 31st AEW, on the morning of 15 March by Colonel Eberhart and Maj "Bro" Broderick (31st AEW's weapons chief). General Leaf gave it a "thumbs up." Presumably, since the current campaign plan called for night operations only, there was no discussion of A-10 AFACs. They were mentioned solely in the context of CSAR. After Bro's briefing, Goldie lobbied hard to include A-10 daytime AFAC missions in Colonel Eberhart's briefing to Lt Gen Mike Short. General Short, as the dual-hatted commander of USAFE's Sixteenth Air Force and NATO's AIRSOUTH, was briefed that afternoon and approved the plan to use F-16s as the primary night AFACs and A-10s as the primary day AFACs. The concept was titled the Combined Air Interdiction of Fielded Forces (CAIFF).

Lt Col Gregory A. "Snoopy" Schulze, my predecessor as the commander of the 81st FS, was then stationed at Ramstein AB, Germany, as the chief of USAFE's flying standardization and evaluation. He had been tasked to take the briefing General Short had approved and make it ready for presentation to Gen John P. Jumper, the USAFE commander, and Gen Wesley K. Clark, who was dual-hatted as supreme allied commander Europe (SACEUR) and combatant commander, United States European Command. During his preparation Snoopy called me at Aviano to get additional details on two unique A-10 target-acquisition capabilities—our binoculars and Pave Penny. Our hand-carried, gyrostabilized 12- and 15-power binos provided a sharper, more color-contrastive, and larger image than the low-altitude navigation and targeting infrared for night (LANTIRN) targeting pod. With the aircraft-mounted Pave Penny laser-spot tracker, we could confirm that another aircraft's targeting laser was designating the right target before we allowed the pilot to release weapons.

Snoopy called later to say that the CAIFF concept was approved. It was great to get SACEUR to buy the concept, but it was another challenge to translate that concept into a coherent tactical plan that would work in flight. Some expressed concern that circling A-10s over known threats—radar-guided missiles, radar-directed antiaircraft artillery (AAA) sites, and an abundance of man-portable missiles—would be asking to get shot down. Those folks thought the best way to attack Serb armor would be to assemble a strike package just to the south of Kosovo. When alerted by JSTARS of the exact location of a convoy on the move, the attack package could push forward and attack. Still other aviators thought A-10s would be particularly vulnerable due to their large size, slow speed, and radar cross section. Jim Bitterman, for example, was an exasperating non-aviator "expert" and Cable News Network (CNN) correspondent who habitually reported from the end of Aviano's runway. He generally provided an informative, accurate, and useful commentary. However, as he observed A-10s taking off, he would invariably intone "the low, slow, vulnerable A-10" and muse that we really had no reason to fly in this campaign. Of course, the media did not yet know that Hogs had successfully led the rescue of the F-117 pilot and that they were getting ready to lead the very first attacks on fielded Serb forces.

We ignored those affronts and continued to work on our plan. We knew that no professional army would drive around in convoys, waiting to be picked off like ducks at a carnival—at least, not more than once. We also knew that even tanks would be very hard to find once the Serb ground forces hunkered down in the hilly, forested terrain spotted with villages. Most of all, we were convinced that any Serb foolish enough to open fire on a flight of Hogs would make himself an easy target and a big loser in any weapons exchange.

The CAOC order, which gave us three days to prepare, stated that day-only CAIFF operations would commence 30 March and would be led by A-10s. We speculated that this decision, more than anything else, reflected the need for positive target identification—a task for which the A-10 and its pilots were well suited. Leading these large force packages would pose a new challenge for the Panthers. Although our weapons officers had led large force packages as part of their USAF Weapons School graduation exercise, no one had ever put a mission like this together—with these kinds of targets and so many NATO participants. By contrast, the F-16CG mission commanders who so ably led the first interdiction strikes on 24 March had been practicing AI packages in Bosnia for weeks, and had even done a couple of "dress rehearsals" for the day-one strikes. We would get no such practice—or so we thought.

Coke, Goldie, Buster, and I, with a lot of help, worked intensely during those few days. We coordinated with reps of all the plan's players: NAEW, ABCCC, JSTARS, tanker, SEAD, jammer, air defender, and striker aircraft. We then put the final touches on our command and control procedures, frequencies, airspace deconfliction, attack coordination, and tactics—basically, all the details a good plan requires. The CAOC directed the force to operate over Kosovo for three hours, an operational constraint which reflected the limited availability of F-16CJ SEAD, EA-6B jammer, and tanker aircraft. The CAIFF mission did not have top priority, so to save on tankers, we used Lakenheath F-15Es. They were there primarily to fly in the air defense orbit that day and would then come down and be our first strikers if we found something. This was a win-win situation, since each of the highly respected Strike Eagles carried six 500 lb laser-guided bombs (LGB) under each wing! For airspace and target-area deconfliction, we split Kosovo into two sectors, with aircraft entering and exiting via Albania into the western half and via Macedonia for the eastern half. We planned to launch a total of eight A-10s. Two two-ship flights would cover the first 45 minutes in each of two sectors, with the other two two-ships swapping in as the first four went to the tanker. We planned to repeat this rotation to cover our 3-hour "vulnerability," or "vul," period. I would be the mission commander on the first day, with Goldie as my deputy leading the second four-ship. On the second day

Buster would lead, with me as his deputy. Coke would fly on day one in my foursome as the element lead in the opposite sector. My wingman would be Maj Wade "Biggles" Thompson.

I walked into the 510th that morning exactly 30 minutes prior to the time of the mass briefing and exactly 12 hours after leaving the afternoon before. That was as late as I could arrive and still be prepared for the briefing and as early as I could arrive to meet "crew rest" requirements. The hubbub in the hallways took on an ominous tone as a breathless major, who worked in the "Wingtip" (31st AEW's planning cell), ran up to us with maps in hand. He said, "The CAOC didn't get approval to use Macedonian airspace to attack Kosovo and you'll all have to go through Albania. I've got some new proposed orbit points on these maps." This was not good news. The F-15Es would be the only fighters that would be allowed to fly through Macedonian airspace, since they were categorized as air defense. Everyone else—the F-16CJ SEAD patterns, the EA-6B jammer orbits, the two dozen strikers, and us (the AFACs)—would all have to assemble in northern Albania. Moreover, our new plan had to be ready in less than 30 minutes. A mission's execution often reflects the quality, discipline, and tone set in the briefing. We started the brief with a punctual time-hack—there was no way we were going to begin our first mission command with a late hack and set a less-than-professional precedent! In short, the planning and briefing worked out fine and we launched on time.

The weather, however, was not going to cooperate. Because of the weather and the day-one rules of engagement (ROE), we were unable to engage any targets. Those ROEs attempted to limit risk in an uncertain threat environment by restricting operations to not lower than 17,500 feet and a penetration of not more than 10 miles into Kosovo. Now, 17,500 feet is fine for an aircraft with plenty of thrust and precision-guided munitions (PGM). Its pilot can acquire the aim point using its targeting pod, fly a straight-and-level weapons-delivery pass, and then release its LGBs. A Hog driver, however, must enter a dive and point its nose at the target to expend weapons. At that altitude, a pilot has to enter a steep dive to acquire the target within release parameters. A jet engine's ability to produce thrust decreases with an increase in altitude, and the thrust required to sustain flight increases with extra weight and drag. It is, therefore, easy to understand why a Hog's maximum employment altitude is reduced when it's fully loaded. So our challenge was to find targets from as high an altitude as possible, maneuver the aircraft to put the nose on that target, get a weapons lock-on, launch the missile, and recover without busting the 17,500-foot "hard deck" (minimum altitude, period—not just the minimum weapons-release altitude). Our choice was to operate within this ROE or be slow-speed cheerleaders. On that first mission Biggles and I were working in western Kosovo, south of the town of Pec. I found a hole in the clouds and, using my binoculars, identified a single convoy of four small, dark-green-painted armored cars driving south with military spacing between them. Leaving Biggles up at 22,000 feet, I gingerly pushed the stick forward, lowered the nose, and attempted a Maverick missile lock-on, but my altitude alert sounded just as I brought the armored cars in my TV screen and before I could slew the missile to get a lock. I had set the alert to 1,000 feet above the hard deck, which reflected the amount of altitude I would lose during my dive recovery. Getting a kill on the first sortie was not worth an ROE violation—that sort of breach in air discipline would mean an instant end to our mission leadership. As I cleared Biggles to try a pass, the Serb convoy went under a cloud deck.

That was the best shot anyone had all morning, and the next day, the weather was completely overcast. After surviving the first several missions, we received permission from General Short to lower the ROE hard deck—first down to 15,000 feet and then to 10,000 feet. (One of the themes in chap. 5, ROE will be discussed there by several people at greater length.)

The weather pattern continued to repeat itself and provided us with six unexpected days to practice and perfect our mission leadership. It was challenging for us to keep track of 40-odd aircraft as they flowed into and out of an engagement area protected by enemy air-defense systems and filled with cloud layers. It was a task we learned to accomplish without incident.

The self-initiated pressure to get results was building. We had drilled holes in cloudy skies for seven days without expending any ordnance or slowing down the Serb ground offensive. Finally on 6 April, we got our chance. The Serbs hadn't started hiding yet. We caught and destroyed several small convoys and other vehicles parked in the open. After landing from that seven-hour sortie, I was pressed to get out the door to comply with crew-rest restrictions (normal crew rest is a 12-hour period that begins when a pilot departs the squadron and ends when he returns for the next day's mission) but took time to do three important things. First, I distributed the prized bits of weapons arming and release hardware to the ecstatic maintainers and weapons loaders. These swivels, links, and bits of arming wire are attached to the aircraft's bomb racks and missile rails and arm the weapons when they are released or fired. The maintainers and loaders are proud when their aircraft returns without its weapons and are pleased to get these souvenirs. Second, I briefed the following day's mission commander on the tactics that worked and those that didn't. Third, I returned a call General Short had made while I was flying. He was very supportive and asked how the mission had gone. He reminded me to keep the target-identification process rigorous and the "kids" above his ROE altitude. I thanked him for the 10,000-foot hard deck and asked him to consider 8,000 feet. He said he'd think about it.

Evolution of the Airborne Forward Air Controller Mission

After the first week of AFAC sorties, the CAOC changed the name of the CAIFF mission to VMEZ (V=VJ [Serb army] and M=MUP [Serb Interior Ministry police] Engagement Zone). About the same time, we were allowed to seek out and destroy targets throughout Kosovo, but still without using Macedonian airspace. VMEZ then changed in mid-April to KEZ, and on 15 April, we finally received clearance to attack Serbia and Kosovo through Macedonian airspace. (For simplicity's sake, the air campaign against fielded forces is hereafter called "KEZ operations" and the area in Kosovo and southeastern Serbia where we engaged fielded forces is "the KEZ.")

During the first week of OAF, daily KEZ operations were limited to a single three-hour period from 0600 to 0900. After our early successes, the CAOC expanded KEZ operations to two three-hour daytime periods, with F-16CG FACs from Aviano joining us. Unfortunately, the Serbs were quick to adapt their operations to ours. We soon noticed that the Serb army simply hid its armored vehicles while we were roaming overhead, and then wreaked havoc on the Kosovar civilians when we left. We saw a critical need to increase our ability to influence events on the ground and sent a proposal to the CAOC to expand our operations to near-continuous coverage. That proposal required more aircraft (how and where we got those Hogs is discussed at length in chap. 3, whose theme is beddown). Eventually, with more A-10s and carrier-based F-14 AFACs, KEZ operations reached a cruising speed of 18 hours daily in late April, divided into three-hour periods. There were two "holes" in the schedule around sunset and sunrise, due to limitations in the availability of some key assets (jammers and SEAD). This 18-hour coverage continued until the end of hostilities. The F-16CGs did most of the FACing at night and were assisted by ANG A-10s after they arrived. At night, A-10s, F-16CGs, and British GR-7s flew with night vision goggles.

Coordination of KEZ Operations

Extensive coordination was required to make the KEZ operations work well. By late April there were dozens of units, from nine NATO countries, which operated from 15 bases and three aircraft carriers to support OAF. Those nations provided aircraft, which regularly flew the indicated missions during KEZ operations (table 1).

Table 1

Aircraft Involved in KEZ Operations

Country	Mission	Aircraft Type
Belgium	Attack[a]	F-16A
Canada	Attack	CF-18
France	Attack	Super Etendard, Jaguar
Germany	SEAD[b]	Tornado ECR
Italy	Attack	Tornado GR.1 IDS, AMX

Table 1 (Continued)

Netherlands	Attack	F-16AM
	DCA[c]	F-16AM
Spain	Attack	EF-18
Turkey	Attack	TF-16
United Kingdom	Attack	GR-7 Harrier
	Support[d]	E-3D NAEW
United States	AFAC[e]	A-10, F-16CG, F-14
	Attack	A-10, F-16CG, F-15E, F-14, F/A-18, AV-8, B-1, B-52
	SAR[f]	A-10, MH-53J (Pave Low) MH-60 (Pave Hawk)
	SEAD	F-16CJ, EA-6B
	DCA	F-15A, F-15C, F-16CG, F-15E
	Support	E-3 AWACS, E-8 JSTARS, EC-130 ABCCC,
		EC-130H Compass Call, E-2C Hawkeye, KC-10, KC-135
	Recce[g]	Predator, Laser Predator, and Hunter

[a] attack aircraft that employed weapons under the control of an AFAC

[b] suppression of enemy air defenses

[c] defensive counterair

[d] specialized aircraft that support operations in areas of command, control, communications, reconnaissance, intelligence, refueling, and electronic warfare

[e] airborne forward air controller

[f] search and rescue

[g] reconnaissance using unmanned aerial vehicles

Keeping these mixed gaggles going the same way on the same day required three levels of planning and coordination. First, CAOC planners would build the packages from the available units to ensure the requisite capability. These packages would be published in the daily air tasking order (ATO) and, more importantly, in the draft ATO. The information in the draft allowed the units to get a head start on planning for the next day's 0600 vul period.

Aviators representing each of the tasked units accomplished the second level of planning in the Wingtip, the wing's mission planning cell at Aviano. They turned the ATO KEZ package information into two-page "coordination cards" to be used in the next day's missions. The cards listed frequencies, code words, types of aircraft, and their ordnance. We always had an A-10 pilot there to put the cards together and send them to us at Gioia del Colle. Maj Peter R. "Bro" Brotherton, one of our guys doing his time at Aviano, was the first to appropriately indicate "lots" under the A-10's ordnance column.

The third level of planning and coordination took place in the units. There, a group of young pilots, under the guidance of a field-grade supervisor, would produce the two-page lineup cards with tasking and tanker information, navigation way points, and weapons parameters. If units wanted to change something on the coordination card or alter their contribution to the KEZ packages, they simply communicated the details to their reps at the Wingtip and the CAOC. This vertical coordination for KEZ operations, after some initial hiccups, ran quite smoothly.

The horizontal coordination among the units participating in hunting fielded Serbian forces did not work as well. During the first week, while most of the "players" were still at Aviano, it was fairly simple for an A-10 AFAC mission commander to drive down the street to pay a visit to the EC-130 ABCCC squadron to work out command and control kinks, or walk down the hall to compare notes with the F-16 AFACs. Once we moved to Gioia de Colle and the F-14 AFACs started flying KEZ sorties off the USS *Theodore Roosevelt* (CVN 71), coordination among the AFAC units consisted of whatever handoff briefings we managed in the air. In general, we relied too much on the CAOC to provide coordination among units. There was no one playing "Daddy FAC" at the CAOC since there were few, if any, senior FAC-qualified pilots. We knew that the F-16 and F-14 FACs had different capabilities and therefore used different tactics. We had no insight into how they were doing—what did not work, or what worked and got results.

Lt Col Paul C. "Sticky" Strickland ably described our initial situation in an article entitled "USAF Aerospace-Power Doctrine: Decisive or Coercive?" He stated that the initial CAIFF operations did not have an air operations directive to guide them—that is, to provide clear, measurable objectives for the CAOC and the units to attain.[1] Our job was simply to hunt down and destroy Serb weaponry within 10 miles of the Albanian border. Although we enthusiastically applied our talents to this nebulous end, our frustration grew as we went out day after day, often without finding and destroying Serb targets and with no way of assessing our contribution. Certainly we were making a difference: after the first two days, the Serbs stopped driving in convoys, and after a week, they stopped driving armored vehicles during the day. After a month, we knew we had destroyed a significant amount of Serb weaponry, but was the destruction sufficient to achieve NATO objectives?

As FACs we became aware during the KEZ operations of what OAF's commanding officers have since made public: Gen Wesley Clark was eager for a major NATO effort against Serb fielded forces, while General Short preferred using NATO's air resources in a concentrated interdiction campaign against Serb infrastructure. (General Short was always a straight shooter with us and essentially explained these preferences during an official visit to Gioia del Colle after the end of the campaign, while graciously praising our contribution to NATO's victory.) Through our contacts at the CAOC, we learned that, despite the good intentions of many superb officers, this tug-of-war for mission priorities had resulted in ambiguous guidance and a lack of overall direction on our ultimate objective.

During late April, Lt Col Arden B. "Surgeon" Dahl, our 52d Fighter Wing chief of weapons and tactics, had a "eureka style" revelation while we Hog drivers discussed this problem at Gioia. Surgeon drew on his experience at the School of Advanced Air and Space Studies (SAASS) and noted that, while KEZ operations attacked ground forces, they did not explicitly seek a ground-force objective, such as "occupy the high terrain by X date" or "reduce the combat effectiveness of (named enemy unit) by X percent." This should have been obvious to A-10 guys from the start, since we had grown up supporting the ground commander's scheme of maneuver from the air. However, we had not been given an "on the ground" objective to achieve in Kosovo. We understood that our KEZ operations sought airpower victory over deployed enemy ground forces, but we did not know what would constitute "victory." Through our chief CAOC representative, Lt Col Craig "Walrus" Heise, we proposed that intelligence experts identify Serb army units and their locations in Kosovo so we could systematically attack them and achieve a yet-to-be-defined joint objective. We also proposed a FAC conference at Vicenza that would allow us to compare notes and hammer out a common way forward. Both of those initiatives won approval. Afterward, our ATO listed the Serb Third Army as our main objective.

Defining our objectives did not make a big difference in our daily results, since KEZ operations did not have sufficient priority on reconnaissance assets to locate and track Third Army command posts and operational units (see chap. 5 for more details). We argued at the FAC conference for the need to develop a joint concept of attacking Serb ground forces that included NATO ground assets stationed in Macedonia and Albania. Later in the campaign, we understood that the CAOC was working closely with Army counterbattery radars. We, however, had practically no contact with our NATO ground colleagues throughout the campaign.

KEZ operations did keep daily pressure on the Serbs, and although some days resulted in very little battle damage assessment (BDA), we often forced the Serbs to make seemingly stupid mistakes. On at least three occasions, Hogs caught and destroyed significant armored forces (10–15 tanks and armored personnel carriers [APC]) congregated in the open. We termed these puzzling groupings of real armor (they burned black smoke or caused secondary explosions) Serb army "picnics" or "meetings" that got interrupted. Continuous AFAC pressure paid off most when the Kosovo Liberation Army (KLA [English] or UCK [Albanian]) started its meager, but certainly effective, ground offensive in the last 10 days of the conflict. When the Serbs came out to fight, there was no place to hide. We were then able to inflict very heavy damage, especially on enemy artillery, mortars, and APCs.

Combat Search and Rescue Leadership

A-10 Sandys had CSAR responsibility for the entire theater of operations throughout the campaign. If required, they could also lead a search and rescue (SAR) mission in friendly territory. The location and reaction time for CSAR alert were two aspects of the mission that did change over time. Friendly forces can make only an educated guess as to where the risk of having one of their aircraft shot down is greatest. Therefore, CSAR is an alert mission that initially has many unknown factors, including the location and condition of the survivor, as well as the enemy threats in that rescue area. CSAR forces can "sit" ground alert or fly an airborne alert. During ground alert, the aircraft are loaded with ordnance appropriate for a CSAR mission and then "hot cocked" by the pilots. The pilots hot-cock the aircraft by starting the engines, aligning the aircraft navigation systems, performing ground checks up to preparation for taxi, shutting down the engines, and then presetting the switches. In the event they are "scrambled," all the pilots have to do is start the engines and go. During an airborne alert, appropriately loaded A-10s take off, fly to, and remain at a specified orbit to cover the time window during which friendly aircraft are flying over enemy territory. Usually, at least two flights of A-10s are tasked to cover CSAR. One flight locates and stays with the survivor; the other escorts the recovery helos and/or relieves the Sandy who is functioning as the on-scene commander when that Sandy must depart the area to go to the tanker for fuel.

The key considerations that drive the decision to use ground or airborne alert are the level of enemy threat, the reaction time to a potential survivor, and the availability of A-10s in the tasked unit. If there were an unlimited number of A-10s and if CSAR were the only mission, all strike packages could have a dedicated airborne Sandy alert. However, flying an airborne alert takes more aircraft than ground alert and diminishes a unit's ability to execute other required missions. Ground alerts were therefore regularly used to allow a squadron to better manage its limited resources to support other important missions during nonstop operations.

One of the thorniest puzzles we faced throughout the campaign was optimizing the available A-10 sorties. We needed to cover the tasked AFAC and strike missions while ensuring adequate CSAR coverage for all other OAF missions being flown.

At the beginning of the air campaign, the 81st was based at Aviano and was expected to reach target areas in both northern Serbia and Kosovo from a single CSAR alert posture. To satisfy this requirement, given the distance to Kosovo and the uncertainty of the surface-to-air radar-missile threat, we insisted on having at least one two-ship airborne over the Adriatic and another on ground alert. We also assigned an experienced A-10 pilot to ride aboard every C-130 ABCCC during the first week of air strikes to help coordinate rescue efforts and minimize the confusion that normally breaks loose when an aircraft goes down. Airborne OAF aircraft would have to be directed to support the CSAR effort or leave the recovery area. We expected our pilots on board the ABCCCs to help with those tasks, as they did on the evening of 27 March, when they helped coordinate the efforts of six A-10s and numerous other aircraft during the successful rescue of Vega 31 (see chap. 7 for a detailed discussion).

We started flying AFAC missions and a heavy schedule against ground targets on 30 March. As a consequence, A-10 Sandys were scheduled for ground CSAR alert at night, instead of airborne alert, to maximize the number of day AFAC and strike sorties. We adopted an innovative scheduling technique to provide CSAR for the hundreds of day missions that took friendly aircraft over bad-guy land. We "embedded" at least four Sandy-qualified pilots in the AFAC and strike-mission schedule to ensure a continuous airborne Sandy presence in the target area. These pilots could easily respond to a CSAR mission should the need arise. When we were not able to schedule a continuous Sandy presence, we provided ground-CSAR alert.

On 1 May, four ground-alert Sandys were launched from Gioia del Colle to lead the rescue of Hammer 34, an F-16 that had been shot down in northern Serbia. While it was successful, the time required for the A-10s to arrive on scene meant that daylight was approaching by the time the pilot was picked up. The additional risk associated with daylight rescues and the response time from Gioia del Colle led the CAOC to decide to open a second CSAR ground-alert base at Taszar, Hungary. The Killer Bees from Trapani graciously accepted the tasking to man this detachment and provide a faster response to a possible CSAR in northern Serbia. The 81st and 74th EFS, under the OPCON of the 40th EOG at Gioia del Colle, retained 24-hour CSAR responsibility for KEZ operations and interdiction strikes in southern Serbia.

Although A-10s had successfully led the CSAR missions for the only two pilots shot down during OAF, nobody knew it. Those recoveries also happened to be the first time that immediate combat rescues had been attempted at night. The press speculated that the Marines, or perhaps the special forces, had been involved. In fact, both special forces and Air Force rescue helicopters did the pickups, but they remained appropriately discreet about who had accomplished the CSAR missions. We would have loved to have called a press conference at the squadron after each pickup and introduce the Sandy heroes to the world. However, it was much more important to maintain the ambiguity. We had little to gain by publicly announcing to the Serbs that Hog drivers would be the first to come to the aid of a downed pilot and were ready to do whatever it took to provide protection and lead a successful recovery. After Allied Force, our Sandys got the rich recognition they deserved. Capt John "Buster" Cherrey received a personalized State of the Union thanks from President William J. Clinton, and the six Sandys who participated in the Vega 31 rescue were given the "Jolly Green Rescue Mission of the Year" award.

Our Assessment of Mission Leadership

We had proved that A-10 drivers could successfully take the reins of major AFAC and CSAR missions. These were notable "firsts" in the history of the A-10, and we owe our thanks to many senior officers who ignored our reputation as a specialized CAS aircraft, recognized our potential, took us off the sidelines, and gave us the chance to lead. Those officers were not in our normal peacetime chain of command and included the USAF leadership in Italy, notably Colonel Eberhart, General Leaf, and General Short. Neither could we have led in combat without the unequivocal support of our home-station and major command leadership: Brig Gen Scott Van Cleef, the 52d Fighter Wing commander; Col Jan-Marc Jouas, the 52d Operations Group commander; and Maj Gen William T. "Tom"

Hobbins, USAFE director of operations (also an "attached" pilot in the 81st FS).

Our general lack of experience in large-force mission command showed at times in the air, and some missions didn't go smoothly. During our unit debrief at the end of the war and thereafter at the Allied Force lessons-learned conferences, we highlighted these shortcomings as important areas for improvement in the A-10 community. We could visualize a future of low- to medium-intensity conflicts in which air dominance was easy to achieve but ground dominance was not. Experts in mud moving, such as Hog pilots, will be called upon in those future conflicts to lead joint and multinational force packages of great complexity.

A lowly squadron can make a big difference in the conduct of a large air campaign—it's not solely up to the component-level or theater-level headquarters to develop tactics and strategy. This lesson repeated itself often during the campaign but never ceased to amaze us. Our inputs to the CAOC on tactics, coordination procedures, ROEs, flying schedules, and package composition significantly changed how the fight was fought.

In the European theater, the best expertise for finding and killing green-painted vehicles in green fields and forests resided in the A-10 unit, first at Aviano and then Gioia del Colle. Ironically, this capability had been developed during what many of us old-timers call "unrealistic" training 15 years ago in the Cold War's European theater. We had cut our teeth on training flights in Germany long ago trying to find a single "tank in the trees." We would complain about having the most unrealistic scenario possible. What enemy would hide his best combat power to begin with, and then, why would we ever waste the time to attack a single tank?

I Feel Lucky

Maj Phil "Goldie" Haun

I feel lucky. After getting weathered out of yesterday's sortie, I was flying back into the KEZ. Maj Philip "Dirt" Fluhr was my wingman and a good friend. Dirt was an experienced A-10 instructor pilot who never lost his cool. That morning I was the mission commander for a 45-ship package of AFACs, strikers, command and control, and SEAD aircraft. Our objective was to destroy as many Serbian tactical vehicles (armor, artillery, and soft-skinned vehicles) as we could find. As AFACs, Dirt and I were to locate, identify, and attack these mobile targets. The entire package provided continuous coverage over Kosovo by splitting the country in two, with two sets of AFACs rotating on and off the tanker to cover our three-hour vulnerability window. On this day, A-10s had the east, code-named NBA, while the F-16CGs had the west, code-named NFL.

For AFAC operations, my A-10 was loaded with two pods of 2.75-inch Willy Pete rockets for marking, four Mk-82 500 lb airburst bombs, two 500 lb air-to-surface Maverick missiles, and over 1,000 rounds of 30 mm GAU-8 armor-piercing and high-explosive bullets. That gave me a variety of munitions not only to mark targets, but to kill them as well. With F-15Es, Canadian CF-18s, and British GR-7 Harriers available to me, I also had a lot of LGBs and CBUs at my disposal. Life was sweet.

USAF Photo by SrA Stan Parker

Crew chief A1C Ephraim Smallridge arming a pod of Willy Pete rockets and two AIM-9s

That day's five-hour mission included an hour's flight to the KC-135 tankers holding over Macedonia for refueling, followed by an hour in-country over Kosovo, back to the tanker for more gas, another hour in-country, and then an hour back to Gioia del Colle—our deployed location in southeast Italy.

The morning's mass briefing was only so-so. The weather looked workable, but our ability to employ weapons was threatened by midlevel cloud decks. On top of that, the bad weather during the last few days had prevented the accumulation of any good imagery, and we were forced to go it alone, looking for Serbian military vehicles with limited help from reconnaissance and intelligence sources.

This was becoming familiar. The Serbs had stopped using the roads during the day so I didn't expect to find anything out in the open to shoot. I had two options available: systematically search the towns for military vehicles or comb the outlying areas for revetments. Visual reconnaissance in urban areas was extremely difficult. In the towns, the Serbs had been parking their tanks next to houses and sometimes *in* the houses. On a previous mission, I had been able to find Serb vehicles, but it had still taken about an hour to locate one target—and the attack had been only partially successful. My second option was to search the hills for revetments and see if any of them contained APCs, tanks, or artillery. The Serbians had hundreds of dug-in fighting positions all over the foothills that overlooked the main lines of communications (LOC) leading south and east out of Kosovo.

I was determined to give some revetments south of G-Town (Gnjilane, in eastern Kosovo) a first look. I knew where to find 20 juicy revetments that were full of APCs and artillery just two days ago. I found the revetments, called for fighters, and was given F-15Es and Belgian F-16s. Waiting for the F-15Es, I attempted to lock up and shoot a Maverick at one of the APCs, but the target contrast was too poor and I came off target dry. As I called to get an update on the fighters, I looked back at the target and saw a long trail of white smoke off my left wing. It had looked like the smoke trail off a Maverick missile, and I had been angry that my wingman had shot one on his own. I hadn't given him permission, nor had I been able to provide cover for him. When he responded that he'd made no such attack, chills went up my spine. The smoke trail was evidence that a shoulder-fired SAM had been shot at my flight.

I didn't have to wait long for the second SAM after I directed my wingman to roll in on the revetments where the smoke had come from. He came off dry with a hung Maverick only to see another SAM come streaking up for him. I called for flares and then held safely to the south until the strikers showed up. The F-15Es called in but were low on fuel. I talked them onto the target, but they bingoed out (reached the amount of fuel required to fly to a tanker and then on to their divert base if refueling proved unsuccessful) for gas before they could splash any of the revetments with their LGBs. Now I was running low on fuel, and before I could get the Belgian F-16s on target, I hit bingo myself. While flying formation on the tanker and waiting my turn to refuel, I plotted my revenge. Unfortunately, while I refueled, low-level clouds moved into the target area, and we had to leave all 20 revetments unmolested. It still burned me that they had been able to take two shots at us without retribution.

I was now eager to wipe the slate clean and start over. Dirt and I took off from Gioia, under the call sign of Cub 31, and headed east towards Macedonia. Coming off a tanker I turned north to see the weather over southeastern Kosovo looking good. I armed a Maverick as we returned to the revetments south of G-Town. Dirt covered me as I rolled in, but the APCs were no longer there and I came off dry—thwarted. The Serbian army had been extremely adaptive to our tactics. We never got a second chance in the same place with these guys.

I was forced to search around G-Town, looking at the hilltops for signs of other revetments. After 10 minutes I found what I was looking for: two groups of revetments three miles east of G-Town in a group of foothills. I put my binos on them and found the northern group filled with eight artillery pieces. In the southern group were two APCs. I called Moonbeam, the call sign for ABCCC, and requested a set of strikers. First up was Merc 11, a two-ship of Canadian CF-18s carrying 500 lb LGBs. I passed them coordinates and gave them an update as they came into the target area. My plan was to drop a single

500 lb Mk-82 bomb on one of the revetments to get the CF-18s' eyes onto the target area and then let them drop their LGBs onto the artillery. Everything went as planned until I rolled in on the target. I dropped my bomb and then came off target, rolling up on my side to see where it landed. As luck would have it, the bomb was a dud. "The best laid plans and all," I said to myself. I asked Dirt if he was in position to drop, but he wasn't. It would take a while to build up the energy (airspeed and altitude) to roll in again, so I began a talk-on.

A talk-on simply describes the target area to the strikers and, with no more than a radio, gets their eyes on the target. It sounds like a much easier task than it is, as both the AFAC talking and the striker listening were flying war birds three to four miles above enemy terrain. At those altitudes, the revetments looked smaller than the head of a pin. Also, since the jets were flying at speeds of five to eight miles per minute and since English is not always the mother tongue of the strikers, (not so in this case but true of many others) a talk-on can easily be more difficult than just "laying down a mark." Over the course of the war, I controlled USAF, United States Navy (USN), Canadian, British, Italian, French, Spanish, Turkish, Dutch, and Belgium strikers.

I responded to Merc 11's check-in: "Copy. We are just east of the target and setting up for another mark. Call visual on the factory that is just east of the huge town that is on the east-west hardball" (*hardball* was our term for a hard-surface road, which we differentiated from a *dirtball* or dirt road). G-Town is the only large town in eastern Kosovo, and since Merc 11 had eyes on my flight, it was the only town they could see. On the east side of G-Town was an enormous factory complex next to the highway leading east out of the town.

Merc 11 replied: "Copy. I see one factory. Large structure has a blue-roof building to the west." Merc 11 not only responded that he saw the factory but confirmed it by giving a positive description of a distinct feature. I had confidence that he had the right factory in sight.

"That's affirmative. Let's use that factory east-west one unit. From the eastern edge of factory go two—let's make that three— units east on hardball. Then use factory from hardball. You'll see a pull-off on the north side of the hardball. Go one unit to the south off the hardball. In between two small towns you'll see some light revetments." I continued the talk-on by setting the length of the factory complex east to west as a unit. I treated that unit as a yardstick to measure the distance along the road to another feature (a pull-off from the highway). I talked Merc 11 down between two towns where the artillery was lying.

Merc 11 responded, "Copy light revetments; there appear to be four to the south and four or five to the north." Merc 11 had the revetments in sight and again gave a description of what he saw. The revetments appeared shallow due to the light, sandy soil in that region of Kosovo in comparison to the darker-green grass of the field where the revetments had been dug.

"Copy. That is affirmative. Say your laser code." I wanted his laser code so that I could use my Pave Penny pod (a laser-spot tracker that can "see" where another jet's lasers are pointed) to ensure that his laser was actually pointed at the right target.

"Laser code is 1633."

I was ready for his attacks now. "Copy, currently I am visual you, and I am under you currently on the west side. I'd like you to take out the far western pit with a single LGB."

Merc 11 wanted one final confirmation. "Copy far western pit. Confirm the line of pits intersects the road at an angle."

I reassured him. "That is affirmative. The road between the two towns is at an angle. And the arty sets almost in a saddle in the ridgeline. Say how long until attack."

"One minute," Merc 11 called as he set up his attack.

I saw him extend to the southeast some 10 miles from the target. Though they move much faster than A-10s, CF-18s take a long time to set up their attacks. I was not used to fighters extending that far from the target and could barely make them out as they turned inbound. I had to make up my mind on whether to clear him to drop. I couldn't pick up his laser with my pod yet, but I was confident from his responses that he had the target. I decided to clear him, and he shacked (made a direct hit) the first artillery piece. He set up for a subsequent attack and took out another piece of artillery before he ran low on fuel and departed.

In the meantime, I was holding south of the target, coordinating with Moonbeam for another set of strikers. Next on the list was Dragon 61, a two-ship of F-15Es carrying a bunch of GBU-12s (500 lb LGBs). While I waited for Dragon, I took out one of the southern APCs with a Maverick. Finally, Dragon checked in and I gave them my position. I got a friendly buddy spike, which meant Dragon had locked me with one of their air-to-air radars. I told him to call me when he had me visual. Normally, acquiring a visual on A-10s is fairly easy. A two-ship of A-10s circling a target looks like a pair of large Xs in the sky. Dragon called visual, and I rolled in to mark, this time with Willy Pete rockets. I shot three rockets, hoping to get them to blossom into small white-phosphorus clouds on the ground. As long as Dragon saw where I was shooting, he could easily see the smoke generated by my rockets.

Original oil painting by Ronald "Ron" T. K. Wong, G. Av.A., A.S.A.A.

An A-10 attacks Serb forces.

"Marks are away. Expect impact in 15 seconds." That gave Dragon a heads up on when he should expect to see the smoke.

Dirt called to me on our internal Fox-Mike (frequency modulated, aka FM) radio: "Your first mark is closest to arty line."

Dragon 61 confirmed the smokes, "Six-One is contact two smokes."

"Copy. Look at the further northeast smoke. It's setting just on the east side of four arty pits south of a road." Even though the smokes were visible, the arty pits were so small that I had to ensure Dragon was seeing them.

Dragon called contact on the target area. I was starting to run low on fuel and wanted to get the F-15Es dropping as soon as possible. Dragon was not an AFAC and could not pick his own target. He could, however, continue an attack once I gave him permission. My plan was to have him take out as many artillery pieces as he could while I was off to the tanker.

I passed control of the targets to Dragon: "You have flight lead control on that target area. I'd like to take out most of the arty sites at that position; two have already been struck. Those are two just north of the east-west road."

Dirt and I left for the tanker that was waiting for us some 50 miles south over Macedonia. While we were on the tanker, Dragon continued his attack and destroyed three more, bringing the total to five artillery pieces and one APC destroyed.

USAF Photo

Artillery attacked by F-15E with A-10 FAC

After a half-hour refueling, we returned to the artillery sites. Dragon had long since departed. A cloud deck had moved in from the northwest and forced us to work east, out of Kosovo and into the southeastern part of Serbia. A large valley wound its way down towards the town of Kumanova in Macedonia. We called it the Kumanova Valley. For several days, we attacked positions in this valley when the weather was not good enough in Kosovo. The Serbs were fortified against a ground attack from the south and had hundreds of defensive positions built into the hillsides overlooking the valley.

Near the border I could hear a couple of A-10s working targets. I called them and coordinated to work well north of their position, 10 miles north of the Macedonian border. I found the town of Bujanovac and began searching the roads and surrounding areas. I worked my eyes south of the town and finally picked up six revetments. They were on a hilltop but were different than any other revetments I had ever seen. They were several miles from any major LOC and well camouflaged but were visible from the southwest. Because the weather had moved in and clouds were just above us, we were now limited to flying below 21,000 feet. I kept Dirt in a trail position and took a good look with the binos. The targets were hard to make out. I could see the ends of large tubes, which I took for long-range artillery tubes, sticking out from both ends of the revetments.

I rolled in and dropped two Mk-82s to mark the targets for Dirt. The bombs hit next to two revets, but I couldn't see any secondaries. I called Moonbeam and asked for Dodge 61, a two-ship of British GR-7 Harriers carrying BL-755 CBUs.

"Two's got both your marks. Two has a series of brown revets," Dirt called.

"Yeah, I got six revets in the triangle area." I made sure he saw all of them.

"Underneath your smoke now?" The smoke from my bombs rested over the revets.

"That's affirm."

"Got'em now."

"Let's extend out to the south towards good-guy land, and I'll work up a five line for these guys." The targets were very difficult to see. I was planning to pass Dodge five pieces of information to help them find the targets: IP (initial point—the place where they should start their attack), heading, distance, elevation, and coordinates. I also gave them a target description once they were within visual range. The Harriers had an electro-optical targeting pod, which they could use to look closely at targets. I was planning to use this device to get their eyes on the revetments.

Dodge 61 came up on the ultrahigh frequency (UHF) radio: "Cub Three-One, Dodge Six-One."*

"Three-One go ahead." Dodge didn't hear my response, and the radio went quiet—but not for long.

While plotting the revets on my 1-to-250-scale map, I dropped the map between my ejection seat and my right control panel. Pushing the jet over with some negative Gs, I tried to get it to fly back up to me, but only got it hopelessly trapped directly beneath the ejection seat. I called Dirt on our Fox-Mike frequency, where no one else was listening: "You are not going to believe this but I just dropped my 1-to-250."

Dirt's response was not at all what I expected: "OK, triple-A now . . . triple-A coming up . . . I need you to come down here southbound." Dirt was trying to keep me clear of the exploding AAA rounds cooking off right underneath us.

---

*A note to our readers who may not be familiar with standard tactical radio transmissions. It is critical that radio transmissions be clear and as short as possible. A radio transmission generally follows a standard format of call sign, call sign, and message. The first call sign in the sequence is normally the person being called, followed by the call sign of the person making the transmission, which, in turn, is followed by the substance of the transmission.

Often, the person making the call omits his own call sign after the initial call in a series of transmissions. The person receiving the call can then recognize the voice of the caller—particularly when the people communicating already know each other. In communications between flight members, the call sign is often abbreviated to just the position in the flight (One [or Lead], and Two) rather than the flight call sign and position (Sandy 51, Two). Another exception is when a wingman acknowledges that he has understood the direction by simply transmitting his position, for example "Two." In the text, all call signs will be capitalized.

Call signs appear in text and quoted dialogue. When a call sign, such as Sandy 31 appears in text, it will be written "Sandy 31." When it appears as a spoken quote it will be written the way it is said, "Sandy Three-One;" its numbers will be spelled out, hyphenated, and capitalized. When a series of communication transmissions are quoted and the call sign is abbreviated, it will be written, "Three-One," or "Two."

"Copy, I got the triple-A now. I'm visual the triple-A now." For a moment I could make out a ridgeline, where I could see the puffs of smoke coming out of the guns in a group of four to six positions. The AAA pits were two miles west of the target we were working.

"I didn't get a good look at the firing position." Dirt had seen the AAA rounds exploding just underneath us but had not seen where the guns were located. The problem with flying over AAA during the day is that they aren't as visible as they are at night. The only evidence of AAA is usually the explosion of the airburst rounds that have been set to detonate after a specific time of flight, or at a specific altitude. This looks like popcorn popping, or, in a group, they sometimes look like a strand of pearls with four to eight rounds going off in a line. Since not all AAA is set for airburst, we assumed that popcorn going off below us meant that unseen bullets were streaking up, around, and past us.

Dodge repeated his call, unaware of the AAA activity, "Cub Three-One, this is Dodge Six-One."

I answered and Dodge continued, "Holding IP Brad; authenticate Alpha, Foxtrot, November." Dodge was following procedure and was authenticating me, using authentication cards that we carry to make sure a Serb wasn't spoofing him.

On UHF I responded to Dodge, "Stand by, I'm taking a little triple-A."

Dirt asked me on the Fox-Mike radio, "Are you seeing it? You get a hack at the firing position?"

"I saw it coming up, but I couldn't get a good hack. These roads have me screwed up, and I have my 1-to-250 dropped." I had been watching so many roads that I was not positive where the AAA was located.

Getting back to business I responded, "Copy, I've found some AAA positions and/or arty. You'll have to stand by for a while. I'll have to get it plotted." I was going to try to take out both the long-range arty and the AAA positions with the CBU. I made a quick guess of where the hillside was on my remaining 1-to-50 map and passed it on to Dodge. "OK, general target area, I'll give you an update later, is Echo Mike six five nine three . . . and I can give you an update now six nine nine six."

"Echo Mike six nine nine six, copied."

I turned my attention back to my flight and planned with Dirt how to carry off the attack: "If you can get eyeballs on the triple-A area, we'll take it out. We know it's active." What I really meant was that I was planning to use Dirt to suppress the AAA while the Harriers were attacking the long-range arty. I turned my attention back to filling in the blanks as I reached the target area: "And Dodge go ahead with your line up." From his call sign I knew Dodge was the two British GR-7s I had asked Moonbeam to send. The ATO stated that Dodge had been "fragged" with CBU, but I wanted to confirm it, find out how much playtime they had, and most importantly, get their abort code.

"C aircraft, four CBU, India Bravo mikes on station . . . Alpha Quebec Uniform, abort code," came Dodge's James Bond response. My supersecret-spy decoder ring told me that Dodge was two aircraft carrying a total of four cans of BL-755 CBUs with 30 minutes of time to work the target. Moreover, if I yelled "Papa" over the radio, they would abort their attack.

As I got back to the target, the weather had deteriorated significantly. The visibility at altitude was decreasing as a high deck continued to move in, making it difficult to find the revetments. Fortunately, I had taken the time to see exactly where they were located in relationship to some distinguishing features. "Dodge, I'm trying to get better coordinates, but call when you are ready to proceed to the target area and I'll plan to mark it with a Mk-82."

Finally I got my eyes on the small, triangular field where the revetments were located: "For a description, I have five to six berms with arty pieces in them." I double-checked the coordinates, and the 69 and 96 grid lines off the 1-to-50 map overlapped the target like a set of crosshairs. "And new update—coordinates I passed you are good."

"Copy. Are we cleared to leave Brad yet?" Dodge was ready to go. He had been holding just south of the Serbian border at the IP Brad and was ready to depart.

"You are cleared to leave Brad and proceed northbound. Be advised you'll be able to work base plus 16 and below in target area. Call when you are northbound." This informed him that the weather is bad above 20,000 feet.

"OK, we're northbound this time."

"Copy that; I am currently base plus 16. Will be holding just south of target. Be advised triple-A in area approximately two miles west, northwest of target."

With the weather and the Harriers' run-in, Dirt and I were forced to overfly the AAA: "Two, any luck picking up triple-A sites?"

"Negative. They have been quiet."

As we were looking for the AAA positions, Dodge broke in: "Dodge Six-One visual with Cub."

I was starting to get impatient. With the bad weather, the difficulty in locating the target, and the amount of AAA, this target preparation had taken way too long. "I will be in out of the east. It's on top of a ridgeline; there are about four revetments. Do you have your targeting pod on that location?"

"Stand by."

"Disregard. As long as you have eyeballs on Cub, I'll just go ahead and mark."

Dodge responded, "I just lost you for the moment."

"Copy. You'll pick me as I'm coming off target. I'm in with a single Mk-82." I would have dropped more, but this was my last Mk-82. As the bomb came off the jet, I called, "Marks away; impact in 10 . . . call visual mark."

"OK, I have the mark."

"Call visual the four berms that are just to south and west of mark."

"Copy. Looking."

"They are just on the west of that dirtball road."

Finally, the words I had been waiting to hear: "Visual the berms."

I wanted the Harriers to start taking out the revetments and planned to cover them on the west side, watching for the AAA to get active again. "Copy, we're proceeding westbound. You are cleared on those positions."

"Cleared on those positions. Do you have another mark available when we run in?"

This was not exactly the question I was hoping Dodge would ask. This would mean another time rolling down the chute. Before I could respond, Dirt called me on FM: "I've got three," which meant, "Goldie, you've been having all the fun while I've still got three of my four bombs left." I quickly answered Dodge's question: "That is affirmative."

Dodge began to prepare for his attack, "I'll call for the mark."

I knew the timing of this mark was critical for Dodge. I wanted the smoke from the bombs to appear in his targeting pod with enough time for him to be able to drop his bombs on this pass. With Dirt marking the site, I figured he would need some lead time to roll in: "I'll need about a minute and a half for that call."

"Copied, no problem."

As I waited just west of the target, I again turned my attention to the AAA pits. I had taken a snapshot in my mind of where the AAA was coming from and the position of the pits. They were visible only when I looked northeast. I did a belly check and saw them directly below me. I called on Fox Mike to Dirt: "OK I know where those triple-A pits are now."

Dodge interrupted my call: "Requesting mark one minute 30."

"Copy that." I turned my attention to Dirt: "Try to put in those Mk-82s, and I'll extend to the northeast."

Dirt called back, "Tell me when you want the roll in."

"Yeah, as soon as you can." Dirt dropped his three bombs for direct hits on two of the revetments. Their explosions caused huge secondaries.

"Visual, in hot." Dodge saw the mark and requested permission to attack. I cleared him and watched as his CBU tore through two more revetments.

As Dodge reset for his wingman to drop more CBUs, I began to focus on the AAA sites. I put my binos on the position and noted four gun pits. They were tiny and impossible to lock up with a Maverick, but I still had my 30 mm gun available for strafing them. As I considered my next move, I noticed a large truck and trailer, not more than 100 meters from the pits. They were barely visible in a tree line down in a ravine. There was only one reason for that type of vehicle to be there next to AAA pits. It had to be the ammo truck, a far more lucrative target.

That decision was easy. As Dodge 62 began his bomb run, I called up a Maverick. The AAA, which had been silent, began to come up as Dodge's CBUs rained down. AAA exploded in a string of pearls just beneath me. This was a pass I wanted to make only once. I got a steady cross on the truck and hammered down on the pickle button. It seemed an eternity before the 500 pounds of missile began to move off the rail. In reality it was less than a second, and as it accelerated towards the target, I pulled off hard and began jinking. It was going to take 20 seconds for impact, so I waited a few seconds before rolling the jet over.

The impact took me by surprise. The missile slammed directly into the trailer and set off a series of secondaries like I have never seen. Fire reached for the sky like the Fourth of July.

"Unbelievable," was all the ever-cool Dirt could muster. Most importantly, the AAA shut down instantaneously and Dodge 62 could call for his next mark. Completely out of bombs, I returned to place two Willy Pete rockets on the site. Dodge 62 dropped good CBUs before the flight returned to base.

Because the British Harriers worked alongside us at Gioia, I was able to compare notes with Dodge flight the next day. Reviewing the film from their EO targeting pods, we made a startling discovery. The long-range artillery tubes we took out were actually launchers for Frog 7 surface-to-surface missiles, similar to Scuds.

It was incredible to watch as the Frog launchers exploded under the rain of CBUs. We counted secondaries off five launchers, all pointed towards the Macedonian border.

All told, Dirt and I, the Canadian CF-18s, F-15Es, and British Harriers destroyed five artillery pieces, an APC, five Frog 7 launchers, and an ammo-storage trailer. Not bad for a day's work.

This Time It's Real

Maj Dave "Devo" Gross

After flying numerous pseudocombat sorties over Bosnia during several earlier deployments in support of the no-fly zone, the 81st FS received orders to return to Aviano AB, Italy, to fight what was certain to be a shooting war over Kosovo. I sat in the back of the 81st FS briefing room on that cold and rainy February afternoon. I listened to the deployment brief, ready to go to war and fight for what is right in the world—but my name was not on the Aviano deployment list.

"What do you mean I have to ask my boss if I can deploy with the squadron?" I asked incredulously.

Lt Col Kimos Haave replied, "Devo, you work for Colonel Jouas (ops group commander) now, and he will decide if you can deploy with the squadron. Of course we would love to have you, along with all your experience."

I had several regrets leaving my job as the squadron's assistant operations officer in November of 1998 and taking over as the chief of the 52d OG's Standardization and Evaluation (Stan/Eval) Division at Spangdahlem AB, Germany. I felt as though I had been set up by being assigned to take over the Stan/Eval shop just one month before a major inspection. I also missed the Panthers' camaraderie and their day-to-day operations. Stan/Eval made it through the inspection with an "excellent" overall, and I still flew training missions with my family—the Panthers. But because of my new job, I was no longer a sure bet to deploy with the Panthers on what was sure to be a great chapter in the history of the A-10. With all the maturity and poise I could muster, I watched my squadron mates deploy to Aviano AB while I stayed behind. My plan, if the war lasted that long, was to swap out in two weeks with Capt David S. "Ajax" Ure, my assistant in the Stan/Eval shop. I had my doubts.

After the longest two weeks of my life spent watching the air strikes on CNN and hearing about the heroics of my squadron mates during the rescue of the downed F-117 pilot, I was afforded an opportunity to go to Aviano for just three days. Not being one to quibble, I jumped at the chance and packed my bags. On 5 April I would fly my first combat mission over Kosovo with Maj Joseph A. "Lester" Less. Due to continuing poor weather over Kosovo, no A-10 pilot had yet been able to employ munitions. As I performed my walk-around, inspecting the live weapons on my Hog, I was more excited than I had ever been about a sortie. I had flown lots of missions over Bosnia with live weapons, but this time it was real. We could actually shoot something today. We launched as a two-ship AFAC mission over southwest Kosovo.

As we flew into Kosovo, the first thing I noticed was how beautiful the country was. The landscape was magnificent—a wide, green, fertile valley surrounded by majestic, snow-capped mountains on all sides. I could see why generations have fought and died over the right to live in this country. The weather that day was exceptional. You couldn't buy a cloud. The sky was clear—except for the smoke from all the beautiful villages 20,000 feet below us that had been set ablaze by Serbian forces. The roads leading to the southern border of Kosovo were jammed with refugees fleeing the country. As they approached the border, they were forced to leave their cars and walk with little more than the clothes on their backs. Their abandoned vehicles stretched from the Albanian border to more than 20 miles into Kosovo. Seeing the villages being burned and the mass exodus of refugees firsthand made me want to aim my 30 mm gun at the ground and kill those responsible for this devastating crime against humanity. But on this mission I didn't get to fire the gun or drop any weapons. Although we saw several vehicles moving in and around burning villages that we suspected were Serbian military and police (VJ/MUP) forces, we did not find any hard-and-fast "military" targets. After two hours of scouring the countryside and witnessing the carnage, we returned to Aviano with all our ordnance. Frustration was mounting in the Panther clan and at the CAOC. After the first day of really great weather in the KEZ, not one bomb had been dropped. Less than 24 hours later, all of that would change.

Kimos "We Are Going to Kill Something Today" Haave

I had never seen that look in Kimos's eyes before. Normally a very mild-mannered family man and exceptional leader, Kimos revealed a different side of himself that day. As the mission commander for the 6 April CAIFF package, Kimos briefed the pilots assembled in the 510th FS briefing room in Aviano like a football coach giving a locker-room pep talk to a team that has narrowly lost every game that season. He was the coach, and this was his final game—he would not retire a loser! After his brief, I was ready to go out and do some damage to some Serbs! After that mission I called him Kimos "we *are* going to kill something today" Haave to the guys assembled around to hear about the first Panther kill. I was proud to be on his wing that day because I knew from the brief we were going to take the fight to them.

We were Bull 11 flight, AFACs for an 18-ship package that included British GR-7s and French Super Entendards as strikers. After the tedious two-hour flight down the Adriatic Sea to Kosovo, we refueled over Macedonia and began searching for targets. The weather was like yesterday's, ceiling and visibility OK (CAVOK). We set up a search pattern around the town of Rogovo. The first target we acquired was a military scout vehicle parked on a hillside. Kimos rolled in and marked the target area with two rockets to allow Cougar Flight, two British GR-7s, to acquire the target and employ BLU-755s. Unfortunately the Brits' bombs hit well short of the target. With the vehicle now on the move, Kimos rolled in and employed a Maverick missile while I covered his attack. He scored a direct hit.

We went on to employ against a petroleum, oil, and lubricants (POL) storage facility and a military-vehicle compound near Pirane (a small town located near a rail line about halfway between Orahovac and Prizren). Kimos coordinated an attack by Griz 81 flight, a second two-ship of GR-7s, on the vehicle compound while I coordinated with ABCCC for clearance to attack the POL site. Griz flight dropped CBUs on the east side of the vehicle compound, which contained about 15 personnel carriers. We dropped our remaining bombs on the west end, destroying all the vehicles in the compound. Both Kimos and I employed everything on the jet that day: Mk-82s, Mavericks, and even the lethal GAU-8 gun. Not a single shot was fired back at us. I started to get a false sense of security. It felt like another routine training mission except for the fact we were dropping live weapons. Unfortunately, the rest of my sorties over Kosovo would not be as easy.

The true significance of this mission was not the targets we destroyed. Those attacks by no means turned the tide of the campaign. The significance was the effect that our two A-10s had on our maintenance personnel when they saw their aircraft pull into the de-arm area with empty missile rails, empty bomb racks, and bullets missing from the gun. The significance was also in an attitude change among the Panther pilots after hearing that we actually employed this time. Things would never be the same. Milosevic's days were now numbered because the Panthers got their first taste of blood and were hungry for more. Me, I had to go back to Spang to an empty base and CNN. But I was there—there, for the first Panther kill!

You Can Run, but You Can't Hide

After two more long weeks back in Germany, my boss allowed me to join the Panthers in their new home at Gioia del Colle. Once again, my first mission back in country was action packed. It was 22 April and I was leading a strike mission with Capt Kevin "Boo" Bullard, one of the 75th FS pilots. Boo and several other Hog pilots from Pope had recently joined us and brought along six additional A-10s to add to our firepower. This was his first sortie in OAF.

You could hear the excitement in Lester's voice: "We have military vehicles down there!" Lester had to be one of the most laid-back pilots in the squadron. Nothing excited him. That's why I knew from the tone of his voice that we had hit the mother lode when he called us in as strikers to work the target area. Lester had found a group of 20–30 military transport vehicles parked in an area around several small buildings near Urosevac. It appeared to be some sort of VJ/MUP headquarters. After allowing his wingman to employ Mk-82s on the south side of the target, he handed the target area over to my flight. Boo and I proceeded to wipe out every vehicle in that compound with our Mk-82s and guns. The Mk-82s' FMU-113 airburst nose fuses caused them to detonate approximately 15 feet above the ground. This made them lethal weapons against the soft-skinned vehicles we were attacking, as well as any troops within 100 yards of the impact area. Deep inside I hoped that this was one of the rape camps I had heard about in the news and that we were making a difference in this campaign.

After Boo made his last pass, we began searching the area for other targets. There was a dry riverbed that ran from the target area down a narrow ravine towards a town. I noticed several peculiarly shaped rocks in the riverbed, too square to be just rocks. From 15,000 feet they appeared to be the same color and texture as the rocks in the riverbed, but their squared edges led me to believe they were man-made. My first thought was that they were cement blocks used to contain the river, but they were not positioned at the edges of the bank. I set my formation up for a reconnaissance pass, utilizing the A-10's top-secret, hi-tech targeting system—a pair of Canon space-stabilized binoculars. My suspicions were confirmed; those shifty Serbs were attempting to hide six tanks in this riverbed by putting them next to rock formations and covering some of them with tree branches. When I keyed my mike to talk to my wingman, I am certain I sounded even more excited than Lester. I talked Boo's eyes onto the tanks and quickly briefed him on my attack plan. I maneuvered into position, rolled in, and fired an AGM-65D Maverick missile on the tank at the north end of the riverbed. As I came off target with flares, I observed a direct hit on the lead tank. I instructed Boo to hit the tank at the south end of the formation to pin them in the riverbed. As Boo maneuvered for his shot, his target began to move in an attempt to escape. Boo scored a direct hit on the "mover," pinning down the other tanks in the riverbed. The rest of the tanks were now urgently trying to escape as we continued our assault.

For some strange reason, the Serbs were getting a little tired of our act and began firing some pretty intense AAA at us. Most of it exploded below our altitude. We changed our axis of attack and continued our assault on the tanks with our remaining two Mavericks and then made one pass with the GAU-8 gun. Out of gas, we reluctantly handed the target area over to another flight of A-10s, who found more vehicles close by and continued the attack. That was my first experience finding concealed armor in an environment other than a desert, be it Iraq or the Nevada/California desert. It was a completely different ball game, but the learning curve was high for most of us. The Serbs quickly learned that they were going to have to do a better job of concealing their fielded forces with A-10s on the prowl. We were patient and persistent in our pursuit of targets. It was a great day for the Panthers!

A Picture Is Worth a Thousand Words

After two all-night squadron top-three tours and a weather cancel on my next sortie, I was starting to feel the fatigue I had seen in everyone's eyes the day I arrived at Gioia. That was the only time I was grateful for my time at home in Germany with my wife and three-month-old son while my squadron was fighting in the skies over Kosovo. We knew we were in this for the long haul. Milosevic would not fold easily.

Since I was not an AFAC, I coveted the sorties when I was scheduled as a striker because I could lead the mission and have more control over the outcome. On 30 April I briefed my wingman, Lt Scott "Glib" Gibson, like I briefed all the other missions. We were going to take the fight to the Serbs as Chili 11 flight. I had demonstrated my ability to find lucrative targets with some degree of success, so the AFAC assigned to my sector allowed me to perform my own reconnaissance, but I had to confirm the validity of targets with him before attacking. This day's weather was forecasted to be "severe clear" over Kosovo. I was climbing up the A-10 ladder to enter my "office" and go kill stuff, when Maj Thomas J. "Bumpy" Feldhausen, the top-three supervisor, drove up and handed me a target photo, complete with coordinates. A "top three" designation is reserved for the squadron commander, operations officer, or another senior squadron member responsible for the execution of the day's operations. The Brits had flown over a small compound southeast of Urosevac that morning and had taken a recce photo of some tanks parked next to a house. Once again, I couldn't believe my luck. I could hardly wait to get across the Adriatic, hit the tanker, and get into theater to see if the tanks were indeed still there.

As I pressed into the area of responsibility (AOR), I called my AFAC and told him about the target area. Since he was busy with his own flight's carnage and destruction, he cleared me to engage that target area. Glib and I circled the area at 15,000 feet and found the house and the tank. The tank was nestled close to the house, so the Maverick was the weapon of choice to prevent any collateral damage. I rolled and acquired the tank in the cockpit's Maverick video display. It was white hot from sitting in the spring sun all day. I locked the target,

USAF Photo by SrA Stan Parker

Lt Glib Gibson inspecting Willy Pete rockets and IIR Mavericks prior to a day-time combat mission

waited for a valid weapons lock, and fired the missile. The Maverick roared off the rail like a locomotive, finding and destroying its target in a blaze of smoke and fire.

Knowing that tanks are usually not solitary creatures by nature, Glib and I searched the immediate area for more targets. Using the binos we could see tank trails running throughout the area. Once again, I noted something peculiar: a mound of hay isolated in a field, surrounded by tank tracks. Having lived in Germany for the past three years, I knew that German farmers piled their hay in stacks close to their barns. I never saw a single pile of hay just sitting in a field alone with no cattle. On my drives to work in Germany, I had watched the hay combines during the harvest season. The machines would pick up hay, "process" it, and drop the bundles out the back without stopping. This resulted in piles of hay in uniform, regularly spaced patterns, quite unlike what I was now seeing from the air.

I dropped down and took a closer look with the binos as Glib gave cover. My suspicions were again confirmed. The Serbs were trying to hide a tank under a pile of hay in the middle of the field. I clearly saw the turret sticking out from the hay. There was only one thing left to do. I rolled in with the mighty GAU-8 gun and put two 150-round bursts of 30 mm armor-piercing and high-incendiary explosive rounds into that tank. In classic Hog fashion, the gun vibrated the cockpit and rudder pedals and filled the cockpit with the sweet smell of gunpowder as the bullets found their mark. The tank went up in bright-red flames that shot 40 feet into the air, and it was still burning and cooking off unexpended rounds when we left the area 30 minutes later.

Glib and I continued our search of the target area; behind a building we found two square, green patches that just did not quite match the surrounding foliage and grass. I rolled in with my Maverick missile to get an IR image of what we were seeing. What started as a reconnaissance pass quickly became an attack as the Maverick's imagery clearly showed two tanks concealed under a camouflage net. After I killed the first tank with a Maverick, I directed Glib to take out the second. He rolled in and took it out with a Maverick missile.

Out of gas, we reluctantly retracted our fangs and headed for home. The next day a fellow pilot on an AFAC mission saw the tank I had shot with the gun: the tank—with its turret blown off—was sitting in the field. For two days following the Brits' discovery of this tank by the house, coalition forces found and killed numerous pieces of artillery and armor hidden in and around this target area. A picture is indeed worth a thousand kills. Once again, I learned that if something on the ground doesn't look quite right, it's probably a Serb hiding from the wrath of the Warthog. Thanks to my British war brethren for the great target.

Break Left! No, Your Other Left!

The first of May began like any other day in Gioia. I was scheduled to fly as Maj Kirk M. "Corn" Mays's wingman on an AFAC mission around the town of Urosevac. Corn was not alone in his feeling of frustration in not being able to find great targets. The Serbs were getting craftier at hiding their fielded forces because the A-10s were locating and killing them daily. Secret funerals were being held in Belgrade so the Yugoslav public would not know how many of their boys were dying in Kosovo. The Serbs were digging in deeper, and we were getting better at discovering their secrets of concealment.

Corn asked me to lead the reconnaissance portion of the mission since I had succeeded in finding some lucrative targets in the past. We flew into theater and began working with the operator of a UAV who had spotted a tank and Serbian troops hidden in a tree line. I searched the area of interest with both binoculars and the Maverick seeker, but could not positively identify the target in question. Neither could I talk to the UAV operator directly because he was located too far from the AOR. Instead, I relayed my radio transmissions through the ABCCC. This process took a great deal of time and required us to stay in the target area longer than I had wished to positively identify the target. I rolled in and put three Willy Pete rockets close to the area I thought the UAV operator was talking about in hopes that the operator would see my smoke and confirm its position in relation to the target. Minutes later I got the confirmation from the UAV pilot via ABCCC that I was looking at the correct target. At this point Corn and I were rapidly approaching our bingo fuel for our next aerial refueling. Corn was coordinating a handoff of the target area with another two-ship of Hogs piloted by Capt James P. "Meegs" Meger and 1st Lt Michael A. "Scud" Curley. I was positioning myself to roll in and drop my Mk-82s on the troop concentration in the trees.

Just as I was about to roll in, I heard, "SAM launch, SAM launch" over the UHF radio. Looking east towards Pristina Airfield, I saw a volley of two SAMs followed immediately by two more. I was amazed at the amount of white, billowy smoke they produced and the rapid speed at which they flew in our direction. All four SAMs were guiding towards us. I began evasive maneuvers and called the SAM launch out on the very high frequency (VHF) radio that all four A-10s were using to work the target-area handoff. All four A-10s began a SAM defense ballet, the likes of which I have never seen and hope to never see again. The sky was full of chaff, and the world's greatest attack pilots were maneuvering their Hogs like their lives depended on it—and they did! A SAM, the second launched, malfunctioned and detonated in spectacular fashion about 2,000 feet above the ground. From my now-inverted cockpit, I could feel the concussion of the warhead detonating in a blaze of orange fire. The other three SAMs continued on course in an attempt to thwart our attack against the troops massed in the forest below us.

All but one of the SAMs failed to guide—and that one chose Scud as its soon-to-be victim. Wouldn't you know it would pick Scud, who was the least-seasoned pilot in our four-ship—a formation that had over 3,500 hours of combined Hog experience. Meegs did an excellent job of defeating the threat, maintaining situational awareness on his wingman, and calling out the final evasive maneuvers that prevented the SAM from impacting Scud's jet and ruining our day. All four SAMs were defeated, and the Serb troops in the forest below awaited the wrath of the Panthers. The Serbs failed to take a lesson from Desert Storm. In that campaign, the Iraqis quickly learned that if they shot at an A-10 they had better kill it because if it survives, it is going to shoot back with a vengeance.

Corn and I were out of gas, so we departed the area with our hearts in our throats and left the counterattack to Meegs. He dropped four Mk-82 airburst bombs on the troop concentration in the trees and eliminated those forces from the rest of the campaign. (I can make that statement with a high degree of certainty. One year later I received an Air Medal for my participation in that sortie. Afterwards a member of the audience approached me, introducing himself as the UAV operator with whom we had worked during that mission. He had personally witnessed Meegs's Mk-82 attack, vouched for the devastation it created, and was pleased to finally meet one of the mission's pilots.)

After getting fuel from the tanker, Corn and I proceeded back into the KEZ to look for more targets in the northern region of the country. We had received numerous intel reports about troops and targets in this region, but we had not achieved much success in finding them. We flew approximately 15 miles northwest of Pristina Airfield and began searching for targets. I found one area of interest that appeared to have mobile AAA and possibly some other military vehicles in a small valley. I was just starting to talk Corn's eyes onto the area to get his opinion when I saw two SAM launches from just north of Pristina Airfield. I thought, "Here we go again." I called out the SAM launch to Corn and directed his break turn to defeat the attack. As I dumped out as much chaff as I could muster and made the appropriate break turn, I looked back to see that Corn had turned in the wrong direction. He was heading straight towards the SAMs, increasing their probability of intercept. Realizing that he did not see the SAMs, I directed him to "take it down! Break right now and roll out west! Chaff! Chaff! Chaff!" As the second SAM guided in Corn's direction, I continued to monitor his progress and update his maneuvers while attempting to talk his eyes onto the threat. I was certain the SAM was going to hit him, and I was just about to call out a last ditch maneuver when it began to drift aft to pass about 1,000 feet behind him.

Once we were clear of the SAMs, I plotted the area from which they were launched on a 1-to-50 map. I passed the coordinates to a Navy F/A-18 flight, which swiftly acquired the SAM system and destroyed it with LGBs within minutes of its attack on our flight. After the attack, we exited the area and headed home. The trip back to Gioia was very quiet. Not until we got to the cash register to pay for dinner that evening, Corn insisting that he pay for mine, did I realize the full magnitude of what had happened that day. Not feeling the effects of combat until hours after the mission and debrief is fairly common. It seemed that after a day of fighting the Serbs, the adrenaline level ran out somewhere between the order of steamed mussels with garlic and butter and the homemade gelato with fresh strawberries and cream on top. Dinner at the Truck Stop (a favorite eatery between Gioia and the hotel) was a savored ritual. The food was Italian standard—excellent—and the meal was a chance to recap the day's events over a glass of wine. That's when everyone seemed to "crash." During those moments, I said a little thank-you prayer and just hoped that somehow what we did that day had really made a difference.

Final Thoughts

I flew several other sorties over Kosovo, fighting the Serbs with the best fighter pilots in the world. Milosevic did not stand a chance. The sorties I have recalled here were examples of the most memorable ones. For me, OAF was exciting, stressful, and frustrating. It was exciting because I finally got a chance to fight in the world's finest attack aircraft with the best-trained and most professional pilots in the US Air Force. It was stressful because we were getting shot at daily and the physical demands of running a 24-hour wartime operation took its toll on all of us. And it was frustrating to see villages burning several weeks into the campaign and not knowing what to do at that moment to stop the carnage. I am grateful to God that he delivered us all home safely to our families and that the air campaign was enough to convince Milosevic to give in. My last sortie in the A-10 was on 17 May, when I took a jet from Italy back to Spangdahlem for required maintenance. Opportunities like flying in this campaign present themselves only once in a lifetime. I am grateful and honored to have been a member of the fighting 81st FS Panthers.

Notes

1. Lt Col Paul C. Strickland, "USAF Aerospace-Power Doctrine: Decisive or Coercive?" *Aerospace Power Journal* 14, no. 3 (fall 2000): 13–25.

3

Beddown and Maintenance

Introduction

Lt Col Chris "Kimos" Haave

The successful around-the-clock attack of the enemy would not have been possible without an enormous and meticulously coordinated effort by a host of highly qualified professionals. The 81st EFS was supported and sustained by personnel of the 31st EOG at Aviano and the 40th EOG at Gioia del Colle. This chapter tells the story of the dedicated airmen in maintenance, logistics, munitions, personnel, services, civil engineering, contracting, communications, air traffic control, weather, photography, security forces, and the chaplaincy who made the A-10's success possible.

In October 1998, Headquarters USAFE ordered the 81st to send six A-10s to Aviano to stand up a CSAR alert posture. That crisis ended after just one month and allowed the A-10s to return to Spangdahlem. Even though the crisis was brief, the 81st still missed its once-a-year deployment to Nellis AFB, Nevada, and lost its chance to participate in Red Flag, Air Warrior, and the Gunsmoke gunnery competition. Little did the personnel of the 81st and other supporting units realize that they would soon have the most intensive large-force employment and gunnery experience of their careers.

In chapter 1, I stated that the 81st started its six-month-long deployment to Italy at Aviano and that it was hosted by the Buzzards of the 510th FS. However, I failed to mention that the two squadrons shared a common heritage. The 510th had been an A-10 squadron at RAF Bentwaters until October 1992 when it moved to Spangdahlem AB, where it remained until it was inactivated in February 1994. In fact, the first time Warthogs went to

Aviano in support of operations over Bosnia, they went as the Buzzards. During the Air Force's reorganization in the mid-1990s, the 510th was reactivated at Aviano AB, flying F-16s. The A-10s at Spangdahlem were redesignated and assumed the name and traditions of the 81st FS Panthers, which had formerly been an F-4G Wild Weasel squadron at Spangdahlem.

Over the years, the squadrons maintained strong ties. The Buzzards exhibited extraordinary hospitality when the Panthers came to town. During the 81st's one-month deployment to Aviano beginning 7 January 1999, the 510th invited the Panthers to use its operations facilities while most of its F-16s were away. On 7 February 1999 we were ordered to remain in place and stand up a CSAR alert. The Buzzards, although now at full strength and in cramped quarters, once again invited us to operate from their facilities.

All of the squadrons in the 31st Fighter Wing, particularly communications, transportation, airfield management, and intelligence, generously supported the Panthers. When we hastily relocated from Aviano to Gioia del Colle in April, commercial trucking was uncertain, and Aviano's 603d Air Control Squadron volunteered its two-and-one-half-ton trucks to take us 400 miles down the road. Although commercial trucks were eventually located, the 603d's sincere offer was indicative of the welcome we had at Aviano. This above-and-beyond hospitality was even more impressive considering the crush of units and personnel that filled every available parking space, hangar, and office on its air patch.

The Desire to Go South

Despite our comfortable arrangements at Aviano, we needed to move south to be more responsive with our CSAR mission. The CAOC proposed that we stand up a CSAR alert at Aviano and another at Amendola AB during our October 1998 deployment. Amendola is an Italian air force training base on the Adriatic coast opposite Split, Croatia; unfortunately, it had no US or NATO infrastructure to support all the communications and weapons requirements for CSAR missions. Although we wanted to move farther south, we rejected the idea of splitting our squadron. We proposed moving our entire CSAR contingent to

Brindisi, where we could work alongside our principal partners in CSAR operations—the special forces' helicopter units. However, Brindisi was already too crowded, and the USAF wanted to leave in the near future.

We continued to look for a more southern location. Amendola was now no longer possible, since the Dutch and Belgian air forces had filled all the available ramp space with a joint F-16 detachment. Goldie and I looked to the Sixteenth Air Force force-structure experts for help and asked to review their aerodrome site surveys. After looking at airfield diagrams in our instrument-approach books, we were most interested in Brindisi and Gioia del Colle. The surveys of the Sixteenth Air Force experts indicated there were too many complicating issues with United Nations (UN) logistics to safely locate even six A-10s at Brindisi. They also told us the Italian government had not given them approval to survey Gioia del Colle.

Our sorties during our first two days of operations (30 and 31 March) were seven and one-half hours long but provided less than two hours of on-station mission time. This proved the need to relocate nearer the KEZ. The physical toll on the pilots was enormous: two hours to get to the KEZ followed by three hours of "one-armed paper hanging" in the target area (including about an hour going to and from the tanker), finished by two hours of struggling to stay awake on the way home. If we flew two long sorties per day, our maintainers wouldn't have enough time to fix any broken jets and still maintain aircraft ready for the CSAR alert. We were faced with limiting ourselves to one sortie per aircraft per day or accepting a continuous lowering of our mission-capable rate. Either choice would inevitably result in a reduction to one sortie per day. At the same time, the CAOC had asked us to increase our sortie rate and the already stretched 31st AEW at Aviano was told to expect another squadron or two of F-16CJs from Shaw AFB, South Carolina. It was time for us to go.

On Monday, 5 April, anticipating that the Italians might say "no," I called the commander of the British GR-7 detachment at Gioia del Colle to ask whether there was sufficient parking space for 18 A-10s. He told me, "Yes, there is. . . . We built our own parking areas and taxiways on the other side of the runway, so we've left plenty of room."

Eureka! I immediately called Col Gregg Sanders, an A-10 pilot and the 52d Fighter Wing's inspector general, who had recently been pressed into service in the planning division (C-5) at the CAOC. I told him about the situation at Gioia and asked if the CAOC would approve the 81st's sending a site-survey team there. Later that day, after coordinating with the local Italian authorities, he called back to say that our team could depart the next day to visit Gioia del Colle and Amendola.

Our team of maintainers, aviators, and support personnel took two days to complete their site visit and returned to Aviano on Wednesday, 7 April. Gioia del Colle was the clear choice. It had more available space on the aerodrome and more obtainable hotel accommodations in the local area. The next day we sent an advance echelon team, comprised of Sixteenth Air Force and 81st personnel, to Gioia to evaluate the facilities and determine what it would take for us to begin to operate. Their initial assessment was that it would require at least one week without flying to get it ready. There was not enough space to build up munitions, nor were there sufficient maintenance facilities. Two floors of an old dormitory (complete with beds), serviced by a finicky and outdated electrical system, would become our operations area. On 9 April we received EUCOM orders to have 15 jets in place at Gioia by 11 April.

The same order requested that Air Combat Command (ACC) deploy four A-10s from the continental United States (CONUS) to augment us. I called CAOC personnel to make sure they understood that the 81st had three additional aircraft at Spang that we could immediately bring to Gioia. They said, "No one here knew that." General Short had asked, "How many A-10s are at Aviano?" After the CAOC told him "15," he replied, "Get four more from ACC." It was too late to turn off the request, but we knew ACC couldn't generate the aircraft and fly them across the Atlantic for at least a week. I tried to get approval to bring in the three 81st FS jets. After I had called the CAOC, Sixteenth Air Force, NATO's Regional Headquarters Allied Forces Southern Europe (AFSOUTH) at Naples, EUCOM, and USAFE, I learned that publishing another EUCOM tasker in less than 24 hours for just three jets was in the "too hard to do" locker. However, I also learned that USAFE could move its own jets within the European theater without higher approval. After getting the CAOC to buy off on the idea, I asked my home wing leadership to weigh in for us. Brig Gen Scott Van Cleef, Col Jan-Marc Jouas, and Col Al Thompson came through, and on 10 April we got USAFE approval to fly the last three Spang A-10s into Gioia on 11 April.

The Move to Gioia

The move to Gioia del Colle on 11 April 1999 involved establishing full-up operations in near bare-base conditions and relocating people, equipment, and aircraft from both Spangdahlem and Aviano. The following week contained one of the least known but most impressive logistics accomplishments of OAF. Maintainers of the 81st FS and logisticians of the 52d and 31st AEWs had only one "down day" to pack up all the tools and equipment, and load them on trucks, "Cadillac bins," or pallets, while still maintaining a full CSAR alert of six aircraft and two spares. Even the right parts arrived at Aviano in time to replace those missing from our cannibalized aircraft (CANN bird), so we could fly it to Gioia. Our weapons loaders added extra bombs and missiles to the A-10s at Aviano to help cover our immediate munition needs. We estimated that it would take the munitions depot at Camp Darby, located on the Italian Riviera near Livorno, Italy, about three days to transport the weapons over the 500 miles to Gioia and begin routine deliveries. Eleven trucks departed Aviano for Gioia on 10 April. The next day, C-130s departed from Ramstein, Spangdahlem, and Aviano, and all 18 A-10s (15 from Aviano and three from Spangdahlem) took off on time and landed on time at Gioia del Colle. Colonel Thompson flew one of the three Spangdahlem A-10s to Gioia, where he established and assumed command of the new 40th EOG.

I arrived in the first jet to land at Gioia and was unpleasantly surprised to find a USAF cameraman filming us as we taxied in and climbed down the ladders. Airlift is a zero-sum game. If something is added, something else must be taken off. I was livid—what was a cameraman doing on the flight line when we barely had enough crew chiefs to recover our jets and enough airlift to move our most critical items? I didn't yell at him; he just got on the returning plane as ordered. I found out later that Ramstein had manifested combat camera personnel

Photo courtesy of author

A-10 with extra munitions deploying to Gioia

and equipment on the first C-130 to land at Gioia. While they were just trying to do their job—document our move and bed-down—they took up limited airlift capacity, and I'd much rather have had more toolboxes.

The maintainers already on site immediately went to work generating the aircraft necessary to bring up our CSAR alert status. We were down for only two hours—but even that delay would have been less if it were not for a fuel truck delay. These maintainers worked through the night—often without enough tools to go around. MSgt Daniel E. "Dan" Weber, MSgt Rod Many, and a number of key maintainers toiled for 24 hours straight to ensure we had jets to meet our tasking. The aircraft were ready for the next morning's AFAC lines, and the first sortie airborne appropriately logged a Maverick kill on a Serb APC.

Operations experts also sprang into action, setting up a functional intel section (crucial for CSAR and AFAC missions), secure telephones, an operations desk, and life support in less than 12 hours. By the morning of 12 April, our combat operations were up and running around-the-clock again.

Integration of the 40th Expeditionary Operations Group

Meanwhile the 74th FS Flying Tigers at Pope readied four aircraft, nine pilots, and 65 maintainers to send to the fight. We had asked ACC to provide pilots with a good level of experience, particularly in AFAC and CSAR missions. Once they arrived at Spangdahlem, USAFE told them they might be used to train the 81st's eight new pilots instead of joining the Panthers at Gioia. USAFE was aware of the capacity to park only 18 A-10s at Gioia, and those spots it knew were being used by the 81st. We had not yet informed USAFE that we had found room for four more A-10s. In a proposal to the CAOC, we highlighted the increased sortie rates we could achieve with those additional aircraft, and its leadership won the Italian government's approval. The Italian base commander wasn't pleased with either the process or the decision, but we didn't want to give him a chance to veto it—and we now had 22 Hogs to unleash in the KEZ. Colonel Thompson, as commander of the newly established 40th EOG, once again worked his magic, soothed hurt egos, and smoothed things over.

After some initial awkwardness, all of the 81st and 74th operations and maintenance functions became fully integrated into the 40th EOG. Flight leads from each squadron flew with wingmen from the other, and a Flying Tiger maintenance-production superintendent ran the daytime-sortie generation for all 22 aircraft. There was some good-natured hazing, particularly on Hog paint jobs. For some months, the 81st had taken care of a 74th jet that had been left in Kuwait after a deployment because of parts problems. It was eventually flown to Spangdahlem to be fixed. When that aircraft (the fifth Flying Tiger jet) arrived at Gioia, it not only had the trademark Flying Tiger shark's teeth on the nose but also huge, black panther heads on the engine nacelles. Soon afterwards, and with the same good-natured spirit, the lower jaws of the panther heads that decorated both engine nacelles were painted over in light gray, making the panthers look like rats.

Backbone of the Mission

All of the flight-line personnel worked together with inexhaustible energy and enthusiasm. After every sortie, crew chiefs and weapons loaders swarmed over the aircraft to prepare it for the next flight. Nothing motivates tired, greasy wrench turners more than seeing their jets—the ones they had launched fully loaded—come home with clean wings. Together, the 81st and

Pope A-10 with the Panther-Rat cowling

74th had a total of 26 A-10s in-theater. Of those, 22 were at Gioia del Colle, and at any given time at least two were undergoing major inspections at Spangdahlem. The 40th EOG normally flew 30 combat sorties with those 22 aircraft during the day between 0600 and 1830, and then used them to generate the six aircraft to stand CSAR alert between 1830 and 0600 the next morning. We launched up to 16 aircraft on each day's "first go" and then turned (postflighted, loaded, preflighted, and launched) 14 of those aircraft on the "second go" each day. The British also flew an aggressive schedule with their one forward-deployed squadron—sometimes launching 10 of their 12 GR-7s. The Italians eventually had 24 Tornados at Gioia del Colle, but we never saw them launch more than six aircraft at a time. As a matter of interest, the 40th EOG flew more sorties and hours in Allied Force than the entire Italian air force. The French air force deployed 15 of their Mirage 2000D strike aircraft to Gioia and, like most European air forces, swapped out their personnel after three to six weeks, flying only six days per week. By contrast the 40th EOG personnel knew we were there for the duration and flew seven days a week. We made an exception on 1 May 1999, the only OAF day we "took off"—even then we still maintained a 24-hour CSAR alert.

There is not enough room here to detail all of the incredible feats of professionalism that molded the 81st FS, 74th FS, 40th ELS, and 40th Expeditionary Air Base Squadron (EABS) into an efficient fighting team. The numerous small things were exemplified by our first sergeant, SMSgt Stanley J. "Stan" Ellington, who went to a local grocery store to buy food on the first day for folks who never left their jets. Chaplain (Maj) Karl Wiersum's frequent visits to the flight line—just to listen to people who needed to talk—made a world of difference in putting jets in the air and bringing them back again. Every member of our team played an absolutely crucial role in carrying out the mission, and the following stories can relate only a small part of it. Every pilot knew that no excuse could justify missing the target when all of those people had done all of that work to put him in a cockpit with an enemy tank in his sights.

USAF Photos

Crew chiefs generating aircraft and finishing the forms

Commanding the 40th Expeditionary Operations Group

Col Al "Moose" Thompson

Operation Allied Force was my first true combat experience, and I was the 40th EOG commander deployed to Gioia del Colle

AB in southern Italy. At our peak, we had 25 A-10 aircraft from the 81st EFS and the 74th EFS and nearly 700 personnel.

USAF Photo

40th EOG Hogwalk

Combat operations began against Serbia on 24 March 1999. The 81st EFS from Spangdahlem, flying the trusty A-10, participated from day one of the air campaign while deployed to Aviano. The 74th EFS from Pope joined us at Gioia del Colle.

When it became apparent early in the NATO air campaign that Aviano-based A-10s could not be optimally employed because of the long distances to Kosovo, they found a new home at Gioia del Colle, an Italian air force fighter base. The 81st was out of the bomb-dropping business for only 36 hours while it deployed forward to Gioia del Colle. By air, it was only about 240 nautical miles (NM) from Gioia to Pristina—the capital of Kosovo province. This record-setting deployment was truly a Herculean effort and significantly increased our on-station time and combat effectiveness.

I faced the opportunity and challenge of a lifetime when Brig Gen Scott P. Van Cleef, the 52d AEW commander, selected me to stand up and command the 40th EOG at Gioia. On 11 April I deployed to Gioia with three A-10s from Spangdahlem to fill out the 81st's 18-aircraft squadron. It may seem unusual for a vice wing commander to command an expeditionary group. Although it did not happen, initial thinking had this group expanding to an expeditionary fighter wing.

USAF Photo

Col Al Thompson and Brig Gen Scott Van Cleef

A Commander's Concerns

I had to set priorities quickly and get organized upon arrival at Gioia del Colle. The first priority was to meet each day's ATO in the variety of missions tasked by Lt Gen Mike Short, the combined forces air component commander (CFACC), at the CAOC in northern Italy. Just as important was mission safety on the ground and in the air. The peacetime rules, of course, did not go away, and a host of new ones for combat operations—known as ROEs—came into play.

My third priority (frankly, they were all nearly equal in importance) was taking care of the men and women charged with performing the mission. I knew I could depend on all of them to do their very best. I wanted to set our basic direction, keep us focused, and rely on the leaders at all levels from my four squadron commanders (two fighter, one support, and one logistics) all the way down to dedicated crew chiefs. None of us knew how long the air campaign would last, so we each had to be prepared for the long haul. There was no time for distractions—we just sent home anyone not pulling his or her weight or not demonstrating absolute professional behavior. While I tried not to add a lot of extra rules for our deployed situation, but those few I did add had a direct effect on the mission and force protection.

Gioia del Colle is a large NATO air base designed to accept other squadrons during conflict. Upon our arrival we were given several ramps for A-10 parking, four hardened aircraft shelters for our maintenance functions, and some administrative space as well. The base is blessed with two long, parallel runways, and the weather in the spring and summer is normally clear except for some morning fog. Since Gioia del Colle is a fighter base, our integration did not pose a huge problem. Because Gioia was so close to Kosovo, many other NATO squadrons still desired to bed down there—even long after we arrived, when it was bursting at the seams.

From day one, the Italian 36th Stormo (Wing) was a great host despite our almost overnight deployment. Although the 36th Stormo provided lots of space and such basics as fuel, electricity, and water, we were on our own for everything else. I spent lots of time maintaining good relations and working particular issues with the Italians and the RAF detachment. The Brits had been regularly deployed to Gioia during the previous five years to support sorties over Bosnia-Herzegovina. The RAF had great insight and experience on how to fit in and work smoothly with the Italian hosts. The Italians flew Tornado fighter-bombers and the older F-104 Starfighters. The British flew the GR-7, more commonly called the Harrier. Challenges with our host wing were frequent; the following account highlights a couple of them.

Our group had most of the functions that a wing would have. Our Air Force security forces, all 13 strong, were forbidden by the Italians to carry weapons. The Italian military had primary responsibility for security both inside and outside the base fence. In the first days after arrival, we found several holes cut in the fence next to our parked A-10s—not a good sign. Shortly after, a bomb threat was directed at our personnel in one hotel. Additionally, our Italian hosts were very concerned about our safety off base and the number and location of hotels we had contracted. Hence we avoided taking military vehicles off base and took other precautions as well.

Another challenge was getting an accurate reading on the weather during foggy mornings to determine if our first-go sorties would be permitted to take off. Leaving out the technical details, the way the USAF computes the visibility and ceiling is slightly different than the Italians' procedure. There is no exactly right or wrong way to do this. If done independently, both national measurement methods and weather minimums would allow aircraft to operate under similar conditions. However, the Italians' methods for measuring ceiling and visibility are more conservative than ours, and our weather criteria are more conservative than theirs. When Italian measurements were applied to US criteria, US aircraft were prevented from taking off under weather conditions that Italian rules deemed suitable for take off. We were hamstrung by this situation on several mornings and, in my view, lost sorties unnecessarily. We worked quickly to find a compromise with the host base and tower personnel. Afterward we essentially used our own weather data for determining take-off minimums; under our Air Force and USAFE regulations, I also had a limited waiver authority, which I exercised on foggy mornings. These alternatives were sound and safe. All pilots had the right to decline to launch if they thought the weather was too bad, but none ever refused.

Driving in southern Italy can be very risky, and, sadly, we had several major car wrecks. Some of the accidents resulted in serious injuries but, thankfully, no fatalities. While I was in command, the most serious accident involved a senior maintenance supervisor who drove back to his hotel alone after a 12-hour night shift. He fell asleep and literally drove a full-size guardrail through the center of his rental car from front to back. Going through, it struck the side of his face and shoulder. If the car seat had not given way instantly to lessen the blow, he would have died on the spot. He received emergency treatment, an immediate operation in an Italian civilian hospital, and was then flown by the USAF Aeromedical Evacuation system (Medevac) to the United States to complete his recovery.

We also had a serious aircraft-parking problem at Gioia with fully combat-loaded A-10s lined up a few feet from each other on two closely spaced concrete ramps. Since we did not meet any of the Air Force weapons-safety criteria, we required a three-star

USAFE waiver just to operate. If a single rocket had gone off or an engine had caught fire on start, we could have lost all of the A-10s and a few hundred personnel in seconds. This situation reminded me of a similarly congested parking problem at Bien Hoa AB, South Vietnam, early in the Vietnam War. The enemy fired mortars one night and destroyed many aircraft. The aircraft vulnerability at Gioia was not acceptable and had to be improved. During the visit of the secretary of the Air Force and the commander of USAFE, I walked them both down the entire ramp to ensure they were aware of the parking situation. More importantly, I briefed them on our plan of action—to quickly build five temporary asphalt parking pads around the airfield so not more than four A-10s would be at risk from any one incident.

The EOG made an incredible effort to get engines, pods, and parts to keep the jets flying at a high rate, and to build and load the bombs, missiles, and bullets. Taking care of the personnel was no easy task either, but it was done with great focus, energy, and class. Our parent wing, the 52d at Spangdahlem, provided around-the-clock support, and no task was too hard for it. I had gained valuable experience, which really helped me accomplish the overall mission by serving as the wing's vice commander and regularly flying with the 81st before the conflict began. General Van Cleef exhibited remarkable leadership and we talked almost daily. Even though he had his hands full as the AEW commander, he still found time to visit us several times and see us in action. General Short's *Air Forces' forces rear* (a term he used to describe the USAFE staff) was also spectacular and provided world-class support.

I tried to fly almost every other day, but that was only one key part of my command. Staying on top of the myriad of issues on the ground was equally important, as was hosting visiting dignitaries and military leaders. We had the press to deal with, but we were not their main interest in Italy or even at Gioia. I visited as many maintenance functions as I could each day, usually on my expeditionary bicycle. As the senior safety officer, I visited each CSAR ground-alert crew and aircraft daily during the entire conflict.

We were essentially on our own to establish and maintain communications with higher headquarters. We had the deployable wing-information communications package that included about 30 high-tech specialists led by a young captain. The package's equipment included a satellite dish, switchboard, and all the key communications capability we needed. The team was spectacular and worked tirelessly to get us set up in a few short days with all the military communications critical to performing our mission. They ensured we had the ATO in time to plan and execute each day's missions.

I was scheduled to fly on 27 missions during the 60 days I commanded the EOG. Three of my sorties were cancelled because of bad weather, so I ended up flying 24 long and hard sorties over Kosovo. My first mission was on 15 April with the 81st EFS commander to southeastern Serbia. I was really keyed up and had much on my mind. The night before I got only about three hours of sleep—not ideal for my first taste of combat. We were on an AFAC mission, primarily working the Kumanovo Valley, a Serb area northeast of Skopje, Macedonia, that includes the towns of Presevo, Bujanovac, and Vranje.

I flew as number two, having the primary responsibility of keeping lead from getting shot down and then attacking the targets he assigned me. His job was to find military targets and then control a variety of NATO fighters during their attacks. We

USAF Photo

Lt Col Chris Haave and Col Al Thompson debrief their mission

launched from Gioia del Colle with a typical combat load. The weather on this first mission was incredible, not a cloud in the sky. We pushed in after "tanking" (aerial refueling) and lots of airborne coordination, and then immediately began searching for ground targets. Since this was the first day we could use Macedonian airspace to fly attack missions, we had not yet worked this valley. Therefore, targets were plentiful, but so were SAMs and AAA. Not long after we entered the area, I called a break turn for a shoulder-fired SAM. I was not sure I called it in time since I saw its smoke trail pass between our two aircraft. AAA was everywhere that morning, most of it well below our altitude. I was excited, to say the least, and felt this would be a long and hard-fought air campaign. We found, attacked, and killed several targets, including some artillery and APCs.

During all of our sorties, our total focus was on the mission. We had no reservations about what our president, secretary of defense, and NATO commanders had tasked us to do. The horror of nearly a million Kosovo refugees fleeing their homes was more than enough reason. I was ever mindful of the great tragedy unfolding on the ground before our eyes. Villages were being burned every day, masses of humanity were camping in the most austere conditions in the hills, and innocent people were being forced to flee their homeland with everything they owned pulled by farm tractors. Families were separated, and, as we learned much later, untold atrocities were being committed.

Our overarching mission was very clear—find and destroy the Serb military in and around Kosovo, reduce its capability, and inhibit its ability to move and operate. The mission was always very difficult since there was no direct threat of a NATO ground invasion. The Serb army and MUP could—and did—hide from us, commandeering and using civilian vehicles to move around. Hence, finding and attacking a massed military ground force in the traditional sense was not in the cards.

Life seemed surreal flying home over the Adriatic after the first mission. Fatigue set in immediately after landing. After over five hours in the air, I felt almost too tired to climb out of the aircraft—I vowed to do better next time.

The most difficult missions were our CSAR or Sandy missions. Capt Buster Cherrey, mission commander on the successful rescue of an F-117 pilot downed deep inside Serbia, was awarded the Silver Star for gallantry. He was recognized by the president of the United States on 27 January 2000 during the State of the Union Address:

> And we should be proud of the men and women of our Armed Forces and those of our allies who stopped the ethnic cleansing in Kosovo, enabling a million people to return to their homes.
>
> When Slobodan Milosevic unleashed his terror on Kosovo, Capt John Cherrey was one of the brave airmen who turned the tide. And when another American plane was shot down over Serbia, he flew into the teeth of enemy air defenses to bring his fellow pilot home. Thanks to our Armed Forces' skill and bravery, we prevailed in Kosovo without losing a single American in combat. I want to introduce Captain Cherrey to you. We honor Captain Cherrey, and we promise you, Captain, we'll finish the job you began.[1]

I flew a mission on 9 June, the last day we were authorized to expend ordnance. We found and attacked several APCs in southern Kosovo near Mount Osljak before my air conditioner control froze in the full-cold position, which forced our return to Gioia. For over an hour I flew in a frigid cockpit and thought my toes would suffer frostbite until the valve somehow freed itself.

By 10 June my AEW commander wanted me back at Spangdahlem, and Col Gregg Sanders, my extremely capable deputy, was ready to take over. I flew home solo in the A-10 on 11 June, after assembling and thanking all of the fine airmen. I could not find the right words of appreciation for their dedication, hard work, and professionalism. What an unbelievable effort by every one of them—I have never been prouder of an all-ranks group of airmen in my entire life! Readjusting to the parent wing—52d AEW—was difficult, and I immediately turned my energy to helping reconstitute our wing's force.

Lessons Learned

It is important to review observations and lessons learned, in many cases lessons relearned, or lessons validated under fire. In no exact order, here are mine:

- With solid leadership, training, and equipment, anything is possible. Any clear mission is attainable over time. No one can precisely predict the time necessary to complete an air campaign or any other type of campaign.

- Realistic training and exercises pay off in combat. Those experiences provide confidence to commanders and airmen at all levels. Realistic training and exercises also help develop tactics and procedures that, in turn, minimize learning on-the-fly and unnecessary mistakes.

- Experienced pilots are a force multiplier. Both the 81st and the 74th were blessed with mature pilots and high levels of A-10 experience. This is not to say that the young pilots struggled—they did not. However, our combat experience was enhanced and our risks minimized by having experienced pilots leading in the air, reviewing all aspects of our daily operations, and then guiding everything from the daily flying schedule to combat tactics.

- Combat is team building and teamwork in its finest hour. Our flying-squadron organization worked in peace and war. It was one team, with one boss, going in one direction, and with everyone pulling his or her weight. There were no divisions, no competition, or conflicts between maintenance and operations.

- Clear communication between the squadron, group, and headquarters is crucial to success. You know it's a "bad day" when the CFACC invites you for a face-to-face talk because someone in your command has failed to "follow his published guidance." Such a communications failure makes his job of commanding the air war more difficult.

- Regular deployments working with allies facilitate future fighter operations in a coalition air campaign against a determined adversary. Knowing and trusting one's allies before the shooting starts are imperative to the successful execution of an air campaign.

- General Jumper's principle of "tough love" saves time and trouble when things get difficult. He emphasizes establishing and communicating expectations and then holding everyone accountable to those standards. Any required action was fair, firm, and quick. I found nearly all of the 40th EOG ready to fight and win; those few that were not were sent packing.

- There should never be an expectation that A-10s can fly 5,000-plus combat hours in a 360-degree threat without a loss. To have flown an entire air campaign without a combat loss is a miracle, unlikely to ever be repeated, and should never be an expectation of war planners, senior leaders, or politicians.

- Pilots will forever resist political restrictions that defy the principles of war and air and space power doctrine. However, they will unhesitatingly follow those restrictions to the letter. These pilots deserve to have the rationale for the restrictions explained, particularly when lives are at stake. They also deserve to have those restrictions regularly reviewed for operational necessity.

- The quality of our parent wing's maintenance, effectiveness of its training, courage of its pilots, and superb quality of its leadership enabled the 52d AEW to fly more than 3,500 combat sorties for over 15,000 hours in F-117s, F-16CJs, and A-10s against a determined enemy and in a high-threat environment without any combat losses and with exceptional effectiveness. But this absence belies the high threat! The Serbs had a fully integrated, robust, and lethal air defense system and used it cunningly, firing over 700 missiles and millions of rounds of AAA.

- Many people sacrificed much to support the air campaign. Our wing had over 1,200 of its 5,000 active duty personnel deployed for up to six months. The families left behind took care of our children, sent us care packages, and prayed for our safe return. I will never forget seeing all the yellow ribbons tied around trees at Spangdahlem AB when I came home.

As everyone should know, freedom is never free—it puts at risk and may cost the lives of our soldiers, sailors, marines, and airmen. There is no better air force in the world today than our United States Air Force; the hardworking, dedicated airmen of all ranks deployed all around the world make it great. Since we are back to our expeditionary roots—not off chasing some new idea—and doing what we have done well for most of our history, we must have an expeditionary mind-set. Finally, NATO's tremendous value and the role it plays in this rapidly changing and dangerous world cannot be overstated. NATO proved false the prediction that it could not stay together until the end—and did so convincingly.

Redeployment, Beddown, and Maintenance

Maj Dave Brown

All those maintainers assigned or attached to the 81st EFS during OAF put forth the necessary effort and were directly responsible for keeping the aircraft flying—24 hours a day for 78 consecutive days. Both obvious and not so obvious things went on behind the scenes during this conflict.

To say we showed up, did our jobs, and went home would in many aspects be correct. However, that statement would not do justice to all the individuals who went the extra mile and gave their all every day. Their total commitment was demonstrated not only during the campaign but also during the months leading up to it. When the 81st FS left Spangdahlem in January 1999 for a 30-day rotation at Aviano to support Operation Joint Forge, our jets were already in good shape. Despite having to deal with serious parts shortages and an aging airframe, our maintainers did everything within their control to keep our A-10s fully mission capable and at the same time support an aggressive flying-training program. Our crew chiefs kept their deferred discrepancies—those identified, noncritical aircraft problems whose correction had been delayed to an appropriate time in the future—to a minimum. Our maintenance schedulers worked our phase flow at a healthy 220-hour average, and our time-change items were all in compliance, with nothing deferred or coming due in the near future.

We usually looked forward to a trip to Aviano. This one was no different. It was to be a short 30 days in northern Italy supporting Bosnian overflights. Aviano was a "full up" air base with nearly all the comforts of home. Maintenance support was available, to include supplies and equipment. Aviano also had a base exchange, commissary, and eating establishments on and off base. As tensions began to heat up in the Balkans, we were extended for an additional 30 days, while political efforts attempted to resolve the crisis. As we got closer to the March deadline, we were extended indefinitely. We immediately added a couple of A-10s to our forces at Aviano, bringing our total to eight; by the time air operations commenced on 24 March, we were up to 15 Hogs on station—all ready for the fight.

Aviano AB was crowded with over 150 airframes of various types on station. We had one hardened aircraft shelter that held two A-10s—one CANN aircraft and usually one that was undergoing unscheduled maintenance due to an in-flight write-up. The other 13 Hogs were parked outside—up to three per hardstand. This created an additional workload for the maintainers by requiring additional tow jobs at the end of the scheduled flying period; it also necessitated some creative planning during launches. We continued to generate more and more sorties, as well as CSAR alert lines. Due to our 24-hour CSAR commitment, we did not enjoy the eight- to 10-hour down period to maintain our aircraft that many of the other units had. We usually flew our tasked sorties during the day and then assumed nighttime (airborne or ground) CSAR alert. Most other flying units had either a day mission or a night mission. Due to our capabilities, we had both. We would postflight our last sorties of the day and immediately start reconfiguring jets to cover the night CSAR alert tasking. This dual tasking presented many challenges and resulted in a full schedule—one that challenged our aircraft, aircrew, and maintenance resources every day.

This pace continued for the next couple of weeks with our pilots flying long sorties—often exceeding seven hours. Aviano continued to receive and bed down additional fighter aircraft. By 7 April, it had over 170 aircraft on station and was looking for a place to park more F-16s. To help reduce our sortie length and make room for more aircraft at Aviano, the 81st looked for a new location further south that would be closer to the KEZ. We were tasked to send a senior maintainer on a site survey trip to several southern Italian air bases. CMSgt Ray Ide, our rep, evaluated three bases during a 12-hour trip on

USAF Photo by TSgt Blake Borsic

SrA Nick Kraska working on a jet

6 April 1999. When he came back he said, "Gioia del Colle will work, but we need about a week to spin it up to minimum standards." There were no munitions on base, no munitions-storage or buildup area, no dedicated facilities for use by maintenance, and virtually no back-shop maintenance support in place. By the next day, rumors were rampant, and most folks anticipated relocation in about two weeks.

Shortly after I arrived at work on Thursday, 8 April, I was tasked to visit Gioia del Colle for a more in-depth site survey. I was accompanied by some Sixteenth Air Force logistics reps. We arrived at our destination late that night and were ready to get busy the next morning. We had all day Friday to look at the base. From a maintenance perspective, I could tell instantly that we had our work cut out to make it suitable. We would be able to use only one of the hardened aircraft shelters for the entire maintenance package—which had now grown to 22 A-10s (18 from Spangdahlem and four from Pope). This increase also meant that additional personnel and equipment would be required. We went toe-to-toe with the Italian air force and were able to gain a second shelter. We would still be a little crowded, but we were definitely much better off with the additional shelter and would be able to set up our back-shop support in one

88

shelter and run the flight-line maintenance-support section and mobility-readiness spares package in the other.

Eventually we would add a small garage-type building that would house our nondestructive-inspection, wheel-and-tire, and repair-and-reclamation sections. This arrangement would be the extent of our shelter facilities for the duration of OAF. Since we were unable to get any more hangar space to work our CANN aircraft or to conduct any heavy maintenance, we would have to be creative with pallet bags and tarps to cover and protect areas of the CANN aircraft from the elements and debris.

On Friday, 9 April, we not only learned that we would redeploy to Gioia del Colle, but also got the other "good news" that we would do it on Sunday—in two days. Our focus instantly changed from the site-survey mode to the advanced echelon (ADVON) mode, and we knew we were way behind the power curve. I now had a day and a half to prepare to receive 18 A-10s with more to follow shortly as the 74th FS Hogs made their way across the Atlantic from Pope to Gioia. To further complicate our planning, we learned that we would have to vacate Aviano on Saturday by 1200 due to a large local war demonstration expected to take place at the main gate that afternoon. Our list of "must haves" was instantly growing. We had located initial work areas, located billeting to accommodate 400 personnel as we stood up an expeditionary operations group, and worked a contract shuttle bus for the one-hour trip between our accommodations and the base. We wrapped up what we could on Friday and Saturday and then proceeded to pick up our ADVON team of aircraft maintainers on Saturday afternoon. Sunday was coming way too fast. We managed to sneak in a pretty decent meal at the hotel before hitting the sack early in preparation for the big day that lay ahead of us.

Sunday the 11th went really well. We recovered (parked and performed postflight inspections) all 15 A-10s from Aviano and three more from Spangdahlem as scheduled. We were now waiting on the transportation system to catch up. Our relocation had not been without problems. Because our initial request for airlift had been denied, we had contracted for commercial trucks to supplement the assets the US Army Transportation Command had in Italy to move our equipment from Aviano to Gioia del

Colle. We had nearly one-half of our equipment on the road by the time we convinced the decision makers that this approach would not get our sortie-generation equipment to us in time to meet the schedule for six CSAR alert lines that night, and our tasked sorties for the next day. We were finally allocated some C-130 airlift and were able to get a limited amount of key equipment to Gioia, but it remained far from an ideal situation. One of the redeployment's most frustrating moments was the excitement of seeing our first C-130 on final, anticipating the delivery of our much-needed sortie-generation equipment, only to find that some of our materiel had been delayed to make room for a combat camera crew. The crew was there to cover our activity at Gioia del Colle as we began to regenerate our jets. Cameramen were absolutely our last priority since they weren't among the things we needed to have on station to get our A-10s ready to fight—but I figured they would at least be able to take some nice pictures of our 18 static-display aircraft the next morning if the stuff they had displaced didn't make it.

The flow of equipment and tools from Aviano could not have been worse. We had gone into great detail in planning the order we needed to receive the equipment at Gioia del Colle, but since the operational methods varied among the numerous transportation contractors we used, some shipments unexpectedly took longer than others to make the trip. Some trucks had two drivers and did not stop en route. Others had only one driver who took two or more days to make the trip due to overnight

USAF Photo

A-10s and crew chiefs at Gioia del Colle AB

stops for rest. It appeared that almost everything showed up in reverse order. The one movement we had control over was the equipment we used to get the jets out of Aviano. After the Panther launch, we loaded that equipment onto the C-130s, and it made it to Gioia shortly after the Hogs arrived. That limited C-130 airlift support probably saved our efforts and allowed us to meet Sixteenth Air Force's aggressive timeline.

Keeping track of everyone was another redeployment challenge. We did not have a personnel accountability (PERSCO) team on hand to track the people who were showing up from Aviano and Spangdahlem. An Air Force PERSCO team would normally complete all personnel actions required to support deployed commanders, such as reception processing, casualty reporting, sustainment actions, redeployment and accountability of Air Force personnel, and management of myriad other personnel-related programs. Without their help, we did everything we could to catch everyone on their way in, get a copy of their orders, and record some basic information that included their room assignments.

The first three days at Gioia del Colle were absolutely the most difficult. Many of us had already put in a few very long days to get the jets from Aviano to Gioia. Those who had worked a lengthy shift to generate and launch the jets at Aviano jumped on the C-130 for a two-hour flight to Gioia and then went right to work to get our Hogs ready to meet the Monday frag. We did our best to ensure that our technicians stuck to a 12-hour schedule, but that didn't always work out. It was easy to have people working over 24 hours with little more than a nap. We cut our maintenance crews back to the minimum necessary to prepare the aircraft to meet our CSAR alert for Sunday and get the first eight aircraft ready for Monday. We prepped six front lines and two spares to cover Monday and put everyone else on shift, letting them get some much-needed and well-deserved rest.

Five A-10s and about 70 personnel from the 74th FS at Pope were headed our way. They had been holding at Spangdahlem until our redeployment fate was decided, and then held a few additional days to let us settle in. With all that was going on with our own redeployment, inheriting additional aircraft and personnel added to my list of things to do and worry about. Some

USAF Photo by TSgt Blake Borsic

A1C David Hatch from the 23d Fighter Group, Pope AFB, and SrA Jeff Burns from the 81st FS, Spangdahlem AB, troubleshoot an IFF write-up

unique maintenance issues had to be resolved as we molded aircraft and personnel from Pope and Spangdahlem into a deployed unit under the air and space expeditionary force (AEF) concept. We did what we had to do by the book and applied common sense as much as possible. We encouraged team integrity by letting the dedicated crew chiefs work their own jets, and we took the team approach to the rest of the maintenance workload. Once we got through the initial growing pains, things seemed to work well. Everyone shared the goals of generating safe and reliable aircraft to support NATO's missions and of bringing all of our pilots home safely.

We faced several other challenges in addition to a hectic redeployment with an almost impossible timeline. We were in a small town in southern Italy with none of the "conveniences" of home. We arrived on a weekend and were pretty much unable to work any support issues that involved the locals, such as portable toilets, bottled water, or any type of eating facility for our troops. The RAF and the Italian air force were gracious enough to allow us to use their facilities to cover our needs for the weekend, and that enabled most of our day shifters to get a good meal. We were able to scrounge up some "meals ready to eat" (MRE) for our

USAF Photo

Fully integrated—81st and 74th jets on the Gioia flight line

night shifters, and a few of the other troops were able to go off base before their shift and find grocery stores or restaurants to meet their needs. Positive attitudes and a strong sense of mission were the keys to making the redeployment work.

We were not able to provide such basic needs as bathrooms, bottled water, and meals for the first three days—even so, I heard absolutely no complaints. For the most part, everyone was too busy and tired to worry about it, and I think just knowing the problem was being worked was enough for the majority. Everyone's dedication was incredible. We had to order some people to leave work because we knew they had been there way over their 12-hour limit. Attitude was everything. I cannot say enough about the effort put forth by the maintainers—those on the flight line and those in support roles. Our liquid oxygen for the first day's flying was courtesy of an innovative liquid-fuels specialist. Our equipment to fill the bottles was still en route. The specialist knew that Brindisi AB was just an hour or so down the road and he took all of our aircraft bottles and brought them back full. Had he not done so, our first flights on Monday would have not made it off the ground. It was this sort of dedication and creativity that kept us in the fight until our cargo caught up with us a few days later.

Once our equipment was in place, we began to settle into a routine. Our hotel was a 75-minute drive away. Adding two-and-a-half hours of driving to a 12-hour shift wasn't the route we wanted to take. Once we resolved some initial scheduling issues and adjusted the shuttle schedule, the bus system worked great. It was definitely the way to go.

A typical day at Gioia was pretty fast paced. At the height of the air campaign, we were launching 16 aircraft on the first go and usually 14 on the afternoon go. We used a UHF/VHF-equipped Humvee as the production superintendent's vehicle. This enabled us to talk to the pilots and "ops desk" to get aircraft status on the inbound so we could begin to line up the afternoon sorties and have technicians standing by to begin to work the inflight write-ups. We definitely had a full plate turning the aircraft from the first go to the second go.

Our configuration was typically four Mk-82 low-drag bombs, two AGM-65 Maverick air-to-ground missiles, 30 mm combat mix ammunition, 14 2.75-inch rockets, two AIM-9 air-to-air missiles, chaff/flare, Pave Penny pod, and an ALQ-131 electronic countermeasures (ECM) pod. Obviously, our crew chiefs,

USAF Photo by TSgt Blake Borsic

Using a bike to get around the flight line at Gioia

weapons loaders, and system specialists were all busy. They worked in-flight write-ups, conducted aircraft postflight inspections, loaded munitions, and refueled—all of this had to come together in about two hours and 30 minutes. Our production superintendents orchestrated the activity on the line, and the troops hustled each and every day of the campaign to make it happen. Both the day and night crews did a remarkable job of keeping track of the frag, necessary configurations, and CSAR alert. We scrambled our CSAR-alert aircraft on the nights the F-117 and F-16 were shot down, and again on several other occasions. We took our CSAR-alert commitment very seriously, knowing that lives depended on it.

We also had to watch each of our aircraft's phase-inspection timeline. Each A-10 must undergo a phase inspection after 100 hours of flying time to discover and repair problems that might have been missed during normal preflight and postflight inspections. We flew about 75 total hours and accomplished one 100-hour phase inspection at Spangdahlem each day at the beginning of the conflict. As the demand for airborne CSAR alert, AFAC, and A-10 strike missions grew, we were soon flying over 100 hours each day. We knew this would quickly become a problem because we were "earning back" only 100 hours per day with our current flow of one aircraft through phase. We quickly elevated the options: we needed to cut back down to below 100 hours a day, perform contingency phase inspections, or bring in enough personnel and equipment from the combat air forces (CAF) to stand up a second A-10 phase dock at Spangdahlem. We chose the third option. Those who stayed behind at Spangdahlem to perform A-10 phase inspections were just as valuable to the effort as those of us who deployed. Without the hard work and long duty hours performing these vital inspections on our A-10s, we would not have been able to keep up with our NATO taskings. Again, it was truly a total team effort, both at home station and Gioia del Colle.

Daily sustainability issues were initially challenging. We had no Air Force infrastructure to support us. Our spares packages were sparse, and any parts coming into country via premium transportation (Federal Express and DHL Worldwide Express) were subject to Italian customs inspectors. This worked well

Monday through Friday, but we had no customs support over the weekend or on Italian holidays. This became frustrating when a part hit the airport on a Friday afternoon and we knew we wouldn't see it before Monday afternoon when the delivery would be made. This was the single biggest issue that we were not able to resolve during the conflict. We learned to live with it but didn't like it because it was often the one part we needed to return a jet to mission-capable status. We did get the luxury of a twice-weekly rotator flight back to Ramstein for ECM pod and precision measuring equipment laboratory (PMEL) support. We also used this flight to get parts and other needed items from home station, especially those short-notice items.

Looking back, I can honestly say that the only reason we were able to maintain our hectic pace was the dedicated team effort by all involved. Although it was a "pilot's war," I was proud to witness the support of the Air Force ground team—flight-line backshop, munitions maintenance, supply, transportation, personnel, administrative, finance, contracting, and the list goes on. They were all there to provide support—and they did it well. Their behind-the-scenes efforts were key ingredients in the success of the A-10s supporting KEZ operations from Gioia.

Getting There from Here

Capt Kevin "Boo" Bullard

My memory of how the 74th FS got involved in OAF is a little hazy, but I think it all started with a planned deployment for the 81st FS to Kuwait. The boys from Spangdahlem were supposed to go down to Al Jaber AB, Kuwait, for a standard desert rotation to participate in Operation Southern Watch, also known as OSW. They were scheduled to arrive in Kuwait around late March or early April 1999, but there was a glitch in the plan.

By early March 1999, the 81st FS had been tasked to be on call for the situation that was brewing between the Federal Republic of Yugoslavia (FRY) and NATO over the disputed region of Kosovo. There was no way the squadron could be on call and still meet its OSW tasking, so reinforcements had to be brought in. This is the point in time when the 74th got involved.

I guess I've heard about a million reasons why the 74th FS was chosen to participate in helping the Spang guys with their predicament, but I think it all had to do with geographical location and timing. Geographically, the A-10s at Pope were the closest to Germany, and it just made sense to me that we should be going. The 75th FS, our sister squadron at Pope, had just participated in an operational readiness inspection (ORI) for our wing at Moody AFB and had been on a pretty aggressive deployment schedule prior to the ORI. I don't think our local leadership at Pope was willing to send the 75th guys after all their recent time on the road. That left us, the 74th Flying Tigers, to foot the bill.

The plan, at least the way it was briefed to us, was for the 74th FS to fly six or eight jets over to Germany to be the "on call" guys for NATO. At this time, NATO was fairly sure that Milosevic would capitulate and comply with all its demands, just like he had done in the past when threatened with military intervention. After we arrived in Germany, the 81st would then move out to the desert for a vacation in exotic Southwest Asia. The 81st could meet its OSW obligation and we could provide immediate help for NATO if needed. This sounded like a logical solution. The hard part would be to decide who would stay home and who would go to Germany.

The "list," as it was affectionately called, contained all the names of the individuals chosen to participate in this pop-up deployment. It was not surprising that every pilot in our squadron wanted to go. We all had visions of flying at low altitude over the entire European continent without any concerns except where we would be eating that night. I was told very early in the process that I was on the list, and I knew it would be a tough thing to relay to my wife. I imagined what her response would be. I could already hear her saying, "You're going where? For how long? Why?" I know the list changed several times, but my name remained. I waited until I knew for sure that I was going to Germany before I broke the news to my wife. During that time, things in Kosovo had taken a bad turn. The Serbs were not going to comply with NATO's demands, and now there would be an armed response.

Obviously, the Spang Hogs were not going to Kuwait with the current situation in eastern Europe, and their immediate priority was to support anything NATO needed. Well, the bombs started dropping on 24 March, and OAF started to take shape. We, the 74th FS, were now told that we would fly four jets over to Spangdahlem to be a "rear echelon" force. Our primary purpose would be to fly with the few pilots of the 81st who were not mission ready (MR) and upgrade them to combat status. This was not the most noble of missions when there was a war to be fought, but that is what we were ordered to do. Certainly they (whoever "they" may have been) would not let a group of fully trained, combat-ready Hog drivers sit around an empty squadron staring at each other across a mission-planning table, wondering what training profile they would fly the next day.

On Sunday, 11 April, the 74th pilots on the list were contacted and told to be ready to deploy to Germany within 48 hours. Our tasking was still a bit nebulous. We were now being told there was a distinct possibility we would be joining the Spang boys in Italy to take part in OAF. It was at this point I felt obligated to let my wife in on the news, and I searched for the right words to tell her.

My wife is always one to worry, so I kept the whole deployment possibility a secret until it became certain I was going. Looking back on it all, I wonder if I should have kept her informed as I received details of the trip to Europe. However, there was no sense getting her upset at the mere chance of going on this thing, and I would do it the same way if I had to do it again.

Of course my wife cried when I told her I was going, but she knew that this was exactly why I was in this business. We had a long night discussing all the potential scenarios, but she kept coming back to a promise she wanted me to make—to assure her I would come back alive without any differences in my personality or demeanor. Basically, she wanted what any normal woman would want from a husband going into combat.

On the morning of 12 April, all the guys who were going to Germany got together in our squadron briefing room and discussed the upcoming events. An air of controlled excitement ran through the entire bunch. No one really knew what was about to take place, but we were certain we were headed for a big adventure. Our group commander eventually came down to the squadron and filled us in on what he thought our role would be in OAF.

The information that our commander gave us could not have been more wrong. He told us that we would be the 74th EFS, flying only with our own squadron mates and in our own jets. He also told us we would be fragged on the ATO as the 74th EFS (not the 81st EFS) and warned us about being pushed around by our new combat leadership once we got in-theater. He was very keen on maintaining our identity as a separate combat unit, complete with our own maintenance and set of taskings. This was indeed a pipe dream, but we didn't realize it at the time. We all nodded and blindly accepted his briefing as gospel.

On Tuesday, 13 April, the day had come for us to depart. I spent all day packing and avoided direct contact with my wife. I figured if I kept busy, I could keep my mind off the moment when I would have to say good-bye. It was very tense in my house. I had my game face on, my wife was on the verge of tears, and my two young daughters still weren't sure what was going on. Around 2000 hours, my wife and kids drove me to our squadron, and the good-bye was certainly something I will never forget. The thought of never seeing my family again did cross my mind, but I quickly reassured myself it would never happen to me. I figured being a prisoner of war (POW) was the worst thing that could possibly happen, and that would be a long shot.

I finally made it to Gioia del Colle on 20 April, having stopped at the Azores and Spangdahlem en route. The flight down from Germany to Italy was truly spectacular with beautiful views of the Swiss Alps and the Italian coastline. It was hard to believe that just across the Adriatic a war was being fought and people were being killed. It was even harder to believe that I would be in the thick of it all in less than 48 hours—but that's another story.

Showing Our Support

Maj Dawn M. Brotherton

I experienced OAF from a different viewpoint than that of the pilots—a support perspective. Support personnel, for example, range from the maintainer who fixes the jet, to the services person who finds places for people to eat and sleep, and to the communications personnel who ensure that pilots can talk to the ground or to a home unit.

When I stepped off the airplane, I was handed three hats. As the chief of personnel for the contingency operations team, it was my job to ensure accountability for all people deployed, to get more bodies when we needed them, and to assist folks with those parts of their professional military lives that extended beyond fighting the war—testing for rank, medals processing, performance reports, and so forth. As the executive officer, my job was to keep things organized and tied together so the group commander could concentrate on the big stuff—bombs on target and winning a war. As the protocol officer, I had to ensure that everything was ready for any high-ranking visitors who would pass through Gioia.

When I arrived at Gioia, about a week after the airplanes landed, I was amazed at the ingenuity of the people already in place. The Italians gave us two floors of an old dorm to use as office space. It was still full of beds, dressers, and nightstands. The members of the 40th EOG had stacked the mattresses in two rooms at the end of the hall, turned the bed frames on their sides, removed the closet doors from their hinges, and laid them across bed frames to form "desks." In some cases the beds were left in one piece behind the desk to act as "chairs." Nightstands were stacked two high and in rows to form a counter for the operations desk.

We all quickly adapted to our new office space, and the mission was unaffected. It was actually nice having everyone together in one location. At a home base, the support guys are rarely around when a jet lands, so they feel slightly removed from the mission. Not at Gioia! The pilots had to walk down the "support" hallway to drop off their flying gear, and the transportation, personnel, and civil engineering troops would come out into the hallway to ask how the flight went. Most of the time the pilots were more than willing to take the time to swap stories and play hero with the younger troops. It really built up camaraderie between the officers and enlisted folks.

Support personnel had to accomplish many tasks while the pilots flew their missions. Being in charge of the comings and goings of more than 900 folks was no easy feat, but the Air Force has a deployable computer system designed for just such a task. Of course, in the 100-plus days we were there, we never received all the parts required to make the system operational. We didn't have to resort totally to stubby-pencil tracking, but I did have to design a database to meet our needs. Support folks fixed thousands of such problems as this with equal ingenuity.

When I wasn't trying to track our people, I was getting ready to host our many visitors. One might think Gioia del Colle was too small for most people to find, but we had our share of "very important people." Secretary of the Air Force F. Whitten Peters and Lt Gen Michael Short, joint forces air component commander, were two of the highest ranking US people to visit. Our visitors were not limited to Americans. The British were on the bottom floor of our dorm/office building, an arrangement that prompted Prince Andrew to pay us a visit as well during his tour of RAF operations. He appreciated the chance to see an A-10 up close and to talk to some of our members. Rock star Joan Jett also made a support appearance at Gioia, puting on a wonderful concert for the troops.

USAF Photo

Capt Dawn Brotherton greets Prince Andrew

As an executive officer, I tried to deal with the minuscule things that go unnoticed to the untrained eye, such as storing mattresses, allocating office space, and playing peacemaker between operations and support personnel when they didn't understand each other. I also dealt with all the administrative paperwork that goes hand in hand with any organization.

There were big problems to deal with and not-so-big problems. One of the funny inconveniences of our deployment was the lack of a place to wash our clothes. The Italians didn't have American-style laundromats, and the hotels charged ridiculous fees to wash even a shirt. The extra money the Air Force was paying us to cover expenses like this wasn't going to hack it. People came up with some humorous solutions to the laundry problem. I heard of some pilots taking showers while wearing their flight suits so they could wash them at the same time. Others discovered the additional floor-mounted sink in their bathroom (known to most European travelers as a bidet) and used that to wash their clothes. Now is that creativity, desperation, or just cheapness? A few people mailed packages of dirty laundry to their wives, who usually returned clean clothes. I wouldn't want to be on the receiving end of those packages! I am sad to say this little problem was never really solved.

There was definitely an upside to being deployed with this group of professionals. Walking around the area and talking to the airmen about their different jobs was enlightening. I'll never forget the looks on the faces of the maintainers when their jet came back clean. The pride was evident: they bragged to one another, just as if they had dropped the bombs themselves. They were also concerned if a jet was late returning or if they could see the bombs still hanging as the A-10 came in to land.

After we had been in place a few months, things slowed down just enough to give the senior leadership a chance to hold a few meetings. Lt Col Chris Haave was the 81st commander, referred to as Kimos in most of this book—but support officers typically didn't call pilots by their call signs. Colonel Haave briefed the troops on how we were doing against the Serbs and what impact the A-10s were making. He showed gun-camera videos that depicted bombs being dropped on targets, and he described a typical mission. Folks were on the edge of their seats. For the most part, these airmen had never been close to combat, and the briefing made it all the more real. Having a lieutenant colonel thank a group of enlisted and support officers, while explaining how they were really contributing to the war effort, made us feel needed and appreciated. It sure made coming to work for 12-plus hours a day more worthwhile.

Notes

1. President William J. Clinton, "2000 State of the Union Address," 27 January 2000, on-line, Internet, 14 August 2001, available from http://www.washingtonpost.com/wp-srv/politics/special/states/docs/sou00.htm#foreignpolicy.

Enemy Action

Introduction

Lt Col Chris "Kimos" Haave

The Serbs who were occupying and cleansing Kosovo of its ethnic Albanian population were cunning, adaptive, flexible, and intelligent adversaries. We felt no particular animosity for the Serbian people or the unfortunate young soldiers who were perhaps pressed into serving in Kosovo. We did feel a singular animosity towards those we witnessed burning and shelling villages, and for those who tried to shoot us down.

The Serb forces' actions and reactions to KEZ operations can be likened to a boxer with a rope-a-dope strategy: unable to defeat NATO with brute strength, they used delaying tactics to parry the allied knockout blow on fielded forces while continuing to land punches in their ethnic-cleansing efforts. Another useful analogy is that of a cat-and-mouse game. The AFAC "cats" took off daily trying to anticipate the moves of the Serb "mice." The Serbs adapted their tactics daily to improve their chances of shooting down an allied aircraft and their own probability of survival, while continuing the ethnic cleansing.

Although it might seem that as AFACs we had all the best cards, we knew the Serbs held a trump card—but a card they could not play unless we first provided the opportunity. If we made a serious tactical error, we could give them a huge strategic or political advantage that might weaken some allies' resolve. This could happen in several ways. By taking unnecessary risks (even within the ROEs), we could provide the Serbs an A-10 and a POW to parade in front of the media. By failing to find and engage Serb forces, we could prolong the conflict beyond the patience of NATO political authorities. Finally, if we rushed or became frustrated, we could inadvertently kill civilian refugees and destroy the homes and villages of non-combatants. Any or all of these situations could unravel the popular support the campaign enjoyed.

This chapter examines some of the actions Serb forces took to counter allied operations in the KEZ. Those actions included Serb attempts to shoot down NATO aircraft, camouflage and conceal forces, and entice us to make mistakes by misleading our intelligence and interfering with our operations—mistakes that could weaken political and public support for our air campaign.

Attempts to Shoot Down NATO Aircraft

It took a while for the Serb ground-based air defenses to react to being attacked. They didn't shoot at us until our second day of KEZ operations. The Serb air-defense weapons employed in Kosovo consisted of the full range of low- to medium-altitude radar- and IR-guided SAMs and 20 mm to 57 mm AAA. Our SEAD aircraft and crews (F-16CJ, EA-6B, and Tornado ECR) earned healthy respect from the Serbs only a couple of weeks into the campaign. Although the Serbs had very lethal mobile SAM systems roaming around Kosovo, we rarely detected a radar lock-on or radar-guided-missile launch. SEAD forces (as well as the air-to-air fighters) orbiting in the KEZ everyday made it possible for us to attack with impunity. Even though they rarely had either the need or opportunity to employ ordnance, they fulfilled their mission, and we never crossed the border without them.

On average, Serb antiaircraft missiles and AAA engaged each 40th EOG pilot about six times—several pilots were shot at much more often. Although some missions were very quiet, on others we spent much of our time reacting to and destroying surface-to-air threats rather than searching for hidden armor. Of course, targets designated with a CAOC-assigned priority were always attacked first. One A-10 AFAC point of pride was that, even though we often took aimed fire in daylight, none of the hundreds of strikers whose attacks we controlled were ever hit, and practically none were shot at. It was our job to ensure that incoming strikers had the safest ingress, attack, and egress routes.

The Serbs quickly learned that opening fire on Hogs with AAA or SAMs made them both obvious and high-priority targets. Serb air defenses attempted to plan their missile and AAA shots to maximize the chances of hitting an A-10 while minimizing their own risks. The "SAM bush" was one such tactic. The Serbs would first fire AAA to make the A-10 jink. When they thought they had the pilot's attention focused, they launched one or more SAMs in the hopes of scoring a hit. The SAM-bush had zero success, and often the A-10s made the Serbs regret they tried it.

Camouflage and Concealment of Forces

After the first week of KEZ strikes, the Serbs rarely drove military vehicles in the open during the day. They became masters of hiding during the day and making full use of night or bad weather. They also built and deployed ingeniously simple decoys to impersonate mortars, artillery, trucks, APCs, and tanks. After noting that the APCs they parked in revetments would often be blown up when discovered by A-10s, they sometimes put a decoy in the revetment and then camouflaged the real vehicle outside. They also parked vehicles in agricultural fields and painted them the same color as the growing crops. They built tunnels, some real and some not.

Nevertheless, they made mistakes and were sometimes caught with their troops and vehicles in the open—usually when bad weather cleared up rapidly, as documented in a couple of the stories in this book. On one occasion, as 36 hours of heavy rain ended, I spied something very unusual through a small hole in the clouds. I soon understood the scene below me—a series of dark, metallic shapes and several bright-white tents of varying sizes in an area that included an asphalt road 500 meters long, bordered on either side by 10 to 20 meters of clearing and enclosed by woods. Using my binoculars I picked out mortars and artillery pieces in neat rows of revetments. Small, taut white tents covered the three revetments on one side of the road, and the three on the other side were in the open. A couple of APCs were visible, one of which was under a large, white tent. Other such tents were pitched in the trees. Taking extra time to rule out collateral damage, I made sure there were no civilian vehicles and no vehicles painted any other color than camouflage green. Why would a professional army use bright-white tents to cover camouflaged vehicles? The strange scene suddenly made sense. Evidently I had found them just as they were breaking camp after the deluge. This was one of the few times I saw a large group of military vehicles unaccompanied by civilian vehicles. They had apparently used the white tents not only to protect their equipment from the rain but also to pass themselves off as civilians to avoid attacks from anyone who might discover them.

It is easier to visually camouflage a professional army than it is to disguise its disciplined routines and habits. When moving, professional armies tend to drive their convoys at a constant speed with military spacing; when encamping, they tend to pitch their tents in neat, military rows. Today, that latter habit betrayed their attempt at disguise.

The hole in the clouds was closing and I reckoned that my airburst Mk-82s would be the most useful weapons to employ. Luck was with me as I rippled two bombs on an imperfect dive angle, on an axis that overlaid the most targets, hitting an APC in the open and another covered by a tent.

All pilots encountered similar situations when, with a little perseverance, they were able to figure out what was real and what wasn't in the pictures they could see. Of course, that savvy improved with experience and after destroying a number of decoys. I certainly blew up my share of fake tanks.

Forcing NATO Mistakes

The Serb-escorted Kosovar refugee convoys comprised a mix of civilian and military vehicles and were a familiar sight from the very first day the weather allowed us to operate in Kosovo. As time went on, we were convinced that the Serb army and Interior Ministry police moved about in the large, white buses we saw everywhere. What Kosovar Albanian civilian would charter a bus to speed north on the highway towards Serbia? However, we never attacked the white buses because we couldn't be sure there weren't civilians in them.

Serb forces used many other unethical tactics to try to fool us and cause us to bomb noncombatant civilians and villages. They parked armored vehicles next to churches and other lo-

USAF Photo

Serb SA-9 decoy

cations, many of which are too sensitive to mention here. Suffice it to say that the rigorous AFAC discipline in the KEZ precluded the Serbs from gaining much advantage from their efforts to trick us into bombing innocent civilians and other inappropriate targets.

Hit by a SAM

Maj Phil "Goldie" Haun

As the 81st FS weapons officer during OAF, I was involved in most operational aspects of our squadron's activities. We performed the Sandy CSAR role, one of our three OAF missions, which most notably included the rescue of an F-117 pilot near Belgrade on 27 March 1999 and an F-16 pilot on 2 May 1999. I had the exhilarating privilege of being the on-scene Sandy flight lead during the pickup of the F-117 pilot. We were also the primary daytime AFACs and strikers over Kosovo, and I flew 25 of those missions from 30 March to 7 June 1999—19 of them as an AFAC mission commander.

The variety of strikers I worked during these missions was truly impressive. I controlled Air Force A-10s, F-15Es, and

F-16CGs (block 40s); Navy F-14s and F/A-18s; Marine Harriers and F/A-18s; British GR-7 Harriers; Spanish EF-18s; Canadian CF-18s; Dutch, Belgian, and Turkish F-16s; Italian Tornados and AMXs; and French Super Etendards. These fighters carried a wide variety of weapons, including LGBs and CBUs, as well as Mk-82 (500 lb), Mk-83 (1,000 lb), and Mk-84 (2,000 lb) general-purpose bombs.

Our AFAC mission wasn't a new one for the Air Force. The first AFACs were the Mosquito FACs of Korea. Using slow, unarmed prop-driven planes, they were extremely successful in flying behind enemy lines, locating lucrative targets, and working strikers on those targets. During Vietnam the fast FAC was born with F-100F Misty FACs driving deep within North Vietnam searching for targets. In the nearly 50 years since the advent of the AFAC, it's evident that FACing really hasn't changed all that much. During Vietnam one key to survival was to stay at least 4,500 feet above ground level (AGL) to avoid AAA. Since Vietnam, with the improvement and proliferation of shoulder-fired, heat-seeking missiles, we now fly at over three times that altitude. The radar-guided SA-2s of Vietnam were also replaced by more capable and mobile SAMs in Kosovo. Given the threats and the operational altitudes these missiles dictate, the toughest task for a FAC remains that of finding the enemy. A good FAC can find viable targets— a skill not so much a science as an art. The good FAC always has a plan and, most importantly, is confident that he will always find something.

I relied heavily on the same skills it takes to stalk a trout. A successful fly fisherman understands the trout, is able to read the water, and therefore knows where to look. Kosovo is shaped like a baseball diamond, about 60 miles long and 60 miles wide. Twenty-five missions provided plenty of time to learn the terrain by heart and to develop a sense of where to search. The Serbs stopped using the roads openly and hid most of their equipment after they had been attacked day and night for close to a month. They even ceased to bring their SAMs out in the open during the day.

I have to admit that I was starting to feel invincible. At medium altitude we had begun to feel immune to the AAA and heat-seeking, shoulder-fired, man-portable air defense systems (MANPADS). On 2 May I went to the squadron to prepare for a FAC mission. It had been over a week since I had located a command post in western Kosovo and FAC'd three sets of fighters onto it. Since then, I had completed an uneventful three-night rotation of CSAR ground-alert and was raring to get back into country.

Arriving at the squadron, I was greeted by a rush of activity. Catching bits and pieces, I found out that an F-16 had been shot down two hours before and that Capt Richard A. "Scrape" Johnson and Maj Biggles Thompson had launched as Sandys for the rescue. I asked Lt Col Mark "Coke" Koechle, our top-three supervisor, if we needed to begin preparing a subsequent rescue attempt, but before that could get under way, we heard that the pilot had been successfully picked up.

I continued my preparation for the day's mission. I would be the mission commander working eastern Kosovo (code-named NBA). I searched through the imagery and found a juicy new picture of artillery revetments in northeastern Kosovo. Other than that, there wasn't much useful imagery. It appeared I would be on the slow side of Kosovo, with most of the Serbian activity being in the west (NFL). Still, I liked the imagery because it was of an area where we had not spent much time, and a tree line next to the revetments indicated a likely hiding place for self-propelled artillery.

As I "stepped" (departed the squadron at the prebriefed time—a critical milestone in the sequence of getting a flight airborne on schedule), the sun was just coming up on a beautiful Italian morning. I watched Scrape and Biggles return from their successful rescue and raised my arms over my head with clenched fists in a sign of triumph as they taxied by. My call sign that day was Lynx 11, and my wingman, Lynx 12, was Capt Andy "Buffy" Gebara. Andy had been a B-52 aircraft commander and had crossed over to fly A-10s. We took off for the tanker, refueled, and then waited.

The rescue delayed the arrival of the SEAD assets, including Navy EA-6Bs. The ROEs would not allow any aircraft into Kosovo without the presence of SEAD. I waited just south of the border for nearly 30 minutes. Finally, Magic (NAEW, NATO's

USAF Photo

Taxiing for a CSAR mission at Aviano AB

version of AWACS) called the SEAD on station, and I turned
north for the target area. The artillery revetments were 30 miles
north of Pristina. As I approached the revetments I took out my
binoculars and spotted a 2S1 122 mm self-propelled artillery
piece parked at the edge of the tree line. At the same time, Magic
reported that the call of "SEAD on station" was only for the
western area and that the NBA was closing down. I knew I had
just one shot at the 2S1 and quickly rolled in from the east.
Locking up the vehicle with my Maverick seeker, I waited for the
steady cross to indicate a valid lock before I launched the missile. Unfortunately, the target was hot enough to lock up but not
hot enough for a steady cross. Knowing that I probably wouldn't
get to work any more targets that day, I decided to test my luck
and launch with the flashing cross. After all, I hadn't missed on
any of my previous Mavericks and knew there was a chance the
missile would guide all the way to the target. So I hammered
down until I felt the now-familiar sensation of a 500 lb missile
accelerating off the rail. I pulled off target, watched the Maverick
impact the 2S1, and proceeded as directed to the south. On
Magic's radarscopes it must have looked like I had simply made
a U-turn.

Photo courtesy of FAS

2S1 122 mm self-propelled artillery, similar to the one destroyed by Maj Goldie Haun on 2 May 1999

The drive south took about 10 minutes. I was concerned about staying well clear of Pristina with its SAMs, particularly since Magic had just announced that I had no SEAD support. Still, my concern did not preclude looking for targets to attack later. As I climbed out to the southeast, I searched the roads and hillside for any signs of military activity.

I was about four miles north of G-Town. To avoid confusion and save time, we called towns with difficult pronunciations by their first letter. Gnjilane became G-Town, Dakovica became D-Town, and Urosevac was U-Town. I noted a narrow, jagged valley with what appeared to be man-made diagonal cuts through the trees alongside the road. I put the binoculars on the cuts and picked out two tanks. I marked my map, and as I continued to the tanker, started to come up with a game plan. While we refueled, I contacted Magic and coordinated SEAD support for a hasty attack. Magic was able to get SEAD but only 20 minutes' worth. By the time I got off the tanker and headed north, I realized I would have less than 10 minutes on station for the attack.

I decided the best avenue of attack would be from the southeast. Due to the narrowness of the valley and the dirt revet-

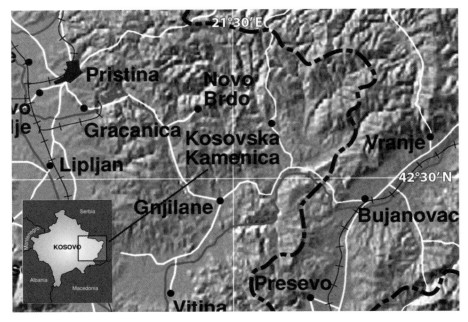

Valley four miles north of G-Town

ments in which the tanks were hiding, the precision-guided Maverick seemed the best weapon. The attack went as planned, except for a small glitch. I had identified the tanks while looking from north to south. Approaching from the southeast, I misidentified the diagonal cutout and rolled in on an empty revetment. I recognized the mistake early and quickly came off target, climbing to the east to regain energy.

After aborting my first attack, I extended for another roll-in. This time I identified the correct cutout and tried to lock up the tank. Unfortunately, the Maverick locked onto a large dirt pile at the rear of the cutout, which was hotter than the tank. It was apparent the Maverick would not work against this target. The remaining options did not appear to have much chance for success. The narrowness of the valley and the protection of the cutouts meant a direct hit with Mk-82s would be required to kill the tanks—and that would be very difficult to accomplish. I didn't have any available fighters with LGBs, and the only other option was to strafe the tanks. This was a riskier choice since I would have to dive to a much lower altitude to get in range.

I decided to let Andy drop two of his bombs to get their heads down, and I would follow up with a strafe pass. I was still low on energy and climbing to the north as Andy rolled in out of the northwest with a tailwind. His bombs landed just north of the tanks with no direct hits. From the radio traffic I knew my time was running out and this would be our last attack. I elected to strafe both targets on one pass, trying to get bullets on both tanks.

USAF Photo

T-54/55 tank shot by Maj Goldie Haun on 7 June 1999, similar to tanks strafed on 2 May 1999

As I (Lynx 11) rolled in for my strafe pass, I turned on my videotape to record the pass. My primary UHF radio was monitoring the NFL frequency. With lots of fighters working in NFL, the radio chatter was constant. I used my secondary Fox-Mike radio to talk to Andy (Lynx 12).

"Lynx 11's in from the west, two-target strafe."

"Magic, Lobo 51 will be Cactus, store in approximately three mike. Lobo 53 will be on station for 20 mike. Do you want to close the NFL or the NBA?" Lobo 51 was the flight lead for a four-ship of F-16CJs providing our SEAD. He was running low on fuel and would be departing Kosovo (code word Cactus) in three minutes. His second element, Lobo 53, had enough fuel to remain on station for an additional 20 minutes. Lobo wanted to know whether to close the western or eastern area.

"Magic, in this case, suggests to close the NBA." All the other FACs and fighters were working targets in NFL. We were the only set of FACs in NBA.

In the meantime, the strafe pass had gone well, with Andy seeing hits on the target. "Lynx 11 en route to NFL now." I had come off target and had begun the excruciatingly slow process of climbing back to altitude.

"Lynx, Bobcat 21. Where you coming into?" Bobcat 21 was a two-ship of A-10s led by Maj Lester Less, the FAC responsible for deconflicting NFL. He was also an embedded Sandy pilot whose job it was to handle the rescue of any downed pilots. I had known Lester for over nine years. We had flown A-10s together as lieutenants at RAF Bentwaters, England.

"Bobcat, Lynx 11. I need to coordinate with you, but I'd like to come in from the south."

"Lynx, Bobcat 21. Yeah, OK, in from the south."

"Lynx 11 copy that. Then, I'll work to the south and to the east." Andy and I began a discussion on our FM frequency.

"Lynx, Two is blind, just west of G-Town." Andy had just lost sight of me, a very common occurrence. A good wingman covers his flight lead as he comes off target by focusing on the ground where the threats (AAA and MANPADS) are likely to be fired. A wingman that never goes "blind" is simply staring at his flight lead and is of no use.

"Lynx 11, copy. One is just west of G-Town climbing . . . OK! I just got hit! I'm turning to the south." I never saw what hit me. As I looked up to find Andy, I felt an incredible jolt to the aircraft on the right side. The nose tried to roll off to the right, and I had to put in full left rudder to keep her from flipping over. I was struggling at this point just to keep the jet flying. Dropping the nose, I started a gradual descent to maintain airspeed. My master-caution panel was lit up like a Christmas tree, and I finally looked over my shoulder to see the engine cowling blown off and the fan blades frozen. Sunlight streamed through the engine inlet. I made sure I was still headed towards the Macedonian border and returned my focus to keeping the jet under control.

"Two copies. Two's blind, egressing south."

"OK, two, I need you to come towards south."

"Lynx 12 is heading south."

"OK, two, where's your posit?"

"OK, two is southwest of G-Town at one six zero."

"OK, copy that. I'm at one four zero descending. . . . I am trailing you. I need you to 90 right." I asked Andy where he was and he informed me he was southwest of Gnjilane at 16,000 feet, while I was at 14,000 feet. I could see Andy about two miles in front of me, and I told him to turn 90 degrees right to get me visual. I felt better having the jet under control and my wingman in sight. However, the severity of the situation had not yet sunk in. I was flying a battle-damaged jet in the heart of the AAA and MANPADS envelope and descending over a heavily defended section of Kosovo. If anything, I was mad—really mad that someone had had the audacity to shoot me. I was also determined that there was no way I was going to eject over Kosovo. I didn't think I'd be able to land the jet, especially since it was difficult maintaining level flight and impossible to make right-hand turns, but I was not going to be on Serbian TV that night and neither were the remains of my A-10. I would nurse the jet into Macedonia before I ejected.

"Bobcat, Lynx 11. Break, break." Still, it was better to be safe than sorry. I wanted Lester (Bobcat 21) to head towards me in case I did have to punch out in bad-guy land, so he could orchestrate the rescue. Thankfully, the jet was hanging in there. The right-engine gauges were showing a severe engine overtemp without producing any thrust. I shut down the engine, and it cooled quickly once the fuel flow was shut off. Gauges for the left engine looked good. Days later, I would find out that the left engine had been severely damaged from ingesting pieces of the right engine and the missile. I had to fly in a one-degree descent to maintain airspeed. Very slow and with no energy available to react to another missile launch, I was a wounded bird.

"Bobcat 21, Go ahead."

"Lynx 11. OK, Bobcat. I've been hit. My right engine has been taken out. I'm single engine. I'm currently south of G-Town, and I'm headed towards Skopje. I've got the right engine . . . looks like the whole engine cowling got hit . . . and I've got no right hydraulics. I've got a wingman with me, and I'm headed towards Skopje. Currently I'm about five miles from the border." I was not afraid, but the adrenalin rush had me excited. Time was distorted, and my world had slowed to a snail's pace. Between keeping the jet aloft and talking on the radios, I clearly pictured myself hugging my kids. I just knew I was going to make it out of Kosovo.

"Lynx, Bobcat 21. Are you still up?"

"Lynx 11, that's affirmative. I'm staying up this freq currently. I am losing altitude, but I think that now I might be able to make it across the border." As I spoke on the radio I had the sensation that this was not really happening to me. I must have been watching some other poor fighter pilot struggling to stay airborne. I had to help him as best I could to get out of these dire circumstances.

"Bobcat 21, understand you are single engine and you've got a hydraulic system out?"

"Lynx 11, that's affirmative. I've got the right hydraulic system out. . . . OK, I feel fairly confident that I'll make it across the border, not sure if I can land. I'm going to set up for Skopje though." By then I could see the border just a couple of miles in front of me. I figured even if the left engine quit, I could still glide to Macedonia. My mind now started to think about what I would do with the jet once I got past the border. The situation was looking better—the left engine was working well and I was getting used to handling the jet. As I descended to lower altitude, she started to perform better, and I began to think I might be able to land her.

"Lynx 12, are you visual? Come right . . . Look at your right three o'clock."

"Two's visual, falling into wedge."

"Lynx 11, OK. I want you to stay high wedge."

"Two's high wedge. Your six is clear." I finally got Andy's eyes onto me just about the time we crossed the border. My mind now turned to how to make a controlled descent for a safe landing at Skopje, some 9,000 feet below. I had Andy come in to give me a battle-damage check. He saw nothing wrong with the jet, except the damage to the right engine.

I proceeded with a controllability check to determine whether I could land the jet and found that I had three problems. First, I could not make right turns into the bad engine. Second, I lowered the gear and received stall indications just below maximum landing speed. This meant I was going to have to land fast. Third, the Skopje airfield was oriented north-south and I was five miles north of the field and much too high to land. I was not sure whether the left engine had enough thrust to go around if I screwed up the approach. I wanted to take my time and do it right the first time. I elected to set myself up for a left-teardrop approach to land from the south. This option gave me the advantage of staying in left-hand turns for the approach and allowed me to gradually lose altitude. Finally, since the wind was coming from the north, I could land with a headwind, which would help decrease my ground speed and landing distance.

The tower at Skopje was very helpful, diverting two heavy aircraft on approach as I started my teardrop turn to final. The jet was flying well in the left turn, and my next concern was what would happen when I rolled level on final approach. I adjusted the pattern to roll out just over the approach-end lights (a normal circling approach would have had me roll out one mile before touchdown). On final I felt the nose start to yaw to the right, and I countered by pulling the power on my left engine to idle. The reduction in thrust on the left side reduced the right yaw, and I began to glide to the runway. I did not flare the jet but "planted" the landing, touching down firmly just below maximum landing speed.

Skopje was a good, long runway, but I was going pretty fast and wanted to get the jet stopped. I aerobraked the damaged Hog as much as I could and finally put the nose down at around 120 knots. Because my speed brakes were inoperative, I relied only on my wheel brakes to slow me down. I waited until 100 knots to touch the brakes and was relieved to come to a full stop with 2,000 feet of runway to spare. Now that I had reached terra firma, I wanted out of the jet as soon as possible. I automatically ran through the bold-face procedure—the ones pilots commit to memory—for "emergency ground egress" to shut down the remaining engine and exit the aircraft. I ran to the side of the runway, turned, and looked at my battered jet.

USAF Photo

Damaged jet at Skopje

Several NATO countries used the Skopje airfield. First, a group of Dutch soldiers came up to see how I was doing. Next, a French officer who managed the airfield showed up. They didn't have any emergency personnel or vehicles, so I ended up having to go back to the jet to "safe up" the remaining munitions and pin the gear. Quarter-sized holes peppered the Hog's right flaps and the tail fins of one of my AIM-9 air-to-air missiles. I got back in the cockpit and rode the brakes as they towed my jet off the runway.

Thankfully, a group of US soldiers from Task Force Able Sentry soon arrived in a couple of humvees. Up to this point I had not seen any civilians or press. The last thing I wanted was my jet on CNN or on the front page of newspapers. I tried unsuccessfully to have the A-10 put out of view in a nearby hangar. The soldiers provided security for the jet, put a tarp over my right engine, and drove me a couple of miles to their headquarters. I called my squadron at Gioia and gave a mission report, which included an update on the condition of the jet.

My biggest concern at this point was getting back to the squadron. When I asked about the next flight leaving Skopje, I was told there wouldn't be one for at least a couple of days. The US soldiers treated me great and took me over to the chow hall. I found myself famished as I sat down next to a big-screen TV. After a while, I realized everyone in the chow hall was watching the TV intently with big smiles. I looked to the TV to see three Army POWs—captured the month before while performing a routine border patrol—being released to Rev. Jesse Jackson in Belgrade. I was eating with members of their company.

When I got back to the headquarters, I found out an Army C-12 was being diverted to Ramstein AB, Germany, to take the ex-POWs' commanders to see their soldiers. They offered me a seat, and I gladly accepted. I thought that it would be a lot easier to get back to Gioia del Colle from Ramstein, where cargo aircraft were constantly departing for Italy. I also didn't want to spend anymore time in Macedonia than I had to, and, more importantly, Ramstein was only a one-and-one-half-hour drive from my home base at Spangdahlem. The five-hour C-12 flight from Skopje to Ramstein felt even longer than my previous flight over Kosovo as I reflew the mission over and over in my head. When I landed at Ramstein, I rushed to base operations and called the squadron at Gioia. My commander, Lt Col Kimos Haave, informed me that a C-130 departing at 0100 that night would bring me directly to Gioia—I then called my wife Bonnie. It was 8 P.M., and she had just gotten home from church. I told her to put the kids in the van and meet me at the Ramstein Passenger Terminal as soon as she could. At base operations, I was greeted by a group of three Air Force Materiel Command officers who needed to know the extent of the damage to the jet. I briefed them as best I could before heading to the passenger terminal.

121

When my family arrived at Ramstein, I got to hold my sleeping two-year-old daughter and watch my six-year-old boy play with the toys in the family lounge. I hadn't seen them for over 80 days. My jaw and teeth still ached from the violent impact of the missile, but I didn't want to worry them and didn't know what I could tell them. So I told Bonnie I had had some engine trouble and landed in Skopje, which she accepted as routine. The Lord had heard me over Kosovo, and 14 hours after I had been hit, I had my children in my arms. I held my wife's hand and talked to her for two hours until the C-130 was ready. She talked excitedly about the rescue of the downed F-16 pilot that day and the release of the POWs, completely unaware of how narrowly I had escaped both fates. Before my C-130 departed, I kissed my wife and sleepy kids and sent them home, not knowing when I'd see them again.

I entered the squadron at Gioia del Colle 24 hours after I had stepped to fly and wanted to get back into the air as soon as possible. The next day, some 48 hours after being hit, I was

Photo courtesy of author

Maj Goldie Haun and aircraft 967 less than 30 days after being hit and landing at Skopje

back in the cockpit. This time I didn't strafe but dropped CBUs. That, however, is another story.

Last Day to Fly—Last Chance to Die

1st Lt Mike "Scud" Curley

It was 9 June 1999, a standard (beautiful) day in Italy and forecasted to be gorgeous in Kosovo. Many of us knew the end was near because we were told Milosevic was going to accept NATO's demands and today would be the last "offensive" day of the air campaign. I was excited because I was flying with Maj James "Jimbo" MacCauley, one of the two pilots from Moody to join us at Gioia del Colle. It was always interesting to fly with folks from another squadron to see if their tactics, or thoughts on the way things should be done, were any different from those of my own squadron mates. He had also flown during Operation Desert Storm and was one of the more experienced pilots with us.

The day, as usual, started off with signing off numerous battle staff directives (BSD) that most pilots dreaded reading because most did not apply to us. It was just one more thing we had to squish in while we were half-asleep before the flight briefing at "o' dark 30." Finally we finished our daily planning routine and started our flight briefing.

Jimbo briefed relatively standard tactics, the same ones we studied and practiced every day; it was good to know that Hog guys from different bases practiced the same stuff our squadron did. I noticed he did do a good job emphasizing the basic communications and lookout duties that he expected of a wingman. Such information sometimes gets left out when flying with many of the same guys, and it is important to have it stressed from time to time. I also thought in the back of my mind, as Jimbo probably did, that this was not the day to become complacent— even with all the talk of things winding down.

We eventually stepped, took off, hit the tanker, and entered the AOR uneventfully. We started looking at the areas of interest that intelligence had briefed us about. There was very little activity, and we found nothing where intel told us to look. Capt Christopher "Junior" Short and Col Al Thompson were the prior AFACs on station, and they were looking at an area in southern Kosovo, 10 miles southwest of Prizren. They thought they had found some APCs or tanks but had to hit the tanker, so they gave us a quick talk-on and left the area.

Jimbo made a couple passes with the binoculars but could not quite make out what was there. He also did a Maverick search but could not tell for sure if the potential targets were live vehicles, decoys, or "tactical bushes." He saw a horseshoe formation around a dirt berm, so he elected to drop his Mk-82s on them to see if we could get some secondaries or movement from them. He rippled his four Mk-82s on the eastern side of the formation. We did not see any secondaries, but the targets did not seem to be decoys because they stayed relatively intact. After climbing back to altitude and joining the briefed formation, he instructed me to drop my Mk-82s on the western side of the formation.

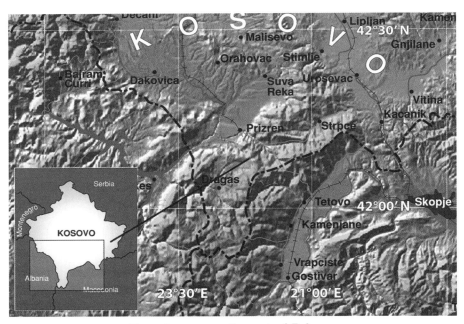

Target area southwest of Prizren

As I rolled in to begin my dive delivery, I saw a flash and smoke trailing a missile quickly climbing towards the spot where I had last seen Jimbo. I immediately broke off my delivery, called out the missile launch, and directed him to expend flares. Shortly after I spit out all the required radio calls, the missile passed behind Jimbo along his flight path. I made sure I knew exactly where the launch came from because I was pissed that they had tried to kill us. There was still a significant amount of smoke in the area from where the missile had launched, and a thick smoke trail lingered in the air—we figured it was not just a MANPADS. We departed the launch-site area and broke line of sight. Meanwhile Jimbo briefed me on a suppressor-bomber attack. I was ready to roll right in and made sure Jimbo knew that. I was excited when I executed the attack, and as soon as I rolled out on "final" I realized that I had not considered the winds. "Final" is the airspace flown through during the few seconds after rolling out of the diving turn and just prior to weapons release. It is where pilots would normally refine their dive angle, airspeed, and ground track so that when they depress the pickle button, they will have the correct sight picture, airspeed, altitude, and dive angle so the bomb will hit the target. As I rolled out, I realized I needed to come off dry—without dropping any bombs—because the wind had blown me too far, and I would not be able to attain the necessary delivery parameters to make a good pass and kill the target. Fortunately, I decided to come off early and had enough energy to expedite the next attack.

Jimbo had suppressed the threat area with the gun before I rolled down the chute. He put a bunch of bullets in the vicinity of the launch site, and I dropped my bombs on a nearby tree line, close to a road intersection where military vehicles appeared to be located. As I recovered from my pass, Jimbo noticed a green, fluorescent flash that indicated I had hit something with rocket fuel or ammunition in it. After this attack we left the target area for the tanker and then headed home.

We debriefed with our intel NCO, SSgt Amos Elliot, on what we saw and what had happened. Amos was very excited about getting all the specifics. BDA is usually very difficult to get, especially on fielded forces, but it is a very important aspect of the entire war effort. After our in-depth discussion, we were pretty sure we had hit a mobile SAM system. While we made sure to report it as "probable," not "confirmed," we also knew there was little chance of its ever being confirmed. The Serbians' standard practice was to haul away the wreckage of targets we had hit to make BDA more difficult. It was another piece of Milosevic's propaganda puzzle that still plagues NATO today.

The Only Sortie as a Wingman

Capt Jim "Meegs" Meger

I "grew up" as a first-assignment FAC at Osan AB in the Republic of South Korea, the "Land of the Morning Calm" or the "Land of the Not-Quite-Right," depending on how I viewed my own situation. That assignment was the best thing that ever happened to me as a FAC. I learned by leaps and bounds from the best fighter pilots and AFACs in the world—the AFACs who carried the revered Misty call sign. While at Osan I listened to the older Hog drivers who had been in Desert Storm, learning from their combat experiences and hoping to have the chance to put my training into the "Big Game."

From Korea I went to the 81st Fighter Squadron at Spangdahlem for my second operational tour. With the Panthers, I gained valuable experience in the A/OA-10's missions and learned how NATO integrated them into an air campaign.

My only sortie as a Panther wingman was the closest I came to meeting a Serb soldier face-to-face. Being in the CSAR rotation as a Sandy 1 and a FAC, I was surprised to see I was on the schedule to fly on the wing of Kimos Haave, the squadron commander. This was a role I had explained to my wingman many times before, and now it was time to walk the walk. Being a good wingman takes discipline, especially since I was used to being a flight lead. It was not my formation to run and I was not responsible for the navigation. My job called for providing support to my flight lead, keeping him in sight, and watching for any threats to the formation or our supporting fighters. With this in mind, I had put away my maps and had zero intention of pulling them back out unless it was necessary or requested by the flight lead.

Kimos, as the mission commander, gave the briefing and went over our targeting information for the day. There had

126

been some heavy activity along the borders, due in no small part to the ROEs that were in effect. I was glad to be flying in the afternoon since the morning fog had delayed or cancelled most of the early packages that week. The afternoon-go also had the benefit of intelligence updates and hot target areas from the morning's sorties.

We stepped to the jets and launched on time across the Adriatic with Kimos as Pepper 01 and me as Pepper 02. Because of some problems with the tanker, the entire package was delayed. We pressed across the "fence" 45 minutes late and began our target search with the imagery we had received. The active ABCCC aircraft was a Navy E-2C Hawkeye, call sign Cyclops, responsible for coordination among all elements to include the CAOC in northern Italy. Shortly after we arrived on station, Cyclops informed us of an active Serb command post west of Urosevac and requested that we locate the target. Kimos found the area and then began a search from medium altitude. He quickly located the command post and several nearby armored vehicles.

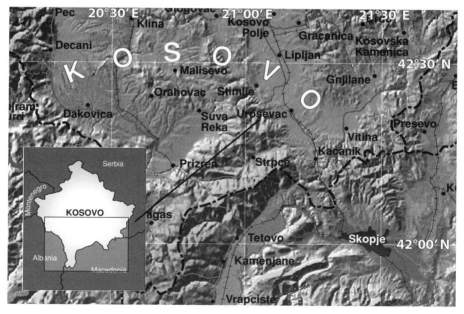

Serb command post west of Urosevac

In accordance with the ROEs, we still had to coordinate for attack permission because of the proximity to the Macedonia border, even though we had been directed to, had found, and had positively identified this target.

After we received authority to strike, we armed up our 500 lb Mk-82s, and Kimos called, "One's in." His bombs hit a tank and a command-post building. He then cleared me in on two APCs slightly to the south.

I returned his call with, "Two's in." With my flight lead in a cover position, I rolled down the chute. The bombs hit on target, but I did not see any secondary explosions because I was maneuvering and ejecting flares as I pulled off target. The E-2C relayed that a set of F/A-18s was en route to the target area. When the Hornets arrived, Kimos gave a quick FAC brief and rolled in to mark with Willy Pete rockets.

"One's off dry, hung rockets," called Kimos. His selected rocket pod had malfunctioned, so he selected his jet's other pod and rolled in again. After his second passed he radioed, "One's off dry, both pods of rockets are hung. Two, you have the lead. Go ahead and mark for the Hornets."

I assumed the lead, maneuvered my jet to a different attack axis, and rolled in. The second smoke was on target and the lead Hornet began to employ his ordnance. The second jet lost sight of the target area and asked for another mark. "Watch the number of passes in a target area" was the lesson firmly planted in everyone's mind after Maj Goldie Haun had been hit by a MANPADS and limped to Skopje only two days prior.

"Two's in."

I hammered down on the pickle button at 17,000 feet above mean sea level (MSL) and was rewarded with a quick, "tally the target," from the second Hornet. When the Hornets departed for the carrier after their attack, we egressed the target area and began a new search.

"Pepper 01, this is Cyclops. We have a two-ship of A-10s with CBU that needs a target." Kimos called them up and decided to have them unload their CBUs on the command-post area.

At this point I was fairly comfortable with the target area. The Serbs had not shot back on their "normal" timing, and I was now lighter and had good energy, having already dropped my bombs. With Kimos in a cover position and the fighters in trail to watch the mark, I began a roll-in to the right on a previously unused attack axis.

"Two, break left!" was the call I heard. I immediately began to dispense flares, turned in the cockpit, and saw two trails of smoke following behind what appeared to be red flares arcing towards my jet. Since I had been in the process of rolling in, I had already committed myself to a right turn—versus the break left—and began to lower the nose while pulling hard on the stick to turn quickly and put the missile at three o'clock. I can still see the red glow of the rocket motors and the way the missiles kept turning with me. I remember thinking that the missiles were rejecting the flares, and my next thought was, "What is three to five seconds?" (Our training tells us that three to five seconds before we think the missile will impact, we should perform a special maneuver to make the missile miss.) I was still breaking into the missiles and ejecting flares when the first missile lost track. I saw it would miss well behind the jet, but the second was rapidly getting closer.

"Two, get rid of your stuff." One of the other A-10s advised me to "combat jettison" all of my ordnance to improve my turn and energy state. It seemed like I had time to think it over and decide that I was okay with just my Mavericks. There was no way I was going to take my hands off the stick or the throttle and the flare button located on it!

As I began a last-ditch defensive maneuver, the second missile began to fall behind the aircraft. I can still see the missile trying to turn and "hack" the corner as it began to lag. With all this defensive maneuvering, I had turned approximately 270 degrees, and I was now looking exactly at where the two smoke trails had started their journey. Time to turn the tables. The GAU-8 30 mm Avenger cannon is the most flexible and formidable weapon on the A-10. Since it was built to destroy Soviet tanks in Germany's Fulda Gap, one can imagine its effectiveness on softer types of vehicles—especially a lightly armored SAM system.

I distinctly remember switching from rockets to the gun in the weapons-delivery mode of my head-up display and then placing the pipper short of the two vehicles where the smoke trail began. I dropped the hammer and began to retaliate in anger. An A-10 driver will normally shoot about 100–200 rounds in a combat burst, attempting to concentrate directly on the target. Passing 300 rounds on target, I kept the hammer down and began to move the pipper around the target area until I saw an explosion—500 rounds later.

"Two is egressing south." With the tables turned and the Serbs diving for cover, I called my flight lead and told him the heading on which I was departing the target area. Looking over my left side, I saw that Kimos was in a solid cover position as we concluded our first vul period, crossed into Macedonia, and began the air-refueling process in preparation for the sortie's second scheduled vul period.

Deep Thoughts

Capt Andrew "Buffy" Gebara

I had to think for a while about what I really wanted to say here. Many of my friends will write about what happened in Kosovo in 1999. I flew 36 combat missions over Serbia, so at first glance the task didn't seem all that tough. I thought about writing about my first-ever combat sortie—we didn't hit anything because we were recalled by the CAOC in what became an almost daily ritual of higher-headquarters mis-/micromanagement. I thought I would write about the time my flight lead Goldie Haun was hit by a SAM and barely made it back over the border. I briefly thought about my most effective sortie, in which Capt Nathan S. "Foghorn" Brauner and I destroyed 14 APCs and eight artillery pieces. To me it seemed like a routine sortie, but we were fortunate enough to get real results. Finally, I thought about the sortie that Lt Col Coke Koechle, my operations officer, let me lead for the first time. A fighter pilot's first sortie in the lead is one that he or she will always remember, and in my case that sortie was in combat over the FRY. As I landed, I felt as if I had genuinely accomplished something.

All of these sorties were memorable, but they didn't really define Kosovo for me. After thinking about it for a while, I finally figured out what I actually took away from Kosovo. Being on the front lines of this war has given me a new perspective and has caused me to view historical accounts through different eyes. From my perspective, Kosovo was weird—just plain weird. Some have written about the delayed stress of combat operations; others have discussed the guilt they feel after taking human life. As for me, I mostly felt, and still feel, that the whole experience was surreal. It didn't seem possible that I was actually in the middle of this whole thing. All my life I had either watched or read accounts of historical events. In Kosovo the Panthers didn't watch history in the making—we made it. We were key players in the first conflict in which the war was fought and won almost exclusively in the air. That I contributed to that victory is a great feeling, but every once in a while I think to myself, "What happened over there, anyway?"

If you get them away from the cameras, many pilots will say that, from a public-support point of view, Kosovo was similar to the Vietnam conflict. The older members of my squadron who had fought in Desert Storm told us of how the support from home had helped boost morale during the tougher times of the war. In Kosovo, we really didn't get much support, and, to tell the truth, we did not even get the animosity I had read about during the Vietnam conflict. It seemed to me that most Americans didn't know that the war was going on, at least at the level of intensity we faced. It becomes emotional when I am asked to risk my life for a just cause. To take such a risk when the cause is controversial is different. It is simply bizarre to do so for a cause my countrymen seem unaware of or indifferent to. Therefore, I often found myself wondering if this war was at all real.

During the first few weeks of the war, we fought out of Aviano. My squadron was housed in a hotel off base throughout the 1990s—ever since Bosnia-Herzegovina really heated up. When we entered the base from the hotel, there would be literally thousands of people outside the gates. We were sure there were Serbian intelligence gatherers in the crowds, and we were concerned about protests. However, it seemed that most of the crowd were made up of people who were little different from those encountered at an air show—teenagers who wanted to see jets launch in the early morning sunrise. I wanted to scream at them, "Do you realize what's going on here?" It was really strange.

We were directed to relocate to Gioia del Colle AB, soon after the war started and Aviano began to get crowded. Gioia was in southern Italy, much closer to Kosovo, which meant an increased sortie rate for us. It also meant we were housed like kings—our enlisted troops were in quarters near the beach, and the officers lived in a great hotel. We would get up around 0100, arrive at work about 0145, brief, launch, tank up, and enter Kosovo around 30 to 45 minutes after sunrise to get the best chance of identifying targets. Of course, that also gave the Serbs the best chance of seeing us—a concept I was to fully understand after my third sortie!

After 45 minutes of hunting, we would leave Kosovo and refuel in Macedonia, and then go back in. After this second vul period, we would head for home, making a total sortie duration of around four and one-half hours. We would land, debrief, eat, and get some sleep before the next day's work. We fought exclusively as two-ships. On most sorties I flew as a wingman but was privileged to lead six.

I was getting shot at daily, but to watch CNN Headline News, Kosovo was a cakewalk, interrupted only by incompetent NATO pilots bombing civilians. Of course, nothing could have been further from the truth. I saw my close friends going to great lengths to avoid harming innocents, often putting themselves at considerable risk in the process. Guys like Capt Francis M. "JD" McDonough have earned my everlasting respect for their actions to keep civilians safe in Kosovo. This is a facet of the war that has been almost entirely overlooked.

We worked under ROEs that severely hampered our ability to attack targets. We were strictly forbidden to engage if there were any chance of collateral damage, no matter how small. That's an important goal, but when taken to extremes, it proved very frustrating. As an example, on one sortie, I saw a red vehicle traveling at high speed towards a village. I paid attention to it because, by this time in the war, we had pretty much destroyed the petroleum reserves in the country. A civilian vehicle racing down the highway was very unusual—especially when the Kosovar-Albanians had been forcibly evacuated and the Serb civilians were given a very low gasoline priority. Anyway, this vehicle stopped in a small village. A few minutes later, the village burst into flames. The vehicle then left the village as quickly as it had come. It seemed obvious that Serbs had torched the village. The Serbs, who, not long into the war, had wisely abandoned their tanks, had taken to driving around in stolen Kosovar-Albanian civilian vehicles. Even though this vehicle obviously was involved with hostile action, we were prohibited from attacking it because it was painted red—not the green of Serb military vehicles!

Now, compare my story to one by Gen H. Norman Schwarzkopf, commander of Central Command. In 1991 he showed the world "the luckiest man in Iraq," using the now-famous video of a bridge being destroyed mere seconds after that Iraqi civilian reached the other side. This video was humorous in 1991, a story told lightheartedly by both the military and the media. In 1999, that same situation would have caused us to abort the attack; or if the attack had continued, it would have generated a huge media uproar. Weird? To me—yes. Nevertheless, it is probably something pilots will have to deal with in America's next war.

After a while, the war's routine and ROEs began to affect us all—but in different ways. Some guys got stressed out while others grew complacent. One of the chaplains on base was quoted in a major newspaper as saying that Kosovo wasn't a real war because of the great conditions in which we lived. That was nonsense to most of the pilots. By this time, two NATO planes had been shot down, several unmanned drones had been blasted from the sky, and two Hogs from my own unit had been damaged. The pilot of one of them, Maj Goldie Haun, was my flight lead the day he was hit. I will never forget conducting a battle-damage check of his jet on the way back over the border and seeing a huge hole where his engine used to be. I could actually see his helmet through the cowling where his engine should have been. Goldie was lucky to make it back to friendly territory before his jet stopped flying altogether. His safe recovery is due to his outstanding flying skill and God's grace.

In some ways though, the chaplain's comments were understandable. Americans see images of World War II and Vietnam, and somehow feel that unless there's mud involved, there is no war. Airpower has changed the reality of warfare—if not the public's perception. World War II bomber pilots fought over Berlin and returned to party in London that night. USAF crews fought in Vietnam from such hardship locations as Guam. So, although the chaplain was dead wrong, I had to admit that the "Cappuccino War," as we came to call it, wasn't what I initially expected it would be. There's something strange about watching my flight lead get smashed by a SAM—then coming back to base and ordering the greatest salmon tortellini I've ever had.

To all of us who fought, Kosovo was an important time—to some, a life-defining event. For example, any hesitation I had about dropping a bomb on another human being evaporated as I flew over Kosovo. Serb atrocities were clearly seen—even from three and one-half miles in the air. The country's highways looked like parking lots as Kosovar-Albanians were forced to abandon their vehicles and walk into Albania. Entire villages were gutted and burned. I quickly learned that no matter what had happened between these ethnic groups in the past, the Serbs were clearly the oppressors now. So the first time I was called on to attack a convoy of Serb military vehicles, just outside a barracks in central Kosovo, I had no moral problems at all. I rolled in, put my pipper on the target, pickled off my bombs, pulled up, spit out some flares, and climbed back into the sun to protect myself from heat-seeking missiles. Just like that.

Due to my younger son's health, I was allowed to return home on the first available transport after the fighting ended. It was a great flight—not in the normal sense, of course, since C-130s are notoriously uncomfortable. No, it was a great flight because I had made it! I had survived the confusing politics, five months of deployment, and almost three months of sustained combat. Not only had I survived, but I had proven to myself that I could perform in combat. That might not seem like much—after all, we fighter pilots like to act like nothing can stop us. But there's always that nagging question, "Do I have what it takes?" I knew the answer, and it felt good!

I returned to Spangdahlem late at night. Our parent wing, the 52d AEW, had been launching, flying, and recovering F-

16CJ and F-117 Nighthawk combat sorties during virtually the entire conflict. I figured that this base would know just how big a deal the fighting had really been. As I drove in the gate, I saw the "Welcome to Spangdahlem" sign. Below it was a message that, for me, truly typified the public's awareness of the combat we had experienced in Kosovo:

CONGRATULATIONS
DENTAL ASSISTANT
APPRECIATION WEEK

5

Target Identification and Rules of Engagement

Introduction

Lt Col Chris "Kimos" Haave

We wrote this chapter with a little trepidation, since it addresses some sensitive and potentially controversial topics. Nevertheless, we think it is important to discuss how the air campaign against fielded ground forces was guided and executed at the tactical level so that readers understand and appreciate the essential war-fighter lessons from our OAF experiences. The authors neither examined all aspects of the air campaign nor attempted to analyze and draw conclusions about the instructions that originated at higher levels of command. We only describe how the ROEs affected our operations—without speculation on the decision-making process that developed them. We discuss how ROEs can best serve an air campaign's objectives, particularly in low- to medium-intensity air operations against ground forces. Our observations and conclusions are from a tactical perspective; from that perspective and at various times, we found the ROEs operationally constraining and war extending.

As the campaign's first AFACs (and the ones who spent the most time over Kosovo), we detected, identified, selected, and engaged most of the fielded Serb forces that NATO engaged. We discuss target identification and ROEs in the same chapter because they had the greatest in-flight influence on determining which targets to leave alone and which to destroy.

Target Identification

Target identification was the critical process through which AFACs located potential targets and determined whether or not they were valid. We used many methods. First, we received a daily list from the CAOC that contained possible targets and their locations, such as "four tanks at coordinates yyyy North and xxxx East." The list was developed during the 12 hours prior to its release, using the best available information. Even so, we quickly learned that it was hopelessly outdated and generally useless. While some of the information may have been incorrect from the start, it was more likely that the Serb forces had moved during the 12–24 hours it took for the data to be gathered, analyzed, and disseminated—and for us to launch, get overhead, and maneuver into a position to attack. The US Army's Hunter UAVs were a much better source of timely information. Their usefulness, however, was still a function of the elapsed time from their observation to our getting overhead.

The crews on the E-8 JSTARS aircraft provided the location of vehicles or convoys that were moving in the KEZ. We found these crews to be very professional and accurate in their assessments of convoy size, makeup, and location. Initially we relied heavily on JSTARS for target information and found ourselves rushing (as fast as a Hog can rush) across Kosovo to identify all convoys, discovering that the vast majority of them were civilian vehicles. The Serbs quickly countered the JSTARS capability by hiding their armored vehicles and mixing their other military vehicles in among the civilian cars, trucks, and tractors that made up the large refugee convoys. Often we were called to identify a convoy while in the process of setting up to attack a valid target. We would abort that attack, fly to the convoy, confirm it was limited to refugee vehicles, run out of gas, and be forced to return to base or go to the tanker. That approach left the original valid targets undamaged. We agreed within the first two weeks to change tactics. The JSTARS crew members would give us an initial target-area briefing, and then we would "pull" information rather than have them "push" it—unless, of course, they saw a particularly interesting target.

There were too few JSTARS aircraft in-theater to provide around-the-clock coverage. The CAOC directed JSTARS to support daylight KEZ operations, which left the night uncovered. We later concluded that the E-8 would have been much more productive had it flown at night. The Serbs generally stopped moving equipment during the day because we had been suc-cessful in acquiring them visually and picking them off. How-ever, they became very active at night—moving and digging like crazy. Every morning artillery had been moved to new pits; more revetments, tunnels, and dugouts had been constructed to pro-tect APCs; and the wreckage of the armor and artillery that we destroyed the day before had been recovered and moved.

Our proposal to switch JSTARS from day to night operations was passed to the CAOC. We reasoned that the JSTARS crews would be able to observe the Serbs' nightly movements and in-form us where they had relocated their weaponry, so that at daybreak we could *schwack* 'em. JSTARS would also be able to assist the nighttime F-16CG and Guard A-10 FACs. The CAOC rejected our proposal, beliving that JSTARS aircraft were needed during the day, when most small Serbian military targets were being struck.

The lack of satellites or drone imagery was also a serious void in our tool kit for locating targets. We did not have a dedicated imagery-production process to provide our unit with photos of the Serbs' fielded forces. Perhaps those targets did not have suf-ficient priority or had been deemed "too hard" to locate. Whatever the reason, the CAOC provided imagery on only a few occasions.

The 40th EOG's operations-intelligence section contained some of the unsung heroes in the A-10's OAF success. This out-standing group was comprised of elements from the 52d FW at Spang and the 23d Fighter Group at Pope, and was well led by 1st Lt Stephen "Al" Smith and Capt Kenneth R. "Ken" Uhler. Their creative response to the imagery problem provided us with many good pictures that resulted in numerous confirmed kills. They fought hard to acquire the equipment necessary to access the Web sites that contained classified US imagery and then spent two to three hours every night searching and downloading satellite target pictures of Serbian forces in the KEZ. They also built a solid working relationship with the British intelligence section located across the street from our operations building. Their GR-7 Harriers often carried photoreconnaissance pods, and our intel counterparts would process the morning's film, an-alyze and enlarge the best prospects, and then bring them over to our unit. From these two sources, Al and Ken built the eagerly anticipated "Hog menu of the day" target list. Some days were richer than others, but the Hog menu usually included at least three and as many as seven targets.

USAF Photo

British GR-7 Harrier

Sadly, there was another source of beautiful imagery for finding Serb army targets that we were unable to exploit. The French army operated ground-controlled reconnaissance drones and routinely collected imagery during the course of the conflict that could have been very valuable. We were unable to use it because we did not even know it existed. I first became aware of this capability a year after OAF while visiting a large open house in September 2000 that was hosted jointly by the French army and the French Joint Defense College. There I met members of the 61st Artillery Regiment as they displayed their CL 289 and Crecerelle optical and IR-imagery drones. They explained that their drones were able to take both day and night pictures, and that they also had data links for real-time imagery transmission. Curious, I asked their leader if they had participated in any recent operations. A lieutenant said, "Yes, Kosovo." I then asked them from where, and they replied "Kumanovo"—which had been our Macedonian entry point into the eastern half of the KEZ. I asked them how they employed their drones, and they said they flew them daily to determine the positions of Serb army tanks, APCs, and artillery—exactly in the areas where we flew our missions. They normally flew them at night so that they would have a good ground order of battle for the beginning of the day. I asked if their operations had been effective. They said, "Yes," and added that they got very good, if not complete, information on Serb army dispositions. I asked them to whom they sent their imagery, and they said to the normal French army-intelligence channels.

I was flabbergasted. As the sun went up each day, we were always the first AFACs across the border, and we desperately needed that kind of imagery to find targets. The French imagery would have been perfect for us since it could have been delivered close enough to real time that the enemy could not have moved his weaponry before we arrived overhead. Someone had it—but we didn't. I can't speculate on where it went or why it never got to us, but obviously every possibility for obtaining crucial target information should be exploited.

Another good source of current target information was the CAOC's force-level execution (FLEX) targeting cell. The FLEX cell fused information gained from various sources, using a variety of methods, and was often able to determine the location of actively operating Serb army units and command posts. For example, when a Serb artillery unit fired on a Kosovar village, the US Army's counterbattery radar could plot the Serbs' position. Similarly, when a Serb command post transmitted orders on its radios, our electronic warfare (EW) folks could triangulate its location. The FLEX cell also received target information from Predator drones. The cell fused all of this information and passed it to the ABCCC, which would then contact the AFAC in the area nearest the suspected target. The AFAC would then take a look, and our experience confirmed that the FLEX information was usually quite accurate. The marriage of drones and AFACs to locate and engage targets was a first for either combat or training operations. Sometimes it worked well, and sometimes it didn't. Our pioneering work with Predator is addressed more fully in chapter 7.

RQ-1A Predator, a long-endurance, medium-altitude unmanned aircraft system for surveillance and reconnaissance missions

Even with all this high-tech help, we still located about 80 percent of the targets we engaged using our Mk-1 eyeballs, augmented by our trusty 12-power gyrostabilized binoculars. A typical OAF AFAC scenario would begin with thorough flight planning using the best target information available from all sources. After takeoff the AFAC would contact ABCCC and/or JSTARS and integrate their updates into his mission planning while en route to the KEZ. He would then proceed directly to the target areas. The AFAC would focus on either the highest priority target or the one that had the highest likelihood of being found. Failing to find anything to attack at the target coordinates and lacking any other good target information, the AFAC would proceed to areas where his experience suggested that he might find something worth attacking.

When AFACs looked for a particular target around a set of coordinates, their observant, naked eyes could often spot telltale signs of other targets—new revetments, tracks leading into the woods, and unusually configured shapes on a hillside. "Well, looky here!" was our normal reaction. The AFAC would then use his binoculars to get a closer look, and if it proved to be a valid target, he'd set up attacks. After our AFACs returned to the squadron, they compiled their own list of AFAC-located (but not destroyed) targets to be included in the daily mission reports to the CAOC and for follow-on AFACs to use in their flight planning.

USAF Photo

Artillery pit found and attacked by an A-10 AFAC. The barrel was blown off and found nearby.

Rules of Engagement

Rules of engagement are exactly what the term implies—rules that limit friendly forces' operations as they engage hostile forces. There were two levels of ROEs during OAF: those imposed by the integrated NATO command authorities and those imposed by nations (or their organic commands) on their own forces. In most cases, national ROEs were more restrictive. For example, out of concern for the vulnerability of their particular aircraft, some nations raised the minimum-attack altitude for their aircraft to above that published in the NATO ROEs.

ROEs were proposed, developed, and changed at several levels within the command hierarchy. In our case, ROEs originated with and were reviewed by political authorities at the North Atlantic Council (NAC) in Brussels; SACEUR at Mons, Belgium; commander, AFSOUTH at Naples, Italy; commander, AIRSOUTH; and the CFACC. We understood that commander of AFSOUTH, at the operational level, was the chief ROE-setting authority.

143

NATO authorities "published" air-campaign ROEs in several documents that were then disseminated to subordinate headquarters and units. ROEs were published in the air operations directive and special instructions (SPINS). Additionally, because ROEs often changed, the CAOC dedicated a section of the daily ATO to list all of the ROEs applicable to that day's sorties. All OAF units reviewed that dedicated section during their pre-mission preparation and found it very useful.

ROEs for KEZ operations fell into three general categories: altitude restrictions, restricted (no-attack) zones on the ground, and procedures to lower the risk of collateral damage. Altitude restrictions were designed to minimize the risk to aircrews from SAM and AAA threats. Higher altitude either puts the aircraft above the enemy's effective capability or provides the aircrew with enough time to react and defeat the surface-to-air threats. On 30 March, at the outset of CAIFF operations, we were given the same minimum-altitude restriction as aircraft flying in interdiction packages—15,000 feet AGL. Although it kept us relatively safe, this altitude made identification of small military vehicles very difficult and rendered A-10 attacks practically impossible. By 6 April the mission-support elements of the standard KEZ package (SEAD, EW, ABCCC, NAEW, and combat air patrol [CAP]) had demonstrated their ability to suppress the most lethal Serb threats, and we were able to convince the CAOC to let AFACs descend to 10,000 feet AGL.

We operated with that minimum ROE altitude until 14 April—the tragic day when a civilian-vehicle convoy was incorrectly identified as a Serb military target and attacked by NATO aircraft. In reaction to this incident, the CAOC changed the minimum altitudes for KEZ operations to improve target confirmation. AFACs could descend to 5,000 feet AGL, and all fighters could descend to 8,000 feet AGL during target attack. These ROEs seemed backwards to us Hog drivers at Gioia. Most enemy missile launches occurred while the AFACs were searching for targets, focused on the ground, and doing very little maneuvering—not during weapons delivery. We immediately directed all of our pilots to conduct target search no lower than 10,000 feet AGL.

144

No-attack zones were geographically defined areas within Kosovo in which we could not expend ordnance. Restricted areas were also geographically defined areas within Kosovo where weapons could be employed only after receiving CAOC permission. Various authorities had established these zones for a variety of reasons. The first such area to appear in the ROEs was the no-attack zone within 10 nautical miles of the Macedonian border. While at first we did not understand, we later learned that the zone was meant to reduce the risk of possible Serb reprisals on NATO troops in Macedonia. Authorities apparently believed that the Serbs might confuse the source of the ordnance raining down on them. Their concern was that the Serbs would ignore the NATO fighters overhead, credit the attacks to NATO artillery to the south, and expand the war into Macedonia. Other restricted areas were created near the end of the campaign, particularly in areas where it was thought the KLA was operating or where refugees were gathered.

Finally, we followed a variety of rules designed to lower the risk of *collateral damage*, commonly defined as the unintentional or incidental injury or damage to persons or objects that are not military targets. The various rules included a temporary prohibition on the use of cluster munitions, the requirement for CAOC approval before attacking targets close to civilian structures, and restrictions on the type and color of vehicles that could be engaged.

Each of these rules had intentional and unintentional consequences for target identification and target engagement. ROEs calling for higher minimum made the pilots' task of judging whether the vehicles on the ground were civilian or military more difficult. The border of a no-attack zone meant the enemy could move from imminent danger on one side of a road to sanctuary on the other side. Other attack restrictions on areas, munitions, and target categories slowed down the prosecution of attacks. During this waiting period targets could escape by moving to a sanctuary area, weather might move in and hide them from attack, or the waiting attack aircraft might run low on fuel and be forced to depart before receiving an attack clearance.

Approval Process

In the beginning of KEZ operations, the ROEs were quite simple: AFACs were their own attack-clearance authority after they had determined that the suspected object was a valid military target. CAOC approval was required only when the AFAC judged that the attack might cause collateral damage—usually to civilian buildings. During the course of the conflict, many additional target types were moved from the discretionary list to one that required CAOC approval. Later, geographic areas were defined, and targets in those new restricted areas required CAOC approval prior to attack.

AFACs often became frustrated when it appeared the CAOC was second-guessing the targets they had chosen to attack. For example, on the second day of KEZ attacks, near the southwestern border of Kosovo, I had located two large, dark-green military deuce-and-a-half trucks, complete with curved canvas tops. They were parked just off an asphalt road on the north side of high terrain, northwest of Mount Pastrik. As I talked a flight of Dutch F-16s through an attack on these two targets, ABCCC called in-the-clear, on strike frequency, and asked whether I had positively confirmed that the target was military. I responded, "Yes." The F-16s had missed on their first pass, so I directed them to make another attack. Apparently my answer to the ABCCC wasn't sufficient for the CAOC. ABCCC then asked me to describe the target—evidently to personally confirm that it was military. Because we had already received AAA fire, I didn't think we should loiter in this area. Barely able to maintain my composure, I described the trucks in detail. After landing I called our CAOC representative who told me that since JSTARS had not detected trucks in that area, the battle-staff director needed additional assurance on the target. In this case, JSTARS could not see the trucks because a high mountain blocked the line of sight between its radar orbit and the trucks. Likewise, the E-8's moving-target indicator would not have highlighted the parked trucks.

We appreciated the CAOC's concern for avoiding civilian nontargets. In a similar manner, I was particularly proud of our pilots' strict discipline, which ensured that their attacks and the ones they directed avoided collateral civilian damage.

If they were in doubt about the military nature of the target or the possibility of damaging a civilian structure, they brought their ordnance home and let the potential bad guys escape. To do otherwise might have cost the lives of innocent people and severely jeopardized the political support for KEZ operations. As CAOC "interference" became routine, I learned to control my blood pressure, jink, and talk to ABCCC.

The CAOC seemed poorly organized to act quickly when the ROEs required its approval. When an AFAC independently found a target in a restricted area or close to a village, it usually took 15 to 20 minutes to obtain approval. For example, using Lt Al Smith's intel imagery, Maj Goldie Haun discovered what he thought to be a radar-missile launcher in an area south of Pristina. I flew there the next morning and found the small, wooded area just on the southern edge of a square village. From 15,000 feet I looked down through the trees with my binoculars and did not see any launchers. I did, however, see about 10 rectangular metal canisters stacked on a flatbed trailer in the center of the woods. They were about 15 feet long and the size of radar-guided missiles. I had two problems: the canisters were less than 100 meters from the nearest house in the village, and a low deck of clouds had begun to move in and would soon block my view of the target area. The trees prevented success when I tried to lock up the trailer with a Maverick, and the low clouds to the east ruled out an airburst Mk-82 attack flying on a heading parallel to the houses—the only attack axis that would minimize the risk to the occupants of the house. I still had my 30 mm cannon, which would work just fine. Moving off to the west to mask my interest in the area, I called ABCCC on secure radio to request approval to attack the trailer and had to wait 25 minutes for a response. During that time, the low clouds moved into the area around the trailer. I made several more calls to help expedite the clearance. I finally got the CAOC's approval to attack, and with it came the direction to "use the gun and not hit any houses!"

The delay and the tactical direction were absurd and a clear violation of the principle of "centralized control and decentralized execution." The expert on the weapon systems' capabilities and limitations had been sitting in the cockpit, looking at the target, fully capable of making a real-time execution decision consistent with ROEs that centralized control had generated. During those 25 minutes, the low clouds moved in and obscured the northern end of the target area. Because the clouds limited my options, the only attack heading I could then use was south to north—pointed directly at the village. My bullets could have ricocheted off the trailer and into the houses. The policy to centralize execution decisions had caused the delay, which had allowed the weather to change, the Serb missile canisters to escape attack, and the missiles in those canisters to remain part of the enemy's combat capability. Perhaps those missiles were some of the many that were subsequently shot at our pilots.

The CAOC's actions indicated that its personnel were under colossal pressure to produce results and avoid collateral damage. They regularly interrupted our attacks—even those authorized by the ROEs. In their zeal to ensure we had the most up-to-date ROEs, the CAOC prompted ABCCC crews to remind us of what and where we could and could not attack. Unfortunately, these calls were sometimes made over the strike frequencies that Serbs monitored, allowing them to hear, "You cannot attack any targets within 10 miles of the Macedonia border," "you cannot attack any trucks, civilian vehicles, vehicles painted white," and other similar transmissions. The unintended consequences of these in-the-clear transmissions were that Serbs began moving their forces south to within 10 miles of the Macedonian border and started transporting their troops in civilian vehicles instead of APCs— we saw white charter buses everywhere.

Even when AFACs were directed to enter restricted areas to find specific CAOC-identified targets, they were still required to receive CAOC approval before they attacked. On one occasion the CAOC tasked Capt Jim Meger to find and destroy a Serb command post. After locating it he requested approval to attack. It then took the CAOC 20 minutes to approve the strike against the command post it had sent him to destroy. These delays not only allowed some targets to escape attack, but also put our pilots at greater risk. On this occasion, it took the

Serbs a lot less than 20 minutes to locate Jim, draw a bead, and fire two missiles at him (see chap. 4).

Our frustrations grew. We were getting shot at while we waited for CAOC clearance to attack, we watched helplessly as Serbs in "civilian" vehicles burned villages, and we were denied clearance to attack enemy troops and equipment in the ROE-designed sanctuaries. I began briefing visiting dignitaries on our successes and frustrations when they passed through our base at Gioia. In late April I described our situation—from our point of view, warts and all—to two very distinguished visitors, Acting Secretary of the Air Force F. Whitten Peters and Gen John P. Jumper, commander of USAFE. I emphasized that, while we thought the current situation was unacceptable, we also understood there were probably some aspects of the ROEs and target-approval process that might justify the delays. So, we thought that informing us of those constraints could make the whole process more responsive and that we could better fulfill our responsibility for identifying valid targets. They listened carefully. General Jumper took a lot of notes, asked who had been working these issues for us at the CAOC, and asked if I knew whether Lt Gen Mike Short was aware of our problems. I told him that, every day, we passed our concerns to the lieutenant colonel who represented our unit at the CAOC. He replied, "Now you've got a four star."

General Jumper suggested that I go to the CAOC to brief General Short personally. I thought that was a good idea and discussed it with Lt Col Walrus Heise, our representative. I expected to be summoned to the CAOC during the days that followed. A few days later our unit got a call to attend a conference at Tirana, Albania, with General Short and Lt Gen John W. Hendrix, the US Army V Corps commander. The purpose of the conference was to discuss employment options with the US Army Apache helicopters. We hoped to discuss the ROEs with General Short while we were there.

Colonel Thompson, Lt Col Coke Koechle, our two squadron weapons officers, and I flew as passengers in a C-21 from Gioia del Colle to Tirana on 1 May. We did not know that General Jumper had sent General Short an E-mail outlining our grievances with the ROEs and approval process. We soon discovered just how unhappy General Short was when he called Coke and me aside at the end of the Apache conference. Coke had worked for General Short at Headquarters USAFE, knew him well, and was not completely unhinged by the dressing-down that followed. General Short detailed for us—with incandescent clarity—that when our commander, a four-star flag officer (Vice Adm James O. Ellis Jr., AFSOUTH and NATO joint force commander) had determined the ROEs, he expected his field graders to understand and follow them, or seek clarification in appropriate channels. He did not need those same officers taking their gripes to another four star when they failed to understand or disagreed with the ROEs. "If you have a problem," General Short said, "then come to Vicenza and see me."

After it was over—and I realized that I hadn't been fired—we all had gained a new appreciation for the source of General Short's ire. He had foreign governments second-guessing his conduct of the campaign; he surely didn't need the same thing from his own squadron commanders and line pilots. Nonetheless, we still hoped something good would result from venting our concerns and our pain.

Something did. Just days later, the CAOC adjusted the ROEs and replaced the 10-mile-deep no-attack border restriction with three zones: from the border to two miles, two to five miles, and five to 10 miles from the border. Attacks on targets inside 10 miles were now possible, and the probability of CAOC approval increased as the distance from the border to the targets increased.

Our AFACs took this change to heart and besieged the CAOC with requests to attack their favorite and previously protected targets. This deluge of AFAC requests generated a negative, unintended consequence. The CAOC began to feel the need to issue a clearance for all attacks—even for those targets where the existing ROEs did not require CAOC approval. Late in the campaign, for example, ABCCC sent Colonel Thompson and me to identify an active Serb artillery site that the US Army's counterbattery radar had located about five miles west of Prizren. It was exactly at the coordinates given, six big tubes parked around a concrete pad facing south. They were not in a restricted area and were well clear of all civilian buildings. We confirmed the target with ABCCC (call sign Moonbeam) and directed that it move our fighters forward. Moonbeam said to stand by for CAOC approval. It was clear that the controller was reading from a checklist he had been directed to use. The radio conversations went something like this:

"Chili 11, Moonbeam, say distance to nearest civilian buildings."

"Moonbeam, Chili 11, this target is not in a restricted area. I do not need CAOC approval to attack it."

"Chili 11, the CAOC will not let you attack the target unless we get clearance."

"Moonbeam, attacking this target will not cause collateral damage. Say reason for needing target approval."

"Chili 11, we know the CAOC will insist on the information. We know we'll get the approval faster if we have it ready."

"Moonbeam, go ahead."

"Chili 11, say distance and direction to nearest civilian buildings."

"Moonbeam, the nearest civilian building is 400 meters to the west."

"Chili 11, describe the building."

"Moonbeam, the building is a farm building about 20-meters square."

"Chili 11, Moonbeam, say type and location of the nearest civilian vehicle."

(I paused to find one somewhere.)

"Moonbeam, the nearest civilian vehicle is a single car parked in the outskirts of Prizren, at least two kilometers from the target."

"Moonbeam copies, stand by."

We productively used the next several minutes (and gas) to locate some mortar pits farther to the south.

"Chili 11, Moonbeam."

"Moonbeam, Chili 11, go ahead."

"Chili 11, the CAOC wants to know if you can attack that target without causing collateral damage to the farm building 400 meters away."

"I can't believe this!" I transmitted privately to Colonel Thompson on the FM radio.

"Moonbeam, Chili 11, inform the CAOC that I can attack this target without causing collateral damage to a building 400 meters away."

"Moonbeam copies, stand by."

We finally got our attack clearance and proceeded to destroy all six of the big artillery pieces, using all the ordnance that was carried by another A-10 flight, a GR-7 flight, and us.

We began to accuse the CAOC folks of trying to FAC from their desks in Vicenza. This time, however, we took a different approach. We submitted a paper to the CAOC on ways to simplify the ROEs and reduce risk to the pilots, while maintaining the zero-collateral-damage safeguards. Col Stu Johnson, the CAOC chief of operations, sympathized with our request but reasoned that the alliance had about all it could take of changing ROEs. He said we'd have to do the best we could under the circumstances and promised to try to accelerate the approval process.

That he did. In the last week or so of the campaign, as the KLA stepped up its pressure on the Serbs, the delay in receiving our target-attack approval was significantly reduced. As noted earlier, this close control by the CAOC violated a basic tenet of air and space power, which calls for centralized control and decentralized execution. Just as centralized planning and control is critical to the proper application of airpower, our *Air Force Basic Doctrine* (AFDD 1) reminds us that so is the concept of decentralized execution—"delegation of execution authority to responsible and capable lower-level commanders is essential to achieve effective span of control and to foster initiative, situational responsiveness, and tactical flexibility"(23). We experienced centralized control and execution. Consequently, our situational responsiveness and tactical flexibility suffered.

I want to emphasize that our discussion of ROEs, their application in OAF, and the influence that they had on our combat effectiveness is not intended to air gripes or to disparage the fine professionals who worked in the extremely difficult circumstances at the CAOC. When we complain about problems with "the CAOC," we do not fix blame but merely identify the CAOC as our immediate contact in the command and control conduit. General Short, Colonel Johnson, and all the battle-staff directors who sat in "the chair" during the nonstop combat operations probably saved our unit from immeasurable pain on numerous occasions—and we never knew it. We did know that we had their support throughout OAF, and we gratefully and sincerely applauded their leadership after the NATO victory.

Nevertheless, we hope that we will never again fight a war with similar ROEs. We had no knowledge of the agendas of, or the interaction and dynamics between nations, heads of state, and our leaders (SECDEF, SACEUR, AFSOUTH, CFACC, and the CAOC). Therefore, we are unable to comment on what the ROEs could or should have been. We did understand that any targeting mistakes that took the lives of innocents could easily have unraveled the international support for the campaign. However, it is our conviction that the war was unnecessarily lengthened and that innocent Kosovar lives were lost because we did not have streamlined ROEs which supported decentralized execution. Our recommendations for the future:

- Push responsibility and authority to the lowest possible level—trust those who are well trained to do their jobs.

- Develop unambiguous target-identification procedures that allow for decentralized decision making at the AFAC level.

- Consider calling a "time out" for a day or two to gather the experts and decide on a best way to go forward when the ROEs adversely affect combat operations.

- Ensure that all war fighters fully understand the ROEs.

When Things Work Out

Maj Pete "Bro" Brotherton

It was a bright, clear morning. We approached our target from the southwest and visually picked up the revetted APC while we were still more than five miles out. We circled south to compare and confirm the target with the photo. I set up and executed a tip-in from the east. It sounds so simple, and sometimes it was if I could ignore the fact that I was being shot at. To get to that point usually took quite a bit of work.

This story really starts one and one-half days prior to that bright, clear morning. Our A-10 squadron was flying from Gioia del Colle AB, where several Italian squadrons, some British GR-7 Harriers, and we were based. The GR-7s occasionally flew with a reconnaissance pod and took pictures of areas of interest. The Brits were nice enough to share those photos with our intel folks. The photo for this mission came in one night while I was working a 12-hour top-three tour. Those of us who pulled top-three duty, especially the night tours, were not thrilled with the task. But this night we were lucky. Pictures of an APC and several other interesting targets came in just after dark, and I briefed them to all the pilots on the morning schedule. At the end of my tour, I went to bed knowing that the guys walking out the door to fly had several good targets. Like everyone who pulled a night top-three tour, I was given a day off to sleep and then scheduled in the first flight of the following day.

I arrived in our operations area at about 0230, sat down for the intel brief, and was handed a couple photos and the usual target list. To my surprise the same photos of APCs were still in the package. Intel said no one had reported hitting the target, so they were passing it out again. The weather had been poor in the area where the APCs were located, and the AFACs had looked for targets in areas with better weather. Although day-old target photos are often worthless, my wingman and I decided we would take a look since we would be the first planes in Kosovo and we hadn't worked that area in many days.

When I studied the targets, including the APCs, I plotted them all on a large Joint Operations Graphic (JOG) map, drawn to a 1:250 scale, that I used in the cockpit to work the entire Kosovo area. I plotted the most promising targets on a smaller 1:50 scale map so I could get a good feel for those areas and accurately determine target coordinates and elevations. (While these maps are normally referred to as 1:50, 1:250, or 1:500, their scale is actually 1:50,000, 1:250,000, or 1:500,000.)

The elevations had to be converted from meters to feet, and the coordinates put in several formats to satisfy the various navigation systems used in the different aircraft we might control. We often did this while circling over a target, but it was much easier to do ahead of time on the ground. I then used a computer that contained photomaps of the area in various scales. With this I could look at each target area from different altitudes. Although neither the photos on the computer nor the maps were current, they gave us a good perspective of the surrounding area—the lay-of-the-land, so to speak. With this situational awareness, we could choose an attack axis that would give us the best chance of success while limiting damage to anything but the target. With our planning complete, I briefed my wingman on the plan to attack this target and search for others in our assigned area.

The flight to the tanker was quiet, and I was encouraged that the weather would cooperate. Our tanker track was over southern Macedonia, and from there I could see that the sky over our target area was bright and clear. We got our gas, departed Macedonia, and proceeded northeast into southeastern Serbia above the Kumanovo Valley. While en route to the tanker, I had tested my two Maverick missiles, and now I reapplied power to start what I hoped would be the last warm-up cycle for at least one of them. We headed for our target, which we expected to find just a few miles west of Vranje. The larger target area was easy to see from far off, and the APC came into view as we drew near. I checked with my wingman to confirm that he saw the target, and then I started to circle south to make a final check to ensure that we were at the right spot. I put the jet's head-up display (HUD) in the proper mode for attack and checked the other settings. The scene below was surrealistic.

A small single-story house was located on a small dirt lane that connected to the valley's main road. The backyard of the house, which the sun was just beginning to hit, was fenced and contained the usual scattering of possessions one has become accustomed to expect. In the front, a dirt driveway led from the road to a small attached garage. I could not detect any movement in the area—not unusual that early in the morning. This was a scene that could have been repeated anywhere in the world, except for two things. This scene matched my target photo exactly, and just 15 to 20 feet north of the driveway was a recently dug revetment in which sat an APC—not your average family roadster. To arm my weapons, I flipped the final switches. I got a good picture and the green lights that indicated the missiles were ready. I checked the position of my wingman and set up for a tip-in from the east. I made one last check of my switches, rechecked the HUD, and rolled into a dive for the attack.

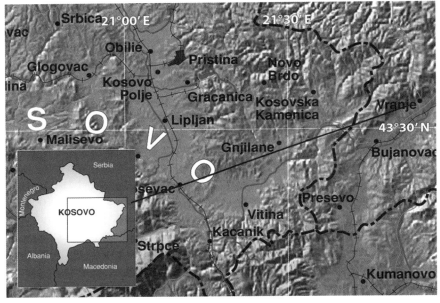

APC just west of Vranje

The IIR Maverick picture that I saw in the cockpit was about what I expected. Different parts of the house indicated various temperatures. The rear wall and one window were cold, while another window and the chimney were hot. Most importantly, the APC was cold—very cold. It had not been run that night. Our observations up to this point indicated that lucrative targets that didn't move were often decoys. However, I was confident that was not the case this time. I slewed the Maverick seeker to the target and got an immediate lock. I waited a moment for the missile's brain to signal me it could distinguish the target from the background. It was ready. I took one last look through the HUD and pushed the pickle button.

The sound of a 500 lb Maverick coming off the LAU-117 launcher is exciting. I shot many of these missiles during the war and still was amazed by each launch. Once it was on its way I started to pull out of the dive. I had lost less altitude than expected during the attack since the missile lock-on process had gone so quickly. The first few seconds of the missile's flight are usually indicative of whether or not it will hit the target. This one flew as expected, and I monitored it until it disappeared below the nose of my jet. I then looked up to locate my wingman to make sure that I would not climb into him. He was where I expected, watching for possible ground fire. I continued to maneuver in the climb although neither of us saw any reaction from the surface. I looked back at the target as it sat there doomed. A Maverick missile never arrives early or even when one expects it to hit. No matter how long I thought the time of flight would be, I would still have to wait when I looked at the target to see the impact. I waited—then it was over. I saw a bright flash of orange and yellow flame followed by a growing cloud of dark gray smoke. A small shock wave emanated from the revetment in a growing circle and quickly dissipated. We saw small flashes at the base of the smoke plume—probably detonating ammunition inside the APC. This was no decoy. The house was untouched.

We proceeded southwest down the valley to move away from the area we had just attacked. The Kumanovo Valley was full of revetments, trenches, and other obstacles the Serbs felt would help them if an invasion came from the south. All of them we saw that day were empty. Forty minutes later, as we departed the area to get more gas, the APC was still burning.

When Things Don't Work Out

Maj Pete "Bro" Brotherton

We pilots lived by ROEs. They told us what we could strike and what we could not. We had to become familiar with a stack of documents several inches thick in order to fly missions over Kosovo. The ROEs were a small—but important—

portion of these documents. Early in the conflict the rules were fluid and changed quite often for many different reasons. After a couple of weeks into the war and a major shift in focus, the ROEs settled down and remained fairly constant except for a few silly, and often politically driven changes. During the last couple of weeks of OAF, the rules again began to change frequently. It was not uncommon when we flew on two consecutive days to use different rules on the second day—sometimes they even changed during a mission.

In Kosovo and during the period from a few weeks after the war started until a couple weeks before it ended, we AFACs were given a fairly free rein to attack whatever military targets we deemed worthy. It was a bold move by Lt Gen Mike Short, commander of AIRSOUTH in Vicenza, Italy, to relinquish control of tactical decision making to the lieutenants, captains, and majors who were on scene and had the best available information. While it was a big responsibility, it was also a godsend and allowed us to kill many more targets than would have been possible under different rules. Our freedom to observe the situation, apply the ROEs, and make decisions was taken away sometime during the last couple of weeks of the war. That change led to the most frustration I experienced during any mission of the conflict.

My wingman and I were on an AFAC mission. We were proceeding from the tanker track into the KEZ when we got a call from a flight of A-10 strikers. They were searching for targets about five or 10 miles north of Prizren, and the flight lead said he had found what he thought were four APCs. Someone next to the APCs had just fired a handheld SAM at his aircraft. He was running low on fuel and wanted to hand the target off to someone before he departed. I led my flight to the target area to take control. A thin, wispy trail of smoke still indicated the missile's flight path, from where it had been launched to where its motor had burnt out. After receiving a good hand-over brief, I used my binos to check out the area. I had some bad news and some good news for the departing flight lead. The bad news—he had found only one APC; the good news—the other three were tanks, and relatively modern models at that. What a find! I began the coordination process for an attack.

We were near the end of the conflict, the ROEs had changed, and we were required to get permission before we could direct attacks on any target. We had operated with these rules for the past couple of days and found that the approval process could be either quick or take many minutes. We soon learned that the best course of action was to find a target, call in the request to strike, and then search for other targets while waiting for approval. At any given time we would have several attack requests in the process of being approved or denied. When we received permission to strike, we had to figure out which of the targets had been approved and then relocate it—hoping to find it where we had last seen it. I was sure that the details of these targets would cause the process to be more responsive. It was a large group of tanks, in the open and far away from any man-made structure. I was excited and decided to stay overhead to monitor their activity while waiting for approval.

I had submitted my target to the ABCCC guys orbiting south of the border, who passed it to the CAOC in Italy. The CAOC, I was told later, had to phone someone even farther removed from the fight. That person would look at a map and decide either to grant or refuse permission to attack. That person was probably away from his desk when the call with our request came in; my wingman and I waited. There was activity down below. The tanks were about 100 feet from a paved road, and a small white car was parked on the side of the road. We suspected that the occupants of the white car were part of the Serb forces associated with the tanks. The Serbs' favorite mode of travel appeared to be stolen Kosovar cars. Their early OAF experience had taught them that civilian vehicles survived when convoys were attacked. At about this time a small civilian flatbed truck arrived from the town located about a kilometer down the road. It stopped near the car, and its occupants proceeded to unload whatever it was carrying.

After five or 10 minutes had passed, I radioed the ABCCC folks to see if they had any news. I told them of the new developments and asked that they check with CAOC to see if more information was needed. From the radio traffic that we could hear, KEZ didn't sound very busy, but one never knew what might be happening in the CAOC. While we waited, I continued to prepare for the attack. I determined the target coordinates and elevation, and checked the winds at our attack altitude. I rechecked our location on a large-scale map and planned where I could hold strikers, if and when they arrived. I wanted to avoid holding a striker directly over a known radar SAM area—that was poor form. I made sure my flight would be ready to attack when the word came down. We spun up our weapons and briefed a plan of action. And we waited.

A flight of A-10 strikers checked in on frequency. They had been released by their AFAC in the west since he did not have any targets for them and had heard that we had tanks. They were each carrying two CBU-87 combined-effects munitions, which were perfect weapons for my group of four armored vehicles parked right next to each other. I brought the strikers in and held them south of the target, briefing them on the situation and asking how much time they had. The flight lead said they had enough fuel to stay on station about 20 to 25 minutes. I told them the approval process was taking longer than usual and asked that they conserve as much fuel as possible. To prepare them for their attack, I deconflicted our altitudes and had them fly over and take a look at the target. This would enable them to attack as soon as the approval came down. We confirmed that we were dealing with three of the newer tank models the Serbs had in Kosovo. We discussed attack plans, munitions placement, and local threats. I then called ABCCC for an update. And we waited.

I sent the strikers south a few miles to resume holding. I scouted the surrounding area for more targets but didn't stray more than a mile or two from the tanks. It had been over 30 minutes since we requested approval to strike, and I was beginning to worry about our fuel state. We could spend between 45 minutes and an hour over Kosovo. This relatively short on-station time would leave us with enough fuel to fly to the tanker track, attempt refueling, and—even if we could not refuel—still be able to return to Italy. We were conserving fuel while we were waiting, but how much longer would it take? Movement on the ground brought me back to the main target. One of the civilian vehicles was departing, and, as I flew overhead, it appeared that the armored vehicles were starting their engines. I excitedly called ABCCC to say it was now or never and told them to tell the CAOC that these vehicles would soon be gone. We waited a few minutes more.

Then things started to come apart. The lone APC moved out onto the road and sat there for a few moments. The three tanks started to move in the opposite direction, through the fields, and deployed in a column formation. I called ABCCC with my last message: "They're moving, they are moving. I'm losing this target." It took a few moments for them to answer, and I assumed that delay was caused by a call to the CAOC. Finally, 40 minutes after my first request, I got what I wanted—clearance to attack. The tanks were now moving slowly through the fields, but the APC was speeding down the paved road towards the nearest town. I decided that I would try to stop the APC first and then bring the fighters up from the south to deal with the tanks. I was sure the tanks could not get far in the time it would take to make one Maverick attack on the APC. It was probably less than a minute from the time I got permission to attack till I rolled in on the APC. I had the right weapons mode set, Maverick video on the screen, and green ready lights. I was ready to kill something.

As I rolled out, pointed at the APC moving down the road, I looked at the TV screen and watched the picture change from crisp and clear to a wavy-lined mess. I couldn't believe it. I thought maybe just the one missile had gone bad and had thrown the switches that called up the missile on the other wing. The picture there was just as bad—the 1960s technology in my TV monitor had failed; maintenance guys say this has been a problem for years. The Maverick pass had taken me too low to be able to switch to the gun, continue the attack, and recover before busting the ROEs' minimum-altitude limit. However, I had developed plenty of speed during that long dive and was able to pull the plane up to near vertical to gain altitude while I set the switches for a gun attack. I was still below the minimum altitude that I generally used for starting attacks—especially for consecutive attacks in a handheld SAM area—but I was mad. I pulled the jet out of its steep climb and pointed its nose at the APC rolling down the road. It was moving faster than any target I had ever tried to attack (moving targets are hard to come by in training). I aimed in front of the APC by a distance I thought would work, and planned to walk my rounds down the road to make sure I got some hits. Because each round from a 30 mm Avenger cannon weighs three quarters of a pound, it doesn't take many hits to destroy an APC. I squeezed the trigger and heard the gun rotate—something was wrong—no rounds came out. I held the trigger down for a while longer, thinking there might be a blank spot in the shell train. I got nothing and was now far lower than I wanted to be. I pulled off target—again trading airspeed for altitude. I was beside myself. I rechecked switches—all were correct. I could not believe what had just happened. All the effort that had gone into this sortie and all the time it took to get approval for the attack would not matter, it seemed, for today was not going to be my day to kill armor.

I had bled off too much energy, so it took a while to climb back to altitude. That gave me time to cool off and decide that, even though I couldn't get a kill today, I could make sure that others would. By this time the APC had escaped. It made it to the safety of the town and was off limits. I started looking for the three tanks that I had last seen moving slowly to the northeast. They were gone. I cursed myself for not assigning the job of watching those tanks to the A-10 strikers holding in the south. Too late now—I had to find them. I did not think they could have gotten far, but the area to the north and east was heavily wooded. I searched for a while before finding one. It had pulled about 20 feet off a dirt road and into some trees. I called the strike leader to bring his flight forward. He told me they were low on gas and had only a little time before they had to depart. I quickly deconflicted our flights and brought him to a point over the target while I worked out a new target elevation. It took a few minutes for the strikers to get their eyes onto the target. They were near their bingo (required recovery fuel), so I told them that my wingman and I could cover their attack. That would allow them to roll in, one after the other, and save time. The leader agreed. He rolled in from the west, and his CBU pattern impacted the ground just short of the target. I passed the correction to the wingman as he rolled out in his dive. His two CBU cans also hit a bit short. The tank appeared to be just in the edge of the bomblet pattern. This was certainly not our best day.

As the strikers departed, I decided we had just enough gas to allow my wingman to try a Maverick attack on the target. I had him try passes from several directions, but the trees prevented him from getting a good lock-on with his missile seeker. We were now bingo and had to depart the area. It was a long, quiet flight home—my most frustrating sortie of the war. We had started with one of the best targets we had seen in a long time and ended up with only the possibility of having damaged one tank.

There were numerous failures. Two different weapons systems had failed on my jet and I had failed to have striker flight track the three tanks as they headed off to the northeast while I attacked the APC. Nevertheless, the biggest failure of all was a process that required us to wait more than 40 minutes for approval to attack a lucrative target located far away from any civilians or buildings. The ROEs that had helped us for much of the war had now—for mostly political reasons—been turned against us. On this day they really bit us.

Humor in the Midst of Controlled Chaos

Maj Pete "Bro" Brotherton

Humor is important. It makes us happy and rejuvenates the mind. We worked hard during the war's 70-plus days, and our minds and bodies were tired. I saw and heard several things that now might seem insignificant, but at the time they were quite funny. One such event, which struck me as very symbolic, said, "This is a team effort; we will make this war work."

A normal sortie profile includes taking off, flying to a tanker and refueling, working in Kosovo for about 45 minutes, taking a 45-minute round-trip flight to a tanker for more fuel, and then working another 45 minutes in Kosovo before going home. Although we often used the same tanker track for both refuelings, we might refuel from two different tankers. It was also normal for us to launch on every mission with all the tanker call signs and air-refueling track frequencies, so that we would have the information if it became necessary to switch to a different tanker while in flight. The tankers launched each day with the call sign and the amount of fuel they planned to off-load to each of their scheduled receivers. This enabled them to manage their fuel and deal with unexpected events. The plan was rather simple, flexible, and usually worked well. Occasionally, however, the refueling tracks became little more than controlled chaos.

On a rather stormy day about halfway through the conflict, my wingman and I were flying an AFAC mission in Kosovo using the call sign Ford 11. As I hooked up to our tanker at the beginning of the mission, I was told by its crew that, even though they were supposed to refuel us again during our second visit to the track, they would not have the fuel to do so. Most pilots like to take on a few extra pounds of fuel when the weather is bad; it seemed that today, because of those extra pounds, our tanker would come up short. The tanker pilot said that he was coordinating with the CAOC for a replacement tanker. I was not concerned since this was not the first time this sort of thing had happened. We took our gas and headed north to Kosovo.

We had some luck: the weather over Kosovo was better than that over Macedonia, where the tanker tracks were located. Eventually we had to depart Kosovo to meet our second tanker. We noticed more radio chatter than usual as we checked in with the area controller. This was to be expected with bad weather, but today the controller was also hard to hear. After trying for several minutes, I was able to get one good exchange with the controller. He said that my new tanker's call sign was Esso 73 and that I would refuel on my original track. That was the last successful contact I had with the controller. That meant we could not have him give us vectors to the tanker, which created a problem since the A-10 does not have an air-to-air radar and the visibility prevented my acquiring the tanker visually. My only other method for finding the tanker was to use my radio's direction-finding capability. That required my being in radio contact with the tanker. While en route to the track I tried all the frequencies but could not contact the tanker. We were now about to enter the track, and our remaining fuel dictated that we either start taking on fuel in the next few minutes or turn for home.

I entered the tanker track and found some clear air in the western end. The tanker pilots had a fair amount of discretion with regard to where they flew in the large tracks—the good ones tried to stay out of the clouds. Lucky for us, most tanker crews were good. As we were about to turn for home, I saw a tanker fly out of a wall of clouds on a heading that I could intercept. We turned to intercept it and started calling again on all frequencies for the track. Normally we didn't talk to the tankers prior to refueling, but we were always on the same frequency and knew each other's call sign. While we were still a mile or two from the tanker, it started a turn towards us, which helped my rejoin geometry and kept us from reentering the clouds before we could join on its wing. We were still about a half mile from the tanker and closing when I saw its flaps come down and the refueling boom lower. This was a good sign. I slid behind the tanker and stabilized next to the boom. From there I could see the boom operator settle into position.

Once connected to the tanker, I was able to talk to the crew on the intercom system. I felt a bit silly but asked, "Hi fellas, are you Esso 73?" As luck would have it, they were, and they asked if I was Ford 11. I guessed they had not received any help from the controllers either. This little exchange made me laugh. In spite of all our planning, our ability to continue with the rest of our mission came down to my plugging into the first passing tanker I saw and asking if it was ours. I then asked the most important question: "Do you have enough gas for two A-10s?" But as I was asking, I looked down and saw that they were already pumping, bringing out an even bigger grin. These guys knew why we were there, how important it was, and got right to it. This was how a war should be run. I had a smile the rest of the day. I took just enough gas to stay above my turn-for-home fuel. I then asked for, received, and passed the tanker's radio frequency to my wingman. I cleared him to drop down and fill up. When he finished, I got back on the boom and took the rest of my gas. It may not sound like much now, but I chuckled about it all the way back to the border. In peacetime, I rarely got near a tanker unless I had talked to the controller, he had cleared me, and I had checked in with the tanker. On this day, the tanker crew didn't care that we weren't talking to them or even who we were. They had a job, and they did it. This war—like all others—was a team effort by all the little guys at the bottom—the ones who made happen those things that the people at the top talked about.

Their Last Gathering

Maj Pete "Bro" Brotherton

Late one afternoon in mid-May, I flew an AFAC mission in southeastern Kosovo. Thunderstorms had built up in the area east of Urosevac where I had planned to spend my second push for the day, so I took my wingman further east into the Serbian Kumanovo Valley. On the whole we spent less time in that valley than we did in Kosovo. Old Milo had been preparing a layered defense within the valley in reaction to the possibility of an invasion. We thought an invasion was unlikely, but if he was willing to provide us targets, we were willing to provide him with incoming ordnance. The AFACs who flew there usually had good luck.

As we entered the valley from the south, I started looking in and around the fortifications at the southern end of the generally north-south valley. The Serbs had done more work since the last time I had visited. During my previous trip, I had stayed at the northern end of the valley near Vranje. My plan was to start in the south, head north, and search for targets as we went. The sun was getting low, and the shadows being cast by the valley's western mountains on its southwestern floor were growing. Because the northern half of the valley was oriented northeast-southwest, the shadows up there would not cover the valley floor as quickly as they did in the south. We had plenty of fuel but would be able to stay only as long as we could see targets in the dusk. By working our way northeast, we could use the last bit of available sunlight.

Dawn and dusk, while the sky is bright and the ground dark, are tactically the worst times of the day for a fighter to strike a ground target. The darkness on the ground reduces the effectiveness of the Mk-1 eyeball, and many night-vision devices are not operable because of the bright light at altitude. Unfortunately, the folks on the ground have no trouble seeing an approaching fighter. These factors usually result in high risk and little success for those who attack targets under these conditions. We flew anyway to keep up the pressure on the Serbs. My wingman and I continued searching up the valley. We stopped once down south to check out a square object up against a house, but it was too hard to identify (ID) in the shadows. I decided to go directly to Vranje since there was still some light on the ground there.

We checked out an area about eight miles west of Vranje where I had found some targets several weeks before. Finding nothing there, we moved in closer to the city and spotted movement northwest of the city. I decided to investigate and could not believe what I saw once I arrived overhead. It was the largest gathering of nonrefugees I had seen during the war. On the darkening landscape I counted well over a dozen military vehicles, at least five of which were APCs, and 75 to 100 troops in three clusters. They were only about a mile out of town in a large field that had been chewed up by the vehicles. My first inclination while I circled overhead was to start bombing immediately. Then I saw some green vehicles parked in the area of the APCs that I could not positively identify as military. I did not want to make a mistake with a group this large. I needed help.

I knew there were some Navy F-14 AFACs working just west of us in Kosovo. Ten years ago, I would have laughed at the thought of the Navy using F-14 Tomcats as AFACs, but then— 10 years ago—the A-10 was also headed for the boneyard. The Navy upgraded the F-14 when it was assigned the AFAC mission. The fighter had acquired a low-light-capable reconnaissance pod whose capability I now needed. I switched to the eastern-Kosovo working frequency, called the call sign fragged for that time slot, and got a quick response. They agreed to help when I asked if they had time to look at a target and learned that they were not having any luck finding targets where they were. I passed the target coordinates in a format they could use, and they were on the way.

None of our pilots had worked with the Navy F-14 AFACs before the war and were a bit leery of them the first few times they appeared in Kosovo. We soon discovered that while they did not have much experience with the AFAC mission, they weren't bad. A few had yet to master the requisite skills, but most were doing fine—and some were quite good. I recognized the voice of one of their better AFACs in the jets headed our way. I deconflicted our flight paths, briefed him on the target below, and told him what I needed. The shadows now covered most of the valley floor. With this lighting I would normally head home—but this target was too good to pass up. From our orbit overhead, I was able to talk the Tomcat crew's eyes onto the targets below. He confirmed that it looked like lots of troops and APCs but was also unsure of the few green vehicles. He decided to make a diving pass near the target to give their pod a closer look. I maneuvered my flight into a position to cover the F-14s as they made their run.

The Tomcats completed the pass and rather excitedly stated they had good pictures of the APCs and confirmed that the few green vehicles were also military. They said there appeared to be more troops in the gathering than first thought. We were running out of both daylight and fuel as I coordinated with the F-14 lead. My wingman and I would make three passes each and then leave the rest to them. He agreed, and they set up an orbit north of us. We made all of our attacks from the south because of some clouds that had entered the area. With the F-14 flight covering us, I reduced the usual attack spacing between my wingman and me. We coordinated our targets and each made two quick Maverick attacks on the APCs. On our third and final pass we each dropped our four 500 lb bombs, offsetting the impact points of our four-bomb sticks so we could cover as much of the area as possible. Anyone dumb enough not to have fled after our four Maverick attacks would not be pleased with the 500 pounders. They were set to explode 15 feet above the ground, and their blast and fragmentation kill mechanisms made them deadly weapons against troops and soft-skinned vehicles.

After our last pass we departed the area for home. The F-14 lead told us that, although our attacks had been right on target, there were still plenty left for his flight to attack. As we departed he was calling over the F/A-18 strikers he was supposed to work with so they could deliver even more ordnance to the area. It was too dark when we left for me to make a valid damage assessment, but I would come back in the next day or so. When I did I was amazed at what I saw. The Navy must have really worked that area over that night—it was a mess—pieces of military vehicles everywhere. I visited the area in the weeks that followed and could see where the Serbs had attempted to clean up the damage, but the ground still bore witness to the beating it had taken. I was puzzled: why, during combat, would anyone without air superiority gather so many troops together in daylight. In war, stupidity rarely fails to get its reward.

The Truck I Couldn't Forget

Capt Ron "Stu" Stuewe

I have several memories of my time in Kosovo. Most are good; some I would rather forget, but all of them are slowly losing their details with the passage of time. Still, one of my most vivid memories involves nothing more than a simple truck.

Maj John "Scratch" Regan, our 74th EFS commander, was on my wing. We had flown some rather effective sorties together during the preceding couple of days. On this particular occasion we had both dropped our bombs on some meager targets earlier in the mission. I say meager because we had direct hits with two tons of Mk-82s with limited secondaries. We were patrolling the western side of the province, just west of Dakovica (D-Town) when Scratch called over the FM radio that he saw a mover. Even during the waning period of OAF, we occasionally saw movers on the roads.

An interesting thing happened during the opening days of the conflict that had a direct impact on our ability to interdict movers. ABCCC had heard someone's description of a convoy of assumed military vehicles that included a white car. ABCCC then said—in the clear over a nonsecure radio—that, in effect, we couldn't hit any white vehicle. As a consequence, during the next few days it appeared that every can of white paint in Kosovo was used on any vehicle that could move.

It didn't take Scratch long to talk my eyes onto the mover. It was immediately apparent that this target was different—big, green, and fast moving. More specifically, it was heading deeper into bad-guy land. I made one low pass behind the

169

mover, and even before I grabbed my 15-power binos, I could tell it was a big truck. With the optics I could clearly see it was a green deuce-and-a-half truck with an open back end covered by a solid-brown object. I couldn't quite make out what was in the back, but I figured it was just a dirty-brown tarp. I immediately brought the nose of my airplane back up to stay behind the truck and to gain back some altitude.

My next move is one that I will regret for quite a while—I called ABCCC for clearance to strike this target. There were rules about what we could and couldn't attack, and, unfortunately, trucks weren't approved. ABCCC's initial reply was to "stand by." So there I was, carving a lazy figure eight at about 14,000 feet behind this truck with Scratch slightly high and behind me. I was all set to roll in from behind, lock a Maverick onto this truck, and blow it to smithereens. A Maverick costs several times more than a truck, and it was certainly not the most cost-effective weapon choice in this situation. However, it would be most spectacular and have the highest kill probability—and the guy driving this truck deserved it.

I was appalled that someone would have the audacity to drive his truck at 80 miles per hour down an open highway in the middle of the day. At the time I was merely shocked; in retrospect I am almost disgusted. I now think about all of the FACs from an earlier time—the Mistys, the Nails, the Coveys. Those guys flying the Ho Chi Minh Trail in their F-100s, O-2s, and OV-10s just hoping to catch a glimpse of a truck through triple-canopy jungle. There I was watching—just watching—this Serb drive down the road like some teenager trying to see how fast his dad's pickup will go.

While I waited several long minutes for approval, the truck made it into D-Town and began winding through some of the lesser streets (the ones without the rubble of destroyed homes). Simultaneously, a voice came over the strike frequency and asked if I could positively identify my target as "armor." Laughingly, I again explained that it was a truck, a military truck, a deuce-and-a-half truck! Immediately, I was informed, "Do not, I repeat, do not strike that target." This was followed 25 seconds later by another voice telling me not to engage the target. Reluctantly, I broke off the attack.

That was my last sortie of Allied Force. Scratch and I went on to find some other targets. I wound up earning a rather important medal for this particular excursion into combat and someday hope to show it to my grandson. I will, however, remember that truck more than anything else we did that day. Even now I often wonder what that driver is doing. Perhaps he told his buddies—at some cheap Belgrade bar—about the day he gave the finger to two A-10s in broad daylight, or how he thinks we were too scared to attack him. Perhaps he never even knew we were there. I knew that with one push of my right thumb, several hundred pounds of missile would have slammed into the top of that truck and cartwheeled it into a fiery heap. It's that image—seen only in my imagination—that I will remember the best.

The Call Sign Was Cub 31

Capt Marty "JD" McDonough

I joined the squadron at Aviano on 28 March and was immediately tasked to go to Vicenza to be one of the squadron's CAOC representatives. Eight days later I returned to Aviano and flew my first sortie. After a couple of weather days, I was selected to be a member of our advance team and was sent to Gioia del Colle.

I will not soon forget my first opportunity to fly after the squadron moved to Gioia. It was 14 April 1999 and only my second sortie of the conflict. I was the flight lead, Lt Col Surgeon Dahl was my wingman, and our call sign was Cub 31. The first half of our AFAC sortie in the eastern half of the KEZ was uneventful. We were flying above a broken deck, which made our search difficult because it was hard to see targets around and through the clouds. After completing our first vul period, we went to the tanker; by the time we returned the weather had cleared significantly. I checked in with Maj Joe "Dice" Kopacz, the other AFAC on station, and learned he was busy dodging AAA. When he finally got a chance to talk, a couple of expletives were quickly followed by a recommendation not to come over to his area. He had found some targets along the Kumanovo Valley road and had, in his words, "stirred up a bees' nest." He suggested I give it a little time to cool down in case I wanted to come over and take a look. I took his recommendation to heart and continued to search for targets south of Urosevac.

Shortly after Dice departed, Moonbeam (ABCCC) transmitted that Bear 21, an F-16 AFAC in the western half of Kosovo, had found and was preparing to engage a large convoy of more than 100 vehicles. Bear 21 had requested that Moonbeam send any available fighters, and I was not about to miss an opportunity to engage some targets. I called Bear 21 and told him that my flight was holding in the eastern half of Kosovo and that we were available as strikers. Since I was fourth in his stack of fighters, I continued to look for targets on my side of the KEZ.

While waiting, I spotted a large truck on the road below me but couldn't immediately confirm whether it was civilian or military. I used my binoculars to investigate, but I still couldn't get a good look because he was moving down the road. I decided to try to stop the truck by firing a couple of rockets. I had previously observed rockets being fired on a range and knew they made a lot of noise but created a very small amount of frag or blast. I estimated the distance in front of the moving truck where I needed to aim so that the impact would occur far enough in front of him to get his attention but avoid hitting him with frags. I set up, flew the pass, and launched two rockets that bracketed his position. The truck immediately came to a stop, and I tried to get a closer look. It appeared to be a deuce-and-a-half military truck—but I wasn't sure.

While I was trying to confirm the truck's identity, I got another call from Moonbeam. Apparently someone at the CAOC had questioned the composition of the 100-vehicle convoy target being attacked in the western half of the KEZ. Moonbeam wanted an aircraft equipped with binoculars to check out the convoy to make sure it was a valid military target. I contacted Bear 21 to get the location of the convoy. I was not sure that I had sufficient fuel to fly all the way to his target, observe the convoy, and still make it to a tanker with the required reserves. I was required to have enough gas when I reached the tanker to be able to recover home in case the refueling was not successful.

USAF Photo

Fuel trucks destroyed by Capt Marty McDonough on 8 April 1999

I communicated my concern to Bear 21 on the common strike frequency. He pushed me to a different radio frequency, checked us in, and said he was sure that he was striking a good target and that he really just needed me to come on over and check it out. I figured it would take me at least 45 minutes to get to the tanker and back, during which time the attacks on this lucrative target would be halted. I had refueled many times before without any problems. I considered the consequences of having a malfunction today and decided that even if we had difficulties, we would still be able to land at a friendly airfield—just not at our home base. We would get refueled on the ground, and with a fast turnaround we could quickly be on our way home. We had Moonbeam confirm that tankers would be available and proceeded to Bear 21's target.

The convoy, which had been heading to the southeast, was stopped near the town of Dakovica, on the main road to Prizren. At 20,000 feet and with my naked eyes, I could tell the target was not military—at least most of it wasn't. It consisted of lots of colorful vehicles. I could see blues, reds, and a lot of bright silver

173

from bumpers reflecting the sun. I let Arden know that I was going heads-down to use the binos. I could then see that a number of civilian cars and tractors had pulled over to the side of the road. I also noticed a couple of larger vehicles leaving the area to the west. One of them was a large charter bus with some colorful paint marks down both sides. There were one or two other west-moving vehicles whose identity I could not confirm before they entered the town of Dakovica and disappeared.

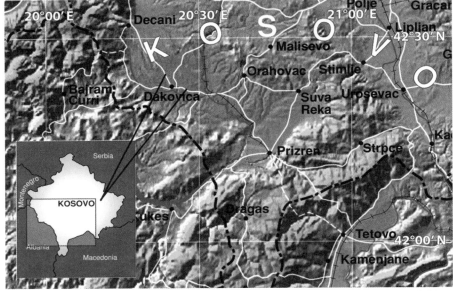

USAF Photo

Convoys near Dakovica on the road to Prizren

I then noticed a strange-looking pattern south of the road and took a closer look. I identified it as a crowd of people who had left their cars and tractors and had run away to a safe distance. They were waiting in the fields for their vehicles to stop exploding. I immediately transmitted that the convoy was definitely civilian. Bear 21 ensured that all attacks and weapons expenditures were stopped. The CAOC quickly closed the KEZ and sent everyone home. We had been trying to extend the target-area time to prosecute this target—that was obviously no longer required.

Our day wasn't over. We flew to the tanker to get a little fuel before going home. I took gas without a problem, but Arden started getting a lot of fuel spray from around the refueling receptacle, the location where the tanker's boom connects to the nose of the aircraft. He disconnected, reconnected, and tried again with the same result. Since the A-10 tech manual recommended that refueling be discontinued in the event of fuel spray due to the potential danger of fuel pooling in the electronics bays, Arden ended up taking on only about 500 pounds of gas. We did the math to figure out if we had enough fuel to get home. It didn't look good for flying straight home, but we could make it to our divert base. While we waited for the jets to be refueled at Brindisi, we learned that CNN was already covering the attack on the convoy. Immediately after landing at Gioia del Colle, Arden and I wrote our reports and submitted them to our CAOC rep at Vicenza.

It was not a glorious moment for either the Air Force or NATO. However, we thought it could be a critical lesson learned and a memorable chapter in Hog history. There are plenty of things technology can do, but experience and training in the basics remain critical. When it came time to confirm a target with vast political implications, it was not a high-tech targeting pod but a set of 12-power binoculars in the hands of an experienced AFAC that provided the accurate and critical identification.

I watched the post-incident briefing at Supreme Headquarters Allied Powers Europe (SHAPE) on public television a couple of weeks later. This was one of the most frustrating aspects of the episode. I wouldn't de-

USAF Photo by SrA Greg Davis

A-10, as seen from the tanker, just prior to refueling. Note the refueling receptacle located in front of the windscreen.

scribe the briefing as misleading, but the description just didn't quite match what we had experienced. Arden and I had submitted our written reports to the CAOC through our rep at Vicenza—but I didn't recognize any of those details in the SHAPE brief. I suspect that our reports were not part, or at least not the focus, of SHAPE's investigation. Its briefing went into much detail on the circumstances of the incident, including identifying Bear 21 and showing his F-16's cockpit video. The briefing appeared to focus on "how" this tragic incident could have happened.

The A-10's role in terminating the attack was understated during the SHAPE briefing. A-10 AFAC expertise did not get credit for its critical role in identifying the noncombatant nature of the convoy, terminating the attack, and preventing further civilian casualties. Like the role we played, our call sign was also abbreviated. We were simply referred to as "Cub flight," which could identify any one of several Cub call signs flying that day. I appreciated our leaders' desire to explain the circumstances of "how" this could have happened to the public, get this tragic incident quickly behind us, and refocus on our continuing combat operations. However, my hope is that we don't forget an important lesson—technology cannot completely substitute for training and experience. This is especially critical in basic tasks like looking at the ground and being able accurately to identify and understand what is really there—particularly when fighting a cynical enemy willing to use civilians as human shields.

The Great Hunt for Radars

Introduction

Lt Col Chris "Kimos" Haave

NATO wanted Montenegro to remain "neutral." Yugoslav forces normally did not use Montenegrin territory for their operations, and our ROEs reflected that Serbian discretion by normally precluding attacks in that territory. Early in the conflict however, the Serbs positioned a long-range acquisition radar on a narrow peninsula on the Montenegrin coast. From that position the radar provided the Serbians important intelligence as it tracked all NATO aircraft flying through the southern Adriatic and Albanian airspace. Serbia's action forced NATO to make an exception to its normal ROEs and directed that the radar be eliminated. Our experiences while we hunted for that single radar on the coast of Montenegro were typical of both our frustrations and our successes during the Hog's participation in Allied Force.

We could not determine whether the Serbs kept the same radar, or even the same type of radar, at that strategic coastal location. At different times it appeared to be a Flat Face (Soviet-built) radar, and at other times it exhibited the characteristics of a Giraffe (Swedish-made) radar. It was clear, however, that the CAOC wanted to remove that Serb capability (no matter what kind or how many radars) to track NATO strike packages and KEZ-bound aircraft.

The Serbs weren't stupid enough to operate their radar continuously and expose it to a classic NATO interdiction attack. Rather, they emitted unpredictably—just long enough to get the information they needed—and then relocated their equipment to a different residential or wooded area near the Mon-

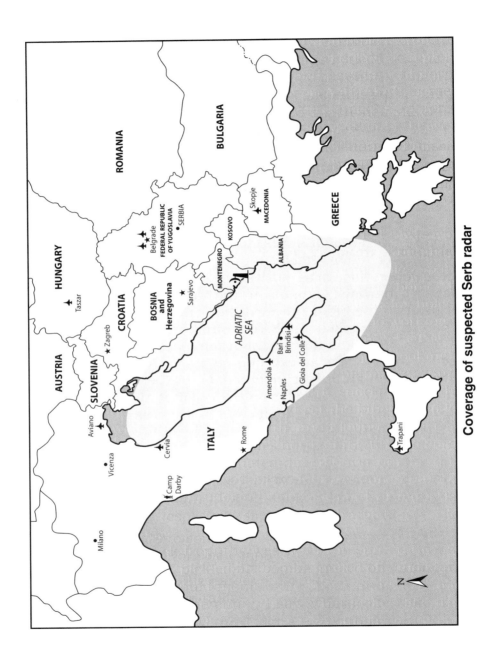

Coverage of suspected Serb radar

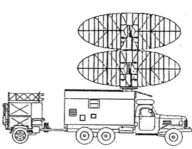

Photo courtesy of FAS

Flat Face radar

tenegrin coast. Therefore, the aircraft that got the opportunity to kill the radar was simply the aircraft that happened to be in the area at the time the radar was detected.

The CAOC, we believed, had decided that our A-10s at Gioia del Colle were the preferred weapon system to kill the radar. We would be able spend more time in the target area, had the best chance of finding the radar, and had a wide range of weaponry with which we could engage it. The radar's location in Montenegro made identifying the target essential and minimizing collateral damage even more critical. The CAOC's choice of the Hog's low-tech binoculars reflected the earlier success that Coke, our operations officer, and others had during Desert Storm knocking out Flat Face radars while they hunted for Scuds in Iraq.

The good news was that we were the privileged few to be allowed to go after this elusive and high-priority prey. The bad news was that it was both elusive and high priority. It was the focus of the CAOC's attention, and that meant we would fly many frustrating sorties without finding it. Some of our pilots started daydreaming about being the lucky one to see the radar in his binos, move it to his gunsight, and hammer down on the trigger.

Fighter pilots are naturally aggressive and generally avoid looking for the definitive answer to an ambiguous rule that would remove all ambiguity—and their flexibility. Thus, most fighter pilots worth their salt have done something in the course of their careers that they would rather not have to explain to their commanders. These natural tendencies, coupled with our pilots' desire to succeed in the difficult hunt for the Flat Face and Giraffe radars, almost resulted in a tactical victory and a strategic disaster.

I began my tour as squadron supervisor at 1800 on the evening of 4 May and would be on duty until 0600 the next morning. The poor weather over Serbia precluded the launch of our normal interdiction strike packages. The CAOC planners, however, had checked with their weather forecasters and believed that the cloud layers over the Adriatic Sea and the Montenegrin coast would be scattered enough for our crews to draw a bead on the Flat Face radar.

Capt Edward D. "Sped" Sommers was a highly qualified weapons-school instructor, generously sent from Nellis to participate in a strategic planning cell headed by Col Daniel "Doc" Zoerb. He also helped our unit representatives at the CAOC explain the finer points of A-10 employment to the CAOC leadership. Sped called from the CAOC to ask if our two CSAR (ground- and airborne-alert) two-ships could be retasked from covering strike packages to a radar-hunting mission. "Yes," I replied. Although in my enthusiasm I may have said something more colorful.

I gathered the four pilots together and told them of their new tasking. Capt Stu Stuewe, who was the highest qualified of the four pilots and had been scheduled as Sandy 1 that night, volunteered to lead the mission.

The weather was the biggest unknown. The forecast for the ceiling on the Adriatic changed several times during the night, but the one I believed that we all had settled on was broken at 4,000 feet. "Broken" denotes at least five-eighths cloud cover—unless the clouds are very thin, it is practically impossible to find and attack a target from above. To attack the Flat Face in that weather meant having to descend through and attack from below the 4,000-foot broken cloud deck. Doing so would directly conflict with our altitude ROE. General Short's exact words on ROEs were seared into my brain, and his voice was still ringing in my ears from my trip to Tirana three days before. Never in my life had my understanding of my superiors' direction been so lucid. Our current ROEs limited our altitude to no lower than 5,000 feet to identify a target and to no lower than 8,000 feet during our attacks.

The following is an example of what Clausewitz meant by "fog and friction." Worried about the weather, Sped, Stu, and I had all independently checked it several times during the two hours from the start of mission planning to the pilots stepping to their aircraft. It was several days later before I was able to piece together each of our differing perceptions of the weather and the ROEs that applied to that night's hunt for the Flat Face radar. I was convinced that the definitive forecast was for a 4,000-foot broken ceiling, which would require the CAOC's approval to deviate below the ROE-established minimums. I told Sped, "Confirm for me that we have been cleared to go below the weather." On the other hand, Sped, who was getting his weather information at the CAOC, was convinced that the ceiling was forecasted for 8,500 feet and saw no conflict staying within the current ROE and operating "below the weather to either identify or attack the radar." Stu, the flight lead, had received several projected ceilings during the planning process from our Gioia del Colle forecaster and stepped with the conviction that the forecasted ceiling was at 2,000 feet. So when I told him, "Go below the weather," he believed that meant he was cleared to operate below 2,000 feet.

There is one recollection on which Stu and I differ. I had required Stu to brief the flight's attack plan to me in detail since I was clearing my guys to descend to low altitude at night, over water, and in potentially cloudy weather. Their plan called for a first pass using Mavericks and, if unsuccessful, a second pass at 2,000 feet for a level CBU attack that Sped and Stu had worked out over the phone. I approved the plan, with an additional restriction of maintaining at least 2,000 feet above the water since three of the pilots in the flight had not yet completed training at night below that altitude. If they encountered weather at 2,000 feet or below, they were to abort the mission and return home. Stu did not recall my 2,000-foot restriction and therefore interpreted my clearance to "go below the weather" as clearance to descend to any tactically safe altitude. I'll leave the details of the mission to the stories in the chapter, but the unsuccessful attacks on this night occurred below 2,000 feet.

When the four intrepid aviators returned from their unsuccessful sortie, they identified the weather as the reason for their lack of success. They did not mention altitudes—there was no reason to mention them since they had adhered to the altitude ROE as they understood it. "Flat Face fever" hit the squadron. All of the pilots eagerly listened to tales about that night's mission and hoped they might have a shot at the radar. A couple of days later, each of the same four pilots found himself leading an element when Stu spotted the infamous radar from medium altitude on the way home. He received CAOC clearance and shifted the entire KEZ package to the west to provide SEAD cover. Once again, there was a low-weather deck. Based on their experiences during that first night attack and their mistaken belief that to kill this radar they had been given an exception to the normal altitude restrictions, they flew another attack below the "real" ROE altitude. On this mission, Stu's gun malfunctioned just as he lined up the enemy radar in his gunsight. We all listened raptly to their mission debrief.

Col Al Thompson (40th EOG commander), Maj Scratch Regan (74th EFS commander), Lt Col Coke Koechle (81st EFS operations officer), and I were the normal ROE gatekeepers at Gioia. Perhaps this sounds like a scenario from *The Emperor's New Clothes*, but none of us had heard about anyone flying below 2,000 feet during that one night mission against the radars or below standard ROE altitudes during the day missions. We learned afterward that those altitudes were well known to the line pilots, who "assumed" it was an approved exception to the ROEs for that target.

The disconnect between what various pilots understood to be minimum-allowed altitude during an attack on the radar site was illuminated as a result of the debrief of a Flat Face mission flown by Scratch and Maj Dirt Fluhr. Due to the weather along the coast and with CAOC direction, they were forced to fly between cloud decks to search for the radar. As they neared the suspected coordinates of the elusive target, they dropped through a thin "scud" layer at about 4,500 feet. Once below the clouds, they searched the area along the coastline for the radar, threats, and a way back up through the weather, which they knew they would eventually need. During this search the Serbs shot a heat-seeking missile at them. Scratch and Dirt promptly defeated the shot, popped up through the clouds, and returned home.

Following their close call, Scratch and Dirt conducted the standard debrief with our squadron's intel personnel. They stated that they were probably at about 4,000 feet at the time of the missile shot. Our excellent intel troops faithfully recorded their details and dutifully forwarded the mission report to the CAOC. That statement of flying at 4,000 feet— below the normal ROEs' 5,000-foot minimum altitude for identifying targets, and 8,000-foot minimum used during attacks—without an operational explanation was certain to draw attention from anyone without our earlier understanding of the ROE "exception." I learned an important lesson and noted that a timely operations review of the unit's mission reports by its supervisors will provide a clearer picture of what is actually taking place and help reduce friction and fog. I had suffered a miscommunication on what I thought was a "one-time exception." to the minimum attack-altitude for that first-night sortie to use while they attacked the radar. I had understood that we were back to adhering to the normal ROE altitudes. If I had reviewed the mission reports, I would have been alerted to the squadron pilots' inconsistent understanding of the ROEs' minimum altitudes. We fixed this immediately. Although it seemed contrary to letting the intel troops do their job, in a shooting war with highly politicized ROEs, it is essential to use every available means to stay informed and ensure a good information flow at all levels.

The lightning bolt from the CAOC was swift and unequivocal. The two pilots involved, plus a supervisor, would be provided a dedicated C-21 aircraft for transport to Vicenza to personally explain the violation of the ROEs to General Short. We understood his concern. He didn't need "wayward aviators" upsetting the delicate politico-military balance and the alliance's commitment to the air campaign. Nevertheless, we weren't looking forward to the encounter, especially since Colonel Thompson, Coke, and I thought we were sitting on a "command ejection seat" with General Short's hand on the handle after our dressing-down in Tirana.

We had to get the details together fast. We heard pilots express surprise that the CAOC was upset about Scratch and Dirt inadvertently flying at 4,000 feet in daytime since the CAOC had already approved flying below 2,000 feet at night on that target. That's when I realized the disconnect between the ROEs the CAOC understood to be in place and the ones our pilots were using. I interviewed all the pilots involved and looked over the mission reports from the previous two Flat Face sorties. They all told the same story—they had assumed that low-altitude attacks on the radar were approved. They had not listed their attack altitudes in their mission reports since that data was normally sought only for weapons-release conditions and threat reactions. These were the same guys who had routinely put themselves at risk to comply with the ROEs—as they understood them. They had enforced the ROEs to ensure that they, and the NATO fighters they controlled, would never come close to hurting civilians in Kosovo. I had no reason to doubt their integrity, professionalism, or sense of duty. When it came to accepting a higher personal risk to take out an important target, they went all out. I concluded that a couple of pilots had let their fangs get a mite too long and had taken unnecessary risks. They were grounded a day or more as a result—not to punish them because they went below any particular altitude but to recalibrate their in-flight and on-scene assessment of risk and payoff. These same great pilots justifiably earned important medals for heroism during other sorties.

Colonel Thompson had to decide who would accompany Scratch and Dirt to see "the Man." I was the commander, present at the beginning of the misunderstanding, and offered to go. Stu nobly offered to explain to General Short his previous sorties and the source of any misunderstanding. Colonel Thompson, although thankful for the offers, doubted General Short would have time to understand all of the convoluted details before grounding our entire group for insubordination. Colonel Thompson had worked for General Short before and decided to lead the two majors to Vicenza. General Short carefully explained to them, Colonel Thompson reported afterward, that he could not tolerate any more ROE deviations, intentional or otherwise. He would expressly approve any exceptions.

Capt Joseph S. "Joe Bro" Brosious's story provides a happy ending to this tale. One of the guys who had twice been after the Serbs' pesky Montenegrin acquisition radar finally strafed it with his mighty GAU-8 Avenger cannon. The Hog had proved its versatility once again, showing that it is well adapted to handle some particularly knotty missions. All the guys who had gone after the radar survived, maintained an aggressive edge, and continued to take the fight to the enemy. However, we all learned an important lesson—we could do the enemy's work for him if we dropped our guard on the ROEs.

The Giraffe

Capt Ron "Stu" Stuewe

I'll warn you up front that this is a long narrative. I've told this story only a handful of times and have found that it's best received at the bar on a Friday night over a couple of beers. Its telling usually involves a lot of fighter-pilot hand gestures, and a good deal of profanity—sometimes it even evokes audience participation. A buddy of mine describes this as a story about a few days of "knife-in-your-teeth combat flying," and the attitude—aggressive or foolhardy—that one can develop while attempting to accomplish the mission. It is an important story, however, that has existed only in the memories and personal journals of a few pilots. Even though it will lose a little in translation, it should be preserved in print.

185

I was "Sandy 1" on the night of 4 May 1999, sitting 30-minute CSAR alert with Maj Dice Kopacz as my number two. I had arrived at the squadron around 2000 hours, in time to be ready for our normal ground alert from 2100 to about 0500. I noticed a buzz in the air about a "priority target," and Kimos, the squadron commander, was on the secure telephone for a long time. Most of the night flyers had already launched on their sorties, and everyone else was in pilot rest for the next day's missions. Finally, after a half hour of pondering, Kimos came to me with a set of coordinates on an orange sticky pad. He simply stated, "There's a Flat Face radar here. Go kill it." As it was shaping up, the only available bodies for this priority target were the guys on CSAR alert.

Attack pilots find nothing better than having their squadron commander tell them to go kill a target. We tried to plot the coordinates on our maps only to learn it was too far west. We grabbed a computer and found out that this early warning radar wasn't in Kosovo, or even Serbia for that matter. It was located on the coast of Montenegro—which, incidentally, was supposed to be a third party during this bombing campaign. Not only did the politically sensitive nature of attacking targets in Montenegro worry me, but also I had concerns about the three unlocated SA-6 batteries that intel claimed were in the area.

I put everyone to work: building maps, working on timing, and getting our night-vision goggles ready. Then I went to the weather shop. The weather forecaster explained that the ceiling was low—real low—2,000-foot overcast with four kilometers of visibility, to be precise. There was not much we could do except fly below the clouds, which would put us well below the altitude prescribed in the ROEs. While I was planning the attack, the weather guy changed his forecast several more times. The lowest forecast was for a 2,000-foot ceiling, and the highest called for a 10,000-foot ceiling. It seemed that the CAOC and Kimos considered this priority target important enough that the normal ROE altitudes would not apply, and I was cleared to go "below the weather." I found out later, however, that the forecast ceilings that the CAOC, Kimos, and I were planning with were all different. Therefore, the attack altitude that corresponded to the below-the-weather approval meant different things to each of us.

Our planning turned to ordnance and formations. Because our Mk-82s were wired for a high-altitude delivery, they would not have time to arm if we dropped them that close to the ground. I therefore requested that the Mk-82s be replaced by CBU-87s on all four of our aircraft because of their low-altitude employment options and their ability to provide us good firepower and mutual support. A well-respected A-10 rep at the CAOC sent down his attack plan. Unfortunately, this particular evening's fog and friction prevented most of his ideas from reaching me.

I launched with Dice on my wing, along with Capt Corn Mays and Capt Joe Brosious as my numbers three and four. Capt Larry D. "LD" Card II suggested a little tactical deception which caused the NAEW to make bogus radio calls that indicated to all who were monitoring the transmissions that Sandy flight was going to rendezvous with a tanker and sit airborne alert. Halfway across the Adriatic, we hit the solid-undercast cloud deck that had been predicted by the weather forecaster. We turned off our squawks, blacked out, and "stealthed up" as much as a Hog can. I led the boys down through the weather and leveled off in a black hole at 1,500 feet on the radar altimeter. NAEW played its role perfectly and began giving us phony traffic advisories and then vectors towards an actual tanker that was airborne over Macedonia. We hit the Albanian coast at our control point (CP) and turned north towards the IP. The IP itself was an illuminated boat dock with a 1,500-foot ridge behind it. Finding the IP would update us on the drift of our navigation systems as well as provide us some indirect terrain masking from any radar. With the poor visibility, I couldn't see the IP until I was right on top of it. I then had to fly a very hard turn to keep from being scraped off on that ridge. Kirk said later that he got much closer to that particular piece of the Balkans than he would have liked. I had the boys throw the master arm switch to "arm" at the IP as we turned west towards Montenegro and the radar.

The ceiling dropped to about 1,500 feet and, with the high humidity and moisture, we couldn't see anything with the Maverick or NVGs except straight down. I nearly passed over the top of the target coordinates without seeing anything. Kirk did likewise one minute behind me. We proceeded out to the rendezvous point over the water. I'm here to say that India ink cannot compare to the blackness I encountered when I pointed my Hog's nose out over an open ocean in the middle of the night below a solid overcast. I flew 500 feet above the cold Adriatic off nothing more than a radar altimeter and a green circle in my HUD that said I was wings level. Due to the outstanding skill of my wingmen, I had to expend only two self-protection flares to help regroup the formation as I turned back towards the coast. At this same time NAEW was rendezvousing our imaginary formation with a tanker 120 nautical miles away. I led us back in on a reattack with CBUs. On the way in I slewed an IIR Maverick missile onto the spot where the target was supposed to be. In the midst of a cold, dark background I found a single hot object. It didn't exactly look like the radar van, but it was in the correct relative position. I locked the Maverick onto the hot object as my thumb gently caressed the pickle button that would unleash the missile.

I don't care much about CNN or the influence the media has on military operations, but there was no way I was going to mistakenly destroy a Montenegrin hotdog stand. It boiled down to the fact that I had a slight doubt as to the validity of my target, so, as a professional soldier, I couldn't proceed with the attack. I learned later that Kirk had also found a hot object, possibly the same one, and had similarly forgone indiscriminately attacking it. I called for yet another "Jake"—the reattack code word that I had named after my three-month-old son. I thought that with one more attack we might just get lucky. Someone, however, without the distraction of having their fangs imbedded in the floorboard, made a wise decision and relayed through NAEW that we were done for that particular night. Feeling rather dejected about not finding the target, I led Dice home. Kirk and Joe Bro—without pretending—flew to the tanker, refueled, and assumed their real airborne CSAR alert. This is where the story gets really interesting.

The next two days passed uneventfully as I finished my turn in the barrel on the CSAR alert schedule. I couldn't forget about that radar because every day ABCCC tasked A-10s with a priority target that had coordinates in Montenegro. On the fourth morning I was the mission commander for the entire KEZ. As we tried to conduct an air war during the Balkan spring, we ended up fighting the weather as much as anything else. The weather was "dog crap," and I started sending the forces, including me, home. As I returned home at 22,000 feet and turned the corner around Montenegro (our ROEs did not allow us to fly over it), I focused my binos on the area where the Flat Face had been previously reported. I began a structured scan pattern when, low and behold, about 600 meters west of the previous location, I found a van with twin horizontal radar dishes turning on it. I called ABCCC and, via secure means, asked if the Flat Face was still a valid priority target. The response was that I could attack as long as I obtained SEAD support. I called all the other A-10s on VHF while coordinating the SEAD on the UHF radio. Within minutes I had eight Hogs lined up, along with four F-16CJs and an EA-6B Prowler. Even Mr. ABCCC came rumbling over to take a look (or get in the way). I took control of my new strike package. By some crazy luck, my new element leads—"three," "five," and "seven"—turned out to be, in perfect order, "two," "three," and "four" from Sandy flight on the first night. Since we all had a full load of ordnance and varying amounts of fuel, I sent the fourth element, numbers seven and eight, to the tanker.

During the time it took to rejoin the formation, line up the SEAD, and coordinate the attack, a small, midaltitude deck of clouds had moved in below us. I was the only one who had seen the target, but I thought it would be "no big deal." I explained to the second and third element leads where the target was in relation to the map study we had accomplished in preparation for the first night's attack. The briefed plan was a ladder of Hogs (two-ship element orbits with vertical separation between elements) with the wingman providing cover on the right side during an attack from southeast with a southwest pull-off. One, three, and five were shooters with Maverick, while two, four, and six (all of whom had no exact idea of what we were attacking) were supposed to provide cover from any threats that popped up. I briefed the plan. When they reached the cloud layer, they would descend through it as fast as possible, acquire and ID the radar, shoot, and recover quickly back to the clear air above the clouds. Everyone acknowledged that he understood the plan.

One of my most distinct memories of OAF is the feeling of adrenaline building up as I prepared for this attack. However, the tight knot that had formed in my chest quickly unclenched and was replaced with pride and awe when I looked over my right shoulder. I wish I had the eloquence to describe what it is like to watch five Hogs follow your every move—all of them hulking with a full combat load that glistened in the midday sun. I noted the awesome firepower we had available: six tons of bombs, 12 Mavericks, 84 Willy Pete rockets, and almost 7,000 rounds of 30 mm combat mix. The sight of those marvelous airplanes and the pilots who had chosen to fly them humbled me.

USAF Photo by SrA Jeffery Allen

A1C Jerry Herron replenishes the A-10's 30 mm ammunition.

I began the attack and realized the weather was slightly lower than I had expected. However, this was the high-priority target we had been gunning for during the last four days. It was the target the CAOC and my squadron commander had deemed so important that they had sent us to attack it (or so I had believed) when the weather was well below the ROEs. During that attack attempt, I had flown over it at a few hundred feet just three nights before. On this day, therefore, I pressed on with the attack despite the weather. I hit the edge of the clouds about four miles from the target. Unfortunately, there was some misunderstanding as to the in-trail spacing I expected between my element leads, which caused my second element lead to pitch back into the third element. My six-ship had quickly turned into a two-ship below the weather.

It took a few seconds to get my bearings below the cloud deck. I found the original position of the radar, worked my eyes from there to where the target should be, and visually acquired the radar site. I stabilized the Maverick on the radar site and tried to lock onto the van. The missile locked onto the cooled van and also on some cold background clutter that would, most likely, have caused a total miss. I attempted once more to lock just the cold van without any luck. I was now getting close enough to start breaking out the hot radar dish and components within the van. I quickly pulled the pinky switch on the left throttle to the aft position to cause the Maverick seeker to look for hot targets. For the third time in a matter of seconds, I couldn't get the Maverick to lock onto the van. I then made an extremely superfluous comment, but one I felt had to get across the radio: "One's going to guns."

I pushed forward on the stick, nosed over slightly, and overlaid the gun symbology on the radar van. Suddenly I wasn't flying an A-10 anymore. I was in a Jug or Spitfire, strafing steam locomotives in occupied France—that's exactly what it felt like. I put my index finger on the trigger, and caught my breath slightly. In that one instant in time I thought to myself, "Oh my God, you're about to long-range STRAFE a real live target!" I lined up my airplane to rip the now large van from one side to the other. All my training and long days of hard work had seemed to build to this one split second. The adrenaline, the ecstasy, the remorse, the fear, and the exaltation of everything in my life seemed encapsulated in the moment I pulled the trigger.

Now I've shot close to 100,000 rounds through the GAU-8 gun without any problem—except for this one particular time. The gun spun up, and the familiar rumbling of the aircraft accompanied it—but something was missing. A fraction of a second later I realized that no bullets were coming from the aircraft. This was accompanied shortly by a "gun unsafe" warning light in the cockpit. I pulled off target and, even with my finger off the trigger, the gun continued to rotate. My wingman and I yanked our jets hard to the left. We were low as hell and we both dropped flares like crazy. I then made one of the worst radio calls of my life: "One's runaway gun."

At that moment Dice, my then number-three man, descended below the weather. Seeing red streaks around my element's aircraft, he called out that we were taking AAA. I then began to jink, while trying to "safe" my gun and talk Dice onto the target. Unfortunately, my erroneous "runaway gun" radio call had focused Dice's concentration more on the nose of my aircraft and getting out of my way than looking for the target. At this point he radioed that it was only our flares and not AAA that he had seen. Needless to say, the attack had turned into a chocolate mess. All four aircraft were within spitting distance of the target, we were looking at each other, and nobody was clearing for any threats. I quickly gathered the four of us together and climbed above the weather.

My wingman was low, real low, on gas, so we climbed to the optimum altitude and slowed to the best airspeed to conserve our fuel and extend our range—we "skyhooked" back to Gioia. I left Dice as the on-scene commander because he had the best situational awareness from going below the weather and seeing where the target should be. Over the next 45 minutes, the remaining three two-ships (seven and eight had returned from the tanker) made three more attacks on the target. Two of them were prosecuted from a low-altitude run-in 100 feet above the water. Unfortunately, due to an inability to acquire the radar, they both were unsuccessful. During the climb out for their skyhook back to Gioia, Joe Bro was able to look through a break in the clouds to see where the van had been parked and noticed the dirt tracks it had left when it drove off.

Explosive-ordnance-disposal personnel SSgt Mike Werner and A1C Joe Deslaurieurs preparing to "safe" a GAU-8 that jammed during a combat mission over Kosovo by using a C-4 explosive charge to "render safe" the stuck 30 mm rounds

USAF Photo by TSgt Blake Borsic

When we got back, I told everyone about the sortie and the lack of results. "Flat Face mania" seemed to grip the squadron. Completely irrational, I had almost convinced Larry Card to hop in a jet, join on my wing, and go back with me to kill that radar right then and there. Everyone shared our disappointment.

The next day Scratch and Dirt went looking for the priority target. The now-familiar midlevel deck of clouds was again present and forced them to drop down through the clouds, which bottomed out at 4,000 feet. The Serbs, having finally decided to defend their radar, shot a manpads missile right between the two-ship of Hogs. Scratch and Dirt defeated the missile and climbed back through the clouds. When Scratch's mission report made it to the bigwigs, the listed altitude of 4,000 feet raised more than a few eyebrows. Scratch, Dirt, and I were called into the squadron commander's office that afternoon. Scratch and Dirt, along with Colonel Thompson, our group commander, had the pleasure of seeing the three-star about breaking the minimum altitudes described in his ROEs.

The trials and tribulations I faced while trying to attack the Flat Face radar taught me some very important lessons. I learned a great deal about the capability and limitations of weapons, tactics, and the effects of weather. I gained a new understanding of mission-essential tasking versus mission requirements. I came to appreciate the occasional discrepancy between tactical leadership and the "can do," "type A" mentality of our typical attack pilot. Finally, I learned what air combat really is. It's not just strategic bombing from 20,000 feet using munitions aided by Global Positioning System (GPS) and delivered against targets whose coordinates had been carefully measured. I now know what it's like to belly up to the table, look the bad guy square in the eye, and be confident that I have the ability, the constitution, and the fortitude to shoot him.

Attack on Montenegro

1st Lt Johnny "CBU" Hamilton

My most memorable sortie had an unsuccessful ending. It started one day when our squadron was tasked to plan an attack on a radar site in the Yugoslav province of Montenegro. The target was a long-range search radar used to track inbound and outbound NATO aircraft. Allied forces had finally pinpointed its location and decided it was time for the radar to go.

I was working in the mission-planning cell (MPC) when short-notice attack orders came down. I would not be a member of the attack force. However, with the exception of the actual flight brief, I was involved with every other aspect of the planning, which called for a four-ship of A-10s to attack at night using CBU-87s, Mavericks, and 30 mm guns. They were to depart Gioia, flying the standard route to Kosovo, and try to employ some tactical deception. The daily operational routine was to fly to a tanker before going into Kosovo, and the Yugoslavs knew it. At about the halfway point, the four-ship made a rapid descent over the Adriatic Sea but kept talking to the NAEW as if they were still cruising at altitude and proceeding to the tanker. The NAEW crew members participated in our deception plan and continued talking and vectoring the imaginary Hogs towards the tanker, even though they were nowhere near the normal routes. This was all an attempt to confuse the Yugoslavs in case they were listening to our radio transmissions and throw them off in case they had not been able to track the A-10s on radar. Unfortunately, the weather was extremely bad, and they were not able to engage the target successfully.

USAF Photo by TSgt Blake Borsic

Lt Johnny Hamilton shows rock star Joan Jett the Maverick missile

Three days later I was flying on the wing of Capt Stu Stuewe on an AFAC sortie in Kosovo. After our two vul periods, we were returning home, and we flew very close to the radar site. We were at high altitude, but the clear weather allowed us look into the area where we expected the radar to be located. At this point, an otherwise routine sortie became interesting. Stu was one of the pilots involved in the first night attack against the radar. He still had the target map with him and, because I had been involved with the planning, I remembered the radar's geographic area and its location in relation to the road that paralleled the coast. Stu immediately located the radar and began coordinating for an impromptu attack clearance. He was able to get approval for the three other returning Hog two-ships to support the attack. Just as Stu had been involved on the first attack, it happened that the other three flight leads had been part of that original four-ship. We had the original four players leading four wingmen with their additional firepower.

We were ready to go after taking about 15 minutes to organize the fighters and get approval for the attack. Our attack force of

195

four two-ships started off in trail at medium altitude with about two miles of separation between the elements. We were trying to attack the radar site quickly, and only Stu had put his eyes on the target. I had seen the target area but had not been able to pull out the binoculars and positively ID its location. The plan was for Stu to hit the target with a Maverick, and then the others would queue off the smoke and flames to find it. My job was to cover for the two of us—looking around for any threats to the formation. As we descended, Stu tried to lock up the target with an IIR Maverick. Because of poor thermal contrast with the surrounding area, the seeker would not lock on to just the vehicle. I was flying with extended spacing off Stu's right wing as we crossed over the coast, flew inland, and rapidly approached the target. My duty was to continuously look for threats to the formation by searching the arc from my right side, through the nose, and on towards my 10 o'clock position to keep Stu in sight. This constant search pattern never allowed me to look for the target. We were two to three miles from the target when Stu radioed that he was switching to guns because the Mav wouldn't lock-on. I started to sense a ground rush now because I hadn't flown this low since the war started. The adrenaline rush was almost unbearable. The flight pressed in. Stu steadied his crosshairs and pulled the trigger. "Runaway gun! One's runaway gun!" is all we heard on the radio. The Gatling gun on Stu's jet had malfunctioned. It had spun up but fired no bullets.

He immediately pulled up and banked hard to the left, egressing over the water. As I heard this I looked out front, curious about the call and expecting to see the gun firing uncontrollably, but in the heat and excitement of the moment, Stu made an incorrect call.

As I looked out in front of Stu's jet, I saw a group of vehicles off the side of the road, and then I saw Stew aggressively turn towards the sea. Since my job was to cover for the flight, I also turned west and egressed with flares. We were both jinking over the water now at less than 1,000 feet AGL. I looked back over my shoulder at the target for any threat reaction. There were no missiles or gun flashes, but I could see the second two-ship running towards the target.

Unfortunately, they never got eyes on the radar, so they aborted their pass. The same thing happened to the remaining two-ships. Because Stu's jet malfunctioned and I was low on fuel, we were not able to reattack the target. The other Hogs were able to loiter for a little longer but never acquired the radar.

I often wonder if I should have hit those vehicles I saw at the last minute. I could have called "contact" and requested clearance to fire. This would have at least marked the target for the remaining Hogs. My job, however, was to clear. With Stu egressing, who would clear for me if I focused on the target? Still, I wish I could have killed that thing!

The Hogs did kill the radar on a subsequent sortie. Capt Joe Bro Brosious finally got it—he strafed it until it wasn't anymore! This was just one more example of the variety of missions the A-10 can fly. Even though it was designed to provide CAS for the Army, it has repeatedly been used successfully in other roles. Hogs have attacked and destroyed radar sites and communication facilities, and have suppressed enemy air defenses—an ability we demonstrated against SA-6 sites in Kosovo. These missions make the Warthog such an exciting plane to fly—I wouldn't trade it for anything!

A Monkey and a Giraffe

Capt Joe S. "Joe Bro" Brosious

"Do you need me to drive?" I yelled from the backseat. I continued, "If you kill us going to work today, I will make sure that you never fly again." I was a scheduler, so this was a credible threat.

In retrospect, the drive to work was the most dangerous thing we did on a daily basis during OAF. The Italians had a knack for turning two lanes of traffic into three, and, depending on which of us was driving, things could get pretty sporty. It was around 0500 when I was rudely awakened by the stunt driving of the lieutenant behind the wheel. The drive to the squadron was the last quiet moment I could expect to have when flying a morning sortie. Everyone was usually too tired (or too tense) to talk, and the ride left a lot of time for reflection—or sleeping, as the case had been that morning. Now we at least had something to keep us all awake, and we spent the rest of our commute expressing displeasure with our young chauffeur's driving abilities. A person normally develops a very thick skin working in a fighter squadron. The ability of a pilot to give someone grief for stupid remarks or actions is almost as highly respected by the pilot's fellow aviators as is his ability to fly the plane. Indeed, it has truly been raised to an art form—a by-product of putting 30 type-A personalities together in the same workplace. It helped take our minds off the three million other things we were supposed to get accomplished during the day besides flying.

Morning sorties were always hectic. We had to get up at four in the morning—arriving at the squadron any earlier was not a rational option. A point of diminishing returns occurs when an alarm clock is set any earlier than around four in the morning (I used to think it was around 0600, but the Air Force recalibrated me). Getting up at 0400 is not something a normal human being should do on a regular basis.

No matter how early we arrived, we were always behind. There was never enough time to wade through all of the information thrown at us during the morning intelligence brief. We had to be very selective about what actions and thoughts we let occupy those precious two hours before takeoff. Mission planning had become a three-step process that was reflected in a series of three questions I asked myself before every sortie: What's out there trying to kill me? What am I trying to kill? How do I accomplish my mission without getting into trouble? The last question seemed like a no-brainer, but it was one of our biggest concerns and something we had to concentrate on during our pre-mission planning. Information about every airborne flight was continuously transmitted to the CAOC and played on the big screen. "Big Brother" was watching, and nobody wanted to highlight himself. Just a week before, two of our squadron majors were ordered to the CAOC to explain an apparent ROE deviation, and they received a tongue-lashing of epic proportions. We all knew that any one of us could have been called up there and nobody wanted to make that trip.

I was scheduled to fly this particular morning with Capt Michael L. "Smokey" Matesick. I was the only one who called him

Smokey. The nickname stems from an antiskid brake-system check that Mike had performed at the request of our maintenance personnel. They asked for volunteers one night when we were sitting CSAR alert, and Smokey, being the youngest, got to volunteer. They had spent the last six hours fixing the brakes and needed them checked. All they wanted was for Smokey to taxi the jet above 25 knots, slam on the brakes, and see that the antiskid engaged. Well that is just what he did. However, out on the runway after he checked the brakes the first time, he realized he still had about 8,000 feet of runway remaining—plenty of room to really check the brakes. After the third test, and as he was pulling off the runway, the Italians in the tower shouted on the UHF radio, "A-10 on taxiway, you smokey!" Sure enough, Mike had severely overheated the brakes and sat there on the taxiway in disbelief as both main-gear tires went flat. If anything made me laugh harder during the war, I don't remember it. Maintenance was not amused.

I liked flying with Smokey—probably more than flying with anyone else. We had flown together enough to know what to expect from each other, and I had good luck finding targets with him. I can't really say I believe in luck or fate—I think people make their own. Strangely, however, I did feel that if I flew with a certain person, I was probably going to get shot at, or if I flew with another particular person it would likely be a slow day. Maybe it was a self-fulfilling prophecy on my part, but I'll bet that most flight leads would admit that they had a lucky wingman.

I got my standard large cup of coffee, and then Smokey and I sat down for our intel brief. Four months into the war, we had a pretty good picture of what was out there and where people had been lucky or unlucky. Intel briefed on an unlocated SA-6 somewhere in Kosovo and SAN-4s off the coast of Montenegro—as they had been the entire war. We were mainly interested in what had happened the day before. Who had been shot at? Where did they find targets? With this information we had the ability to make our plan of attack. Included in our mission planning materials was a list of about 50 targets (some days more, some days fewer). Our first job was to look at the list and guess which ones were valid and which were bogus: 20 tanks just outside of Prizren (most likely bogus),

200 infantry with vehicles (probably bogus). We decided on a handful of targets that looked promising and rank-ordered them. One interesting target, with imagery, was two tanks parked next to a tree line. The picture, from a British Harrier, looked too good to be true. We assumed they were decoys, but they were a possible dump target if it turned into a slow day. I briefed about 30 minutes on flight contracts and other required items, and then we were out the door to fly.

The mornings stopped being hectic when we finally got airborne. I hated waking up at 0400, but there is nothing better than taking off at sunrise and being the first flight into the area of operations (AO). We hit the tanker inbound, refueled, and made our way across the border. We were slotted as an air-strike control (aka AFAC) sortie working in the western half of Kosovo, using Swine 91 as our call sign. We were more like "killer scouts" running down through a suspected target list. We searched each set of coordinates with handheld binoculars for any sign of the Serbian military. While scrutinizing our third target, I struck gold.

Two artillery pieces were backed against a tree line overlooking the border town of Zur. Closer investigation revealed what looked like a deuce-and-a-half truck parked nearby with the cargo cover pulled off. Smokey didn't have the target but was more than happy to provide cover while I rolled in with an IIR Maverick air-to-ground missile. I was unable to break out the artillery pieces due to poor thermal contrast, but the truck showed up beautifully in my cockpit picture. I locked on and hammered down on the pickle button. My Maverick came off like a freight train, but then just as suddenly it pointed vertical and went blitzing off towards some unknown, unsuspecting piece of dirt.

"Two come south, my Maverick just went 'stupid,'" I warned. Things were bad enough; I certainly didn't want Smokey in the same piece of sky as my missile. We watched and waited for what seemed an eternity. A thousand horrifying scenarios flashed through my brain in a matter of seconds. Maybe I would be on the next plane to the CAOC after all. Luckily the Maverick splashed down on the eastern bank of a river just to our north. Crisis averted!

Smokey wasn't exactly sure where the target was, and by this time we were well north of it. No problem, I thought. I've got another missile, so I'll set up for a pass from the north. I found the truck again and pickled off my second Maverick. This one came off the rail and did a direct nosedive underneath my aircraft. I had never had a Maverick missile go stupid on me before, and here I was at 10,000 feet praying that my second stupid missile of the day would not find an inappropriate impact point. Performing a classic posthole maneuver, this missile hit much quicker than the first, coming down in a field just outside a small village. I searched the area for any signs that something other than dirt had been disturbed and found nothing.

Since Smokey had seen where my nose had been pointed, he now attacked the target. I covered our flight while he rolled in with one of his Mavericks. Shack! We had now expended three Mavericks for one truck, not a very good ratio, but I was glad I had my lucky wingman with me (luck doesn't always come in the form of targets). While Smokey was setting up for his Maverick pass, two Belgian F-16s checked in, with each aircraft carrying one Mk-84 2,000 lb bomb. I gave them our coordinates and cleared them into the area at high altitude. Once they were overhead, I marked the artillery pieces with three white phosphorous marking rockets. The Vipers could still not acquire the target. Since my third rocket had landed directly on the southern artillery piece, I finally got to say the only three words that a FAC in any war has ever wanted to say: "Hit my smoke!"

An Mk-84 exploding is one of the most violent things I have ever witnessed. I can't imagine what it is like to be near its detonation on the ground, but I never tire of being safely overhead and watching one explode. The entire hillside erupted as the F-16s dropped one after the other on the two artillery pieces. We thanked each other for the work, and Smokey and I headed back to the tanker.

It had been a successful morning so far. We got our fuel, and I was excited to get back in the fight. After being back in the area for no more than 10 minutes, I received a call from Magic, the ABCCC C-130. He said that the KEZ would be closing to facilitate the search for a priority target—a radar somewhere on the coast of Montenegro. I argued with Magic to allow at least one section of the KEZ to stay open. "Stand by; checking," came the reply. Simultaneously we could hear what seemed like hounds being turned loose, as every Hog driver in the area jockeyed for position to get a crack at this target. It was no great mystery what we were going after. I had been in this situation twice before. The first was a night CSAR alert period that turned into a low-altitude, below-the-weather sortie searching for the proverbial needle in a haystack. The second occurred about a week later—a day sortie in which they had also closed the KEZ down and turned the Hogs loose. That one ended with Capt Ron Stuewe suffering a gun malfunction with the target in his crosshairs. We were "zero for two," and the CAOC wanted this radar badly. It was being used as the eyes of the enemy's early warning system and covered the approaches over the Adriatic that funneled jets into Kosovo. They knew when we were coming and how many of us there were. Someone at the CAOC had the destruction of this radar on the top of his "to do" list.

Magic came back, "Swine 91, you are directed to leave the area. The KEZ will be closing in five minutes."

"Magic, Swine 91. I'm requesting to leave the western half of the KEZ open." There were already three flights headed in search of the radar, and I now had the entire western half of the country to myself. I didn't want to go anywhere.

A new voice came across the radio, this one much older and much more perturbed at my request: "Swine 91, you are ordered to exit the AO. The KEZ will be closing in five minutes." Good thing they were broadcasting this to the world over an open frequency. That was good enough for me and I started outbound. But I realized we were right near the target we had identified during our mission planning that morning—the one that was too good to be true. I altered my course outbound to the west slightly and spotted it—exactly like the picture and it certainly did look too good to be true. Somebody had to pay for those decoys though, and if I'm getting kicked out I may as well take the decoys with me. I relayed my plan to Smokey and we were in 30 seconds apart on the two, what appeared to be, tank decoys. Both passes were good and we rippled four Mk-82 500 lb bombs on each of the tanks. They weren't very tactically significant targets, but those decoys had to cost at least 10 grand apiece. I thought it was a fair trade on that day, and I think Smokey agreed. Information in a subsequent Kosovo after-action report revealed that two tanks had indeed been found destroyed at those coordinates.

We headed south and came up on the frequency being used for the priority target. This was the same one that the two majors were going after when they got into trouble. They were diverted to go find and attack this radar and then got the free ride up to the CAOC for their efforts. After that happened, I swore to myself that I would never go after that radar again—yet here I was, headed for the coast, flying towards the unlocated SA-6 and SAN-4 missile systems. That radar had become a monkey on the back of the 81st FS. We checked in just in time to hear the talk-on from Magic. To say it was confusing would be a gross understatement. In fact, we could hear the confusion from the other flights even though they weren't saying a word. I don't remember exactly what Magic said, but I do recall that it was one long sentence without punctuation—something like, "There are two castles one is in the water one is on the land with the distance between the two shores one unit go one unit south from the castle you come to a road go south on this road which puts you in between two roads that form a V which is open to the target area south along the road."

The first time I heard Magic's talk-on, I couldn't follow it close enough to understand what the controller was trying to say. The flights already in the target area asked Magic to "say again." I was a bit apprehensive, to say the least. I had coordinates inputted into my inertial navigation system (INS) to get us close, but the target radar was so far north this time that it was off all the maps I carried with me (we usually didn't launch with the intention of attacking Montenegro). In summary: I had no map, my INS had drifted at least three miles when I compared it to known ground references on the way out of the KEZ, there were still two flights left looking for the radar, and we had a target-location description that seemed to make matters worse. What I did have on my side was time. We still had about 15 minutes en route to the target area. The next time Magic gave the talk-on, I wrote the entire thing down on my canopy with grease pencil. If someone reads a paragraph without using punctuation, or using the wrong punctuation, it can change the meaning completely—or even make it incomprehensible. I broke the talk-on into what I thought were reasonable sections. It was still confusing without having my eyes on the target. Nevertheless, it seemed to give me a much better mental picture of what I was looking for.

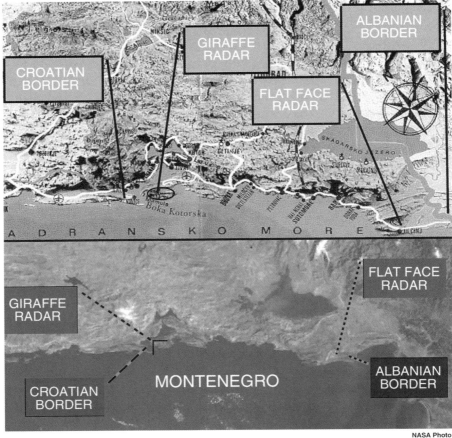

Map and photo of area containing suspected Serb radars

We arrived at the target area just in time for the flight on station to give us an orientation. We could definitely see the ruins of two castles. One was indeed on a tiny island in the middle of a small bay. The other was about a kilometer away on the shore to the south of the first one. The departing flight talked me onto the area they had been searching. They were using the distance between the far shore on the north side of the castle in the water and the shore to the south as one unit. This seemed reasonable enough and is what I would have thought. Next they were going one unit south along a road running away from the castle on the shore. At that point another road branched off from the main road; together they formed a "V." It seemed perfectly logical that the target was in this area, and I took over the search. Ten minutes later I wasn't so sure. I decided to start over. I ran through it one more time and ended up in the same location. The possibility that it wasn't even out there crossed my mind.

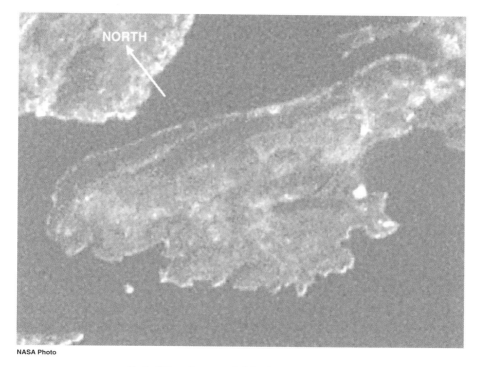

NASA Photo

Satellite photo of Giraffe radar area

It then occurred to me that we had to be trolling around in some pretty unfriendly territory and that the radios had been quiet for some time. With the KEZ closed, surely this effort would have had all the available support dedicated to it. I queried Magic for the status of any SEAD and jamming assets. We had no jamming assets, and our SEAD was on a different frequency, headed for the tanker. I requested that Magic have all players come up on a common victor (VHF-AM) radio threat frequency. A quick check-in revealed that we actually did have two F-16 CJs covering the area and one EA-6B about five minutes out to provide jamming. It felt good to know the CJs were above us, holding in their SEAD orbit while the Hogs were taking care of the destruction of enemy air defenses (DEAD) (with *destruction* being the key word). Things seemed to be in order, so I went back to the beginning of my talk-on.

Nowhere did it say to go one unit from the southern castle. I decided I would try going one unit south from the castle in the water. That put me just on shore, a little south of the southern castle. There I noticed a small road that ran out from the other side of the castle that I had not seen before. This road formed a V with the larger dirtball, and going one unit south put me right smack dab in the middle of that V. There was also a small road that ran from the larger dirtball into a large grove of trees that was covering the entire inside portion of the V. I put my binoculars up to the point where that small road disappeared in the trees and saw . . . nothing. However, there was a small concrete pad with what looked like a small hardened shelter close by. I swung my aircraft back around, refocused my binos, and got a closer look. There it was—sticking out of the tops of the trees—the upper half of a Giraffe radar. Not believing it, I checked at least two more times. It was

Photo courtesy of FAS

Giraffe air-defense-system radar

definitely the Giraffe. Smokey did not have the target in sight—there was no way he could have. I directed him to continue to cover us, and I quickly set up for a gun pass on the Giraffe.

"Magic, Swine 91. Confirm we are cleared to engage this target," I queried, almost wishing I hadn't asked and fully expecting him to deny me.

"Swine 91, you are cleared to expend 30 mm on that target," Magic quickly replied.

I found myself about 10 seconds later hanging in the straps on about a 70-degree diving delivery. In my excitement I had failed to do the most important thing—fly the jet! I was able to shoot only about 50 bullets, not anything close to what I wanted to put down. They did impact the immediate target area, however. I asked Smokey if he had seen my bullets hit so that I could clear him in on a pass of his own. He came back with a negative, so I climbed back to altitude. This time I made sure that I was in a good position to roll in, and with two bursts—about 300 rounds—from the mighty GAU-8 the Giraffe slumped over, smoldering and resting on the same trees that had just provided it cover. The 81st had stuck its finger in Milosevic's eye, and the monkey was finally off our back. It was nothing new for the A-10. As it has done in every war in which it has been involved, the Hog proved it had the ability to adapt to nearly any mission at a moment's notice and have success, leaving some other high-tech jets stuck in orbit.

USAF Photo by TSgt Blake Borsic

Crew chief cleaning the canopy after the GAU-8 cannon had been used on a mission

7

Tactical Innovation

Introduction

Lt Col Chris "Kimos" Haave

The A-10 was a ridiculously simple fighter aircraft in its 1999 configuration, as well as the one used in OAF. When measured by twenty-first-century standards, its avionics suite lacked the gadgets that are standard in most modern fighters. There is a long list of what it did not have: GPS for precision navigation; a targeting pod for target identification or laser designation; a data link for receiving or passing target coordinates; a high-speed data bus for a moving map display; precision survival-radio-finding equipment for CSAR; and radar to provide precise target elevations for medium-altitude attacks or to find a tanker at night or in the weather. Its engines, not having been updated, continued to limit the Hog's maximum airspeed to less than 225 knots at 20,000 feet. Even with this long list of have-nots, the A-10 retained some distinct advantages.

The Hog had abundant cockpit space for stacks of maps, mission materials, and gyrostabilized binoculars. It also had a big canopy on which to write, with grease pencil, the target area and striker information. We had a great mix of weapons, particularly the 30 mm gun and the Maverick missile, both optimized for our targets. We had great logisticians and maintainers to keep the jets in top shape and fully loaded. We had pilots who trained daily in a European environment and learned to capitalize on the A-10's strengths, compensate for its shortcomings, and skillfully evaluate the ground situation. Notwithstanding these strengths, we still had to refine and develop a few new tactics and techniques during the course of our OAF operations.

Efficient cockpit organization was critical to expeditious target identification and attack. Each pilot had his own techniques and habits that worked best for him. These evolved as we compared and adopted each other's tricks. For example, we needed a faster method to determine and pass target information critical to incoming fighters. After an A-10 AFAC located a lucrative target, he had to develop the data necessary for the FAC-to-fighter brief. To do so, while flying the aircraft, he would have to use a sequence similar to the following:

1. Find the general target area on a large-scale map (1:250) that had markings for each of the smaller-scale maps (1:50).

2. Determine which 1:50 to use.

3. Find the correct 1:50 among the stack of 16 such maps.

4. Study the terrain, roads, forests, power lines, and houses marked on the map to match the target area on the ground.

5. Read the coordinates, in Universal Transverse Mercator (UTM) format, from the scale on the map.

6. Write these coordinates on the inside of the A-10's canopy in grease pencil.

7. Go back to the 1:50, follow the contour lines to determine the target elevation in meters, and write that on the canopy.

8. Use the Inertial Navigation System to convert the UTM coordinates to latitude and longitude, and write those on the canopy.

9. Use the HUD to convert the elevation from meters to feet, and write that on the canopy.

10. Finally, read the target information to the incoming fighters over the radio.

By contrast, F-16CG and F-14 FACs with targeting pods could simply point their laser designators at a target to determine its relative range, direction, and elevation. The aircraft's avionics automatically integrate that information with its GPS information and instantly display target coordinates and elevation in the desired format. If the incoming fighters are equipped with a compatible data link, they could pass the information without even using the radio.

We could often get around the need to "pull" coordinates off the map by directing strikers to rendezvous at a known point and then talking the striker's eyes onto the target, usually with the aid of a mark. Generally, the striker would still need the target elevation.

Several of our Allied Force innovations were genuine "Air Force firsts." For instance, Lt Col Coke Koechle described the first cooperative employment of an A-10 with a USAF Predator drone. When we understood what had happened and what was possible, we asked for more interactive targeting. Sometimes it seemed rather comical when CAOC personnel, without FAC expertise, tried to use the Predator's camera feed to describe a tank hiding in the woods. The Predator camera has a very narrow field of view (FOV), similar to looking through a soda straw. The discrepancy between that narrow FOV and the wide FOV an AFAC has when looking out of an A-10 canopy flying at 20,000 feet often resulted in lengthy and frustrating talk-ons. The CAOC transmission would sound something like "the tank is in the woods near a dirt road," reflecting the only tank, woods, and dirt road the Predator feed displayed. However, the AFAC saw dozens of woods and dirt roads from 20,000 feet and was still no closer to finding the tank. The problem was amplified further when the target descriptions were passed through the ABCCC to the AFAC.

The CAOC recognized the problem, and talk-ons improved when it tasked a pilot with FAC experience to man the microphone. In an attempt to further improve the speed and accuracy of passing target locations, the CAOC directed that a Predator be modified to carry a laser designator. Late in the campaign Capt Larry "LD" Card, one of our weapons officers, flew a test sortie on the Albanian coast to validate the concept. The Predator marked a simulated target using its onboard laser. That spot was visible to LD using his Hog's laser-spot-tracking pod, which proved that Predators and Hogs could operate efficiently together. The Predator's laser could nail down a target location very quickly and avoid the lengthy talk-ons. We were eager to use this new tactic to locate and schwack hidden Serb tanks. However, we were never able to record a successful combat mission with Laser Predator due to the combination of poor target-area weather, limited Laser Predator availability, and—thankfully—the end of the conflict.

Hog success in CSAR included leading two immediate night rescues—the first in US combat history. Our CSAR experts were visionaries and had laid the right foundation to prepare us, and our allies, for this particularly tough mission. Our success reflected those efforts, the participants' stupendous seat-of-the-pants flying, and their ingenuity. Goldie exemplified that ingenuity when he shut down Serb radars by making "Magnum" calls—those that normally accompany the launch of a high-speed antiradiation missile (HARM)—during rescue of the pilot of Vega 31.

We also put tactical deception to good use. During the first week of KEZ operations, ABCCC announced in the clear over strike frequency, "The KEZ will close in 10 minutes," followed later by, "The KEZ is closed. All aircraft must depart the AOR." We understood that the CAOC had directed ABCCC to make those calls. We suggested to the CAOC that code words should normally be used for "KEZ open" and "KEZ closed," particularly when they were used in the clear. We then worked through our CAOC rep to set up a "head fake"—that is, announce that the KEZ would close and then go back in to look for any targets that might think it was safe to move and had broken cover. Capt Michael J. "Hook" Shenk Jr. describes that mission well.

Capt Ripley E. "Rip" Woodard's story has nothing to do with employing ordnance, but is simply a feat of courageous airmanship that saved an aircraft with a dual-engine flameout under particularly harrowing circumstances. It is a must-read—twice—that makes it easy to understand why he won the Koren Kerrigan Safety Award in 1999.

One tactical innovation that had enormous potential and just didn't work out was the employment of a joint A-10 and Apache helicopter team. The US Army had based Apaches in Albania. We had worked with these helicopters before and had some joint tactical-employment doctrine, but some tactical concepts needed to be adapted to reflect the Serbs' 360-degree, ground-based threat to aircraft. Because the CAOC's Apache and A-10 reps assumed we would operate together, they worked out a few "practice" sorties during the last week of April. We also looked for additional opportunities to further our orientation. Without compromising our planned KEZ missions, we attempted radio or visual contact with the Apaches as they progressively flew more ambitious training sorties in northern Albania.

To form an effective team, we needed to discuss several issues in detail: CSAR procedures, target identification, and responses to particular threats. We looked forward to the Tirana conference to hammer out those tactical details. As it turned out, Tirana was an operational-level decision meeting between general officers and not one where worker bees could engage in stubby-pencil work. Regrettably, the Apache briefers were not familiar with our KEZ operations and briefed employment concepts and tactics that had been developed during the Cold War. General Short was understandably uncomfortable; he and General Hendrix decided, at that time, not to go forward with Apache operations.

The A-10s and Apaches didn't fly together in combat; therefore, their potential for success in the KEZ remains pure speculation. Our opinions differed significantly on whether we could have developed workable tactics, but most of us thought it would have been worth the try. The level of military pressure necessary to force a Serbian capitulation was eventually applied to the Serb army by the KLA during a two-week period in early June. Perhaps that same level of pressure could have been applied by the Apaches within days or hours in early May.

Some people may consider the A-10 a Stone Age jet, but its very limitations may have been the catalyst that led to our success. When human ingenuity, born out of necessity, is combined with a cultural desire to find creative solutions to difficult tactical problems, tremendous feats can be accomplished. Such feats accounted for a lot of destroyed enemy armor in the KEZ, and the Hog community should never forget the human traits that led to those results.

The First Night CSAR

Maj Phil "Goldie" Haun

Day 4: 27 March 1999. So far so good, if flying an A-10 for seven hours behind a KC-135 in a holding pattern over the Adriatic, while NATO's air armada wreaked havoc over Serbia, is "good." The really sad part was that flying nighttime airborne alert was a great mission compared to what most of my squadron mates were doing. They were either sitting ground alert or just watching the war go by from the sidelines at Aviano. We had only been tasked to provide CSAR support as Sandys. Our job was to respond to a jet being shot down and to be overhead in the A-10—one of the most lethal war machines ever created—to orchestrate the pilot's rescue. So far no one had been shot down, which was a very good thing, and, as a consequence, our operational involvement had been limited.

That night I was scheduled to fly during the graveyard shift. My wingman, Capt Joe Bro Brosious, and I were to take off at midnight. As we traveled from the hotel to the squadron, NATO cancelled its strikes for the night because of bad weather. The CAOC then cancelled our first airborne-alert CSAR two-ship and placed the squadron on ground alert. Capts Buster Cherrey and John "Slobee" O'Brien had been scheduled to fly first and were now pulling ground alert as Sandy 30 and 31.

I turned my attention to more interesting work. In two days our squadron would begin leading daytime attacks on the Serbian army deployed in Kosovo. I was in charge of planning those attacks, so I drove over to wing intelligence, on the other side of the Aviano runway, to review its information. I had just started looking at some Kosovo imagery when an airman in the room yelled, "An F-117 has been shot down!"

That couldn't be right! The strikes had been called off for tonight. We didn't even have Buster and Slobee airborne. Later I would learn that, although the NATO strikes had been cancelled, the F-117 was part of a US-only strike.

Someone handed me a set of coordinates and the pilot's name and rank scribbled on a yellow sticky. I raced back to the squadron and pulled up as Buster and Slobee were stepping to their jets. I gave them the information I had and talked

214

USAF Photo by TSgt Blake Borsic

Weapons troop inspecting an IIR Maverick and IR illumination rockets prior to a night mission

strategy with Buster for about 30 seconds. We decided to have the MH-53J Pave Low helicopters launch when Sandy 41, our second set of A-10s flown by Capts Meegs Meger and Scrape Johnson, were refueling on the tanker. Sandy 41's job would be to contact the helicopters, update them on the rescue plan, and then escort them to the survivor.

I craved more information. The F-117 had to be a Black Sheep from the 8th FS, the only F-117s deployed at Aviano at the time. I grabbed Lt Glib Gibson and sent him to the 8th to get as much information as possible. Glib quickly procured copies of the pilot's (call sign Vega 31) route of flight and, most importantly, his ISOPREP card, which contains personal data that only the pilot knows and won't forget even under a lot of pressure. A pilot reviews that information prior to each combat sortie. Glib, acting on his own initiative, made the important decision to drive out on the flight line to give the ISOPREP-card information to Buster right before takeoff.

Meanwhile I was performing my cat-juggling act at the squadron. I had intelligence pull maps and plot the survivor's

215

Capt Meegs Meger gets ready to take off in the rain at Aviano.

coordinates. I was relieved when I saw that he was within 20 miles of the Croat-Serb border and well clear of major threats. CAOC personnel were on the phone wanting to know our plan. I told them the time we wanted the helicopters to launch and that they should muster as many air-refueling tankers as possible. Gas equals time in operations such as this, and there was no way to know how long it would take us to complete this mission. The F-16CG (Block 40) and F-16CJ (Block 50) squadrons had volunteered an additional six jets apiece for the mission. Thirty minutes after first notification of the shoot down, I was giving the most important briefing of my life, informing the F-16s on their roles in what proved to be the largest CSAR since Vietnam.

The F-16CGs carried targeting pods and could drop laser-guided bombs. My intention was to slow down the Serbian army's search for Vega. I selected the intersections of major lines of communication, near where I believed the survivor to be located, as potential strike targets. Still, I was concerned about the availability of gas on the tankers and didn't know when we would need the strikes, so I decided to keep the F-16CGs on ground alert until we needed them. From Aviano they could hit those targets within an hour. As it turned out,

Plot of initial coordinates for Vega 31

we never launched the F-16CGs because low-level clouds over Serbia would have made it impossible for them to see their targets and the initial survivor coordinates proved to be in error by more than 40 miles.

The F-16CJs carried the HARM and had the "Wild Weasel" defense-suppression mission. It was their job to keep the radar-guided SAMs in the belt around Belgrade from shooting us down. I wanted the F-16CJs to launch ASAP. Those six jets would join the eight F-16CJs already airborne that had been a part of the strike package when Vega 31 was shot down.

I concluded the briefing in 20 minutes. Joe Bro and I then powwowed and updated our information before we stepped to our jets. Our job was to support Sandy 30. My individual call sign and, since I was the flight lead, our flight call sign was Sandy 51; Joe Bro's individual call sign was Sandy 52. Joe Bro and I planned to come off the tanker with a full load of fuel just as Sandy 30 flight would be reaching its bingo fuel and required departure for the tanker. We had no idea how long the rescue would take. Using this strategy, Buster and I could swap out being the on-scene commander and ensure that a Sandy flight would always be with the survivor.

217

Joe Bro and I stepped just as Buster and Slobee, Sandy 30, were taking off. I thought that the timing should work well. Meegs and Scrape's two-ship, Sandy 41, would get airborne in another 30 minutes. I performed the preflight inspection on my A-10. The jet was configured with two IIR Maverick air-to-surface missiles, seven white-phosphorous (also known as Willy Pete) rockets, seven night-illumination rockets, and 1,000 30 mm rounds for the gun. We were not carrying any bombs, but Meegs and Scrape had CBU-87 cluster bombs if we needed them. I climbed into the jet, and, while performing my cockpit checks prior to takeoff, I heard Meegs relay on the victor radio that Buster had contacted the survivor and had an updated position for him. When I pulled out my map and plotted this new set of coordinates, my heart sank. Vega was south of Novisad and just west of the suburbs of Belgrade—in the heart of Serbia.

Actual location of Vega 31

My heart was pounding a mile a minute as I took off from Aviano AB. This base in northern Italy, located at the foot of the Dolomite Mountains, provided a spectacular view at night, particularly when I put on my NVGs. The weather was clear, with a big full moon overhead. Unfortunately, the weather did not remain clear for long. Twenty miles south of the field I entered very thick clouds as I continued my climb to altitude. Looking at my wing, I could see that I was picking up some light rime ice. Though not dangerous to flight, the ice was degrading my weapons as it covered the seekers on my Mavericks and AIM-9 air-to-air missiles. I continued my climb to flight level (FL) 290 to get above the clouds and start subliming the ice off my missiles.

Magic, the call sign used by the crew of the NAEW, gave me a vector to the air-refueling track. I sent Joe Bro over to a separate frequency to contact Moonbeam for an update. Moonbeam was the ABCCC EC-130 aircraft that also served as the airborne mission coordinator during CSARs. It had responsibility for coordinating with the CAOC and Magic to ensure the timely flow of all the resources the CSAR operation needed.

Except for the icing and the survivor being in the suburbs of Belgrade, things were going pretty well. However, I was in for a shock when I keyed the mike to transmit on my UHF (uniform) radio—it was dead. I desperately tried to reset it by switching it off and on. Nothing. This was not good since the UHF was my primary radio and the survivor had only a UHF radio. In frustration I beat on the radio trying to pound it into life. Nothing.

I was over Bosnia—cruising at 300 knots in silence. I turned my radio off, raised my eyes up to the stars above, and prayed, "Lord, I've never prayed to you like this before, but I need your help like I've never needed it before. There is a man on the ground out there who needs me, and I can't help him if this radio won't work. Lord, I need you to fix this radio, because I can't do it by myself." I gently turned the radio back on and heard the angelic voice of Magic, wanting to know why I hadn't responded to his radio calls.

Under my breath I said, "Thank you, Lord," and keyed the mike to respond. Once again the UHF radio went dead. The A-10 carried three radios: UHF, VHF-AM, and FM. The UHF and VHF radios have good range, but the FM was good for only a few miles and useful only between jets in the same flight. I called Joe Bro on our interflight Fox Mike: "Two, my UHF is dead. I need you to talk to Magic." I left my UHF off for a couple of minutes and then turned it back on. I could hear Joe Bro talking to Magic. At least I could monitor UHF. This was going to be painful but workable. I could hear what was being said on the radio, but I had to call Joe Bro on Fox Mike and have him relay my calls on UHF. This just proved what the Rolling Stones said: "You can't always get what you want, but if you try sometimes, you just might find, you'll get what you need."

We continued to the tanker track located over the center of Bosnia. The A-10 was not designed for high-altitude flight. Loaded with munitions, we could not refuel above 20,000 feet. Fortunately the KC-135, Franc 74, was at FL 200. Descending out of FL 290, I picked up Franc going in and out of a broken cloud deck. We pulled in behind him just as he reentered the clouds. My refueling went without a hitch, but Joe Bro had trouble opening his air-refueling door. He had some icing around it and couldn't get the handle to move. I still don't know how he did it. We were flying at night, in the weather, and he was on the wing of that KC-135. While still flying the aircraft, Joe Bro unstrapped from his ejection seat to get better leverage on the handle and somehow forced the air-refueling door open.

Coming off the tanker, we climbed out of the weather, leveled off at FL 270, and turned east towards Serbia. I contacted Sandy 41 (Meegs) on victor, and he told us to continue to the Bosnia-Serbian border. Meanwhile Sandy 30 (Buster) had located Vega 31 and had everything ready for the rescue—everything, that is, except the helicopters. We were still waiting on the two MH-53 Pave Lows and, as I learned later, an MH-60 Pave Hawk. Initially Meegs had not been able to get hold of them, and when he finally raised them he discovered that the helos, call sign Moccasin, did not have the fuel on board to execute. The helicopters had been airborne about as long as Buster had been. Instead of launching at the time I had passed through the CAOC, they launched 90 minutes earlier and had been holding in Croatia, just east of the Serbian border near the first set of wrong coordinates. Later I learned that the time passed by the CAOC had been given in local time instead of Zulu time (Greenwich mean time). Local, or Central European, time is two hours ahead of Zulu time in March, so Moccasin thought he was already half an hour late and requested permission to launch immediately. This simple mistake, by someone not familiar enough with combat operations to know that all times in combat are expressed in Zulu, turned the rescue into an all-night affair and nearly cost the survivor his freedom.

Buster aborted the pickup and sent everyone to his respective tanker—everyone but Joe Bro and me. The survivor, Vega 31, was concerned with the life of his radio's battery and turned it off for 45 minutes while the helicopters refueled. Joe Bro and I were the only ones with gas, so our job was to monitor the survivor's frequency in case he needed to talk to us. I set up a north-south holding pattern just west of the Serbian border, where we listened and waited. We were in dangerous territory, near the place where an F-15A had shot down a Serbian MiG-29 Fulcrum just two nights before. I focused my attention to the east, where the MiG bases were located. Although the weather over Bosnia was bad, I could see into Serbia and make out the lights from the villages and towns all the way to Belgrade. A thunderstorm was building over Belgrade, which prevented me from making out the lights of that city. As the minutes ticked away, I watched the weather rapidly deteriorate. It appeared that the clouds over Bosnia were now pouring into Serbia. A very low cloud deck was moving east, and I could see town after town disappear beneath a blanket of clouds. Why did Moccasin have to launch early? We'd have had Vega 31 out of there by now. There was no way an A-10 Sandy could fly beneath that cloud deck—nor was I sure that even Moccasin could still make it.

While I was contemplating such negative thoughts, Joe Bro added a new thought: "Hey, what's that to the west?" I looked up to see two contrails heading our way. They had to be a set of friendly NATO fighters from the Bosnian CAP. We watched as they began to perform a classic pincer maneuver. I thought they must have been committing on some MiGs, although I hadn't heard any warnings from Magic. It soon became apparent that they were really interested in us, as my radar-warning receiver screamed at me, and the lead aircraft began a descent and turned our way.

I was in no way interested in being a part of a friendly fire incident, so I turned to put the fighter on the beam and kept turning to keep him in sight as he converged within a mile. As the fighter continued to converge, I saw a bright flash coming from his jet. Thinking the worst, I immediately started putting out chaff and flares as fast as I could push them out. Joe Bro was behind me doing the same thing. I was relieved when I realized the fighter had only ejected a flare and had not launched a missile at us. When he came alongside me, I saw that it was an F-16CG. The pilot had on NVGs and had pulled up to identify us. Satisfied, he climbed and departed to the west, leaving Joe Bro and me to clean out our flight suits and refocus on the task at hand.

Meanwhile Sandy 30 had refueled and was heading our way. Buster saw the flares and wanted to know what was up. I calmly said that all was well, passed on-scene command back to him, and turned towards the tanker for my second refueling of the night.

I gave the lead to Joe Bro since I couldn't talk on the UHF radio. I slid back to a position about three miles behind his jet and let him work for a while. Magic's crew members were in over their heads on this one. It seemed that they had no idea how many jets were out here, and they could not provide us any help in locating our tanker. This was going to be sporty since the A-10 has no radar. Fortunately our tanker, Franc 74, was awesome and held in a sucker hole for us. I was running really low on gas. I saw the tanker first and called his position to Joe Bro. The tanker was below me going in the opposite direction, so I executed a descending turn and joined on the boom. Joe Bro finally spotted the tanker and informed me that some jet was already on the tanker. That jet, I told him, was mine. He then joined on the tanker.

I salute the bravery of that night's tanker crews. Unarmed and unafraid they brought us fuel well within the range of Serb MiGs. We completed the refueling without a hitch. Joe Bro's refueling door worked fine, and within 20 minutes we were on our way. Unfortunately, things were not going so well for Buster.

Buster had finished his coordination and had everyone ready for the pickup. Meegs had Moccasin in position and everything looked good except for one thing. The survivor, Vega

31, had not checked in on the radio, and it was now nearly 10 minutes after the time we expected him to reestablish contact. Moonbeam then relayed a message from our intelligence folks that the Serbs were claiming to have picked him up—not exactly the news we wanted to hear. It was time to start worrying. This was by far the low point on the emotional roller coaster that I had been riding all night. We sat in silence for what felt like an eternity and listened. Every minute or so Buster called for Vega—no response.

This couldn't happen. We had worked too hard to lose him now. For over six months, we had trained over Bosnia, developing and refining our skills at CSAR in preparation for this moment. There was no way we are going to leave Vega to the Serbs.

Just when I couldn't take it anymore, Buster made another call, "Vega Three-One, Sandy Three-Zero."

In response was the weak but extremely calm reply, "Sandy Three-Zero, this is Vega Three-One." The roller coaster was on its way back up.

Buster's next concern was the possibility that Vega 31 had been captured and the Serbs were now luring us into an ambush. Buster asked Vega another question from Vega's ISOPREP card, and there was a pause.

"If you do not authenticate, we'll have to wait a little while." Buster was trying to give Vega 31 the option of calling off the pickup. If Vega came back with the wrong answer, we would know the Serbs had him. Vega, however, quickly answered the question and told us it still looked good for the pickup.

"All players, all players, execute, execute, execute." This was the call we had been waiting for Buster to make all night. It was time to move the helos forward and get on with the pickup. Buster prepared Vega for exactly what he was to do when the helos approached.

"Sandy, Vega Three-One, you want me to stay up?"

"Affirm, affirm," Buster replied. Vega was a bit confused about what was going on. He wanted to know if he should continue monitoring his radio or not. I considered this a good sign. If Vega didn't have an idea of when we were planning the pickup, the Serbs should also have trouble figuring it out.

Buster then called us: "Sandy Five-One and Five-Two, I want you to come in and anchor 10 miles southwest of objective and provide mutual support until Sandy Three-Zero, Three-One bingo."

"Copy, en route to 10 miles southwest objective now," I answered. Joe Bro and I were holding on the border, and Buster wanted us to move forward and hold southwest of Vega. Buster and Slobee were running low on gas and would soon have to go searching for another tanker.

"With your eyeball out and your raw up. Confirm your raw is up," I transmitted to Joe Bro.

He replied, "That is affirmative. Raw is up, chaff flare and pod is on." Before we entered Serbia we double-checked our jet's self-protection equipment. The radar warning receiver (RWR, pronounced *raw*), chaff, flares, and the ECM pod are the systems we would use to defeat any SAMs the Serbs might launch.

"Sandy Three-Zero, SAM reported active BRA, north 10." Magic was reporting that a nearby SAM was trying to track Buster and Slobee.

"Five-One, Four-One and Four-Two are in trail on you. We're about 700 pounds above bingo before tanker." Meegs and Scrape, Sandy 41 flight, had joined in behind Joe Bro and me and were following us into the heart of Serbia. They had enough gas to hang around for another 15 minutes.

"Five-One, Three-Zero; we're going to have to bug out for gas. The signal is standard; confirm you have the information to give that signal." Buster was flying on fumes and had to return to the tanker. He was making sure that I had all the info to get Vega to signal the helos at the right time.

"OK, you got the helos up SAR bravo?" I hadn't heard the helicopters on "bravo" frequency yet. I was trying to act like I was in charge now.

"They're coming up SAR bravo now." Meegs interjected.

"Sandy, Moccasin Six-Zero on PLS bravo." The helos were finally up on the bravo frequency associated with the personnel-locator system.

"Magic, Three-Zero is going to have to RTB for gas. Moccasin, Sandy Five-One now OSC." Buster had finally turned west. He informed Magic that he was returning to base (RTB) due to low fuel. In reality, Buster was so low on fuel that he had to find a tanker or divert to Tuzla, Bosnia. He also informed Moccasin that I was the OSC.

"Sandy Five-One, Moccasin is up—can you hear that on uniform?" I hadn't responded to Moccasin's first radio call. Meegs knew I had been having uniform-radio problems and was asking on victor to make sure I could hear him.

"That's affirmative, Five-Two is going to have to answer, I'm UHF receive only." I responded to Meegs using victor. This is where it was going to get hard. Up until now, I had been able to make most of my radio calls on victor. Moccasin and Vega had only uniform radios, and I would have to relay the info through Joe Bro.

"Two, One, Fox plain. I want you to call when you hear Moccasin call two miles out. That is when I want you to call the number." I began briefing Joe Bro on when Vega should turn on his signal.

"Let's go secure." Joe Bro transmitted; he wanted to talk on our Fox-Mike secure radio.

"OK, have you got me secure?" I replied.

"I've got you loud and clear. Confirm the number." Joe Bro was on another frequency when Buster told Vega that he would use a number off Vega's ISOPREP card as the sign for Vega to begin signaling the helos.

"The number is three, how do you copy? Number three?" I asked. The response from Joe Bro was nothing but static.

"One, Two, fox in the plain I'm not getting you secure now. We're going to have to find some way to pass that because I don't [have it]." Joe Bro was saying that the secure function on his radio had failed. I had to figure out how to get him the number three without compromising it on a nonsecure frequency.

"Ok, I've got it. If I'm pulling supervisor what am I called?" One of my additional duties back at the squadron was pulling supervisor duty during flying operations. The Air Force calls this job "top three," because, by regulation, only the top-three positions in the squadron are permitted to be supervisor.

"OK, gotcha," Joe Bro responded, indicating he understood.

"OK," I directed, "check Moccasin in on this freq." We had not yet spoken to the helos, and I wanted to make sure they recognized Joe Bro's voice and knew who the OSC was.

"Moccasin, Sandy Five-Two, SAR bravo."

"Sandy, this is Moccasin. Go ahead, sir."

"OK. Like a two-mile out call."

"Moccasin copies, two miles out."

"Two, One. I want you to check in Vega. Make sure he is still there." Now that we had coordinated with the helos, I realized that we hadn't heard from Vega in quite a while. I wanted to make sure nothing had happened to him.

"Vega, Sandy Five-Two."

"Sandy Five-Two, Vega Three-One."

"OK, got you loud and clear. Stand by for my number." Everything was going great. Maybe this wouldn't be that hard after all. Before I could even crack a smile, Moccasin broke in.

"Climb! Climb! Climb!" Moccasin was flying low-level at night across unfamiliar enemy territory. Electrical lines suddenly appeared and one of the helos had directed they climb immediately to avoid them.

Joe Bro broke in, "I've got a weird looking smoke trail to the west." I looked to the west and saw it as well. Having never seen anything like that before, I assumed it was a SAM the Serbs had snuck in to the west of us.

"Copy, we might have to fight our way out." Even as I was saying these words, the smoke trail continued overhead and into Belgrade. We had seen our first night HARM shot from the F-16CJs. Whew, that made me feel much better.

"OK, Two is spike—Mud SAM 150." Joe Bro informed me that his RWR showed him being tracked by a SAM.

"One, same, . . . Five-One defending SAM south." The SAM was tracking me now. I passed the information to Magic on victor. I hoped he would pass it to the F-16CJs on a separate frequency.

Now we were in the hornets' nest. We had made it to Vega's position on the outskirts of Belgrade. The Serbs had been waiting for us to come in with the helos, and now our RWR showed that their SAMs were lighting us up. What was worse, the thunderstorm building over Belgrade was just south of our position. We would not be able to see any SAMs launched from that direction until they broke out of that weather and were right on top of us.

"SAM active BAT 320/32." Magic informed us that another SAM was active. It was just northeast of our position.

"Sandy Five-One defending SAM east, 280/14 bull." I was being tracked by the northeast SAM. I put out chaff, checked to see that my pod was working, and turned to put the new threat on my beam.

"SAM BAT 195/25 now reported as active." The Serbs were turning on their whole SAM belt for us.

"Sandy Five-Two is defending SAM north."

"Sandy Five-One is Magnum SAM north." Magnum was the call the F-16CJs used when they fired a HARM. I remembered hearing that, during the first three nights of the war, the Serbs had shut down their SAMs when they heard Magnum. I didn't have any HARMs on board, but that didn't prevent me from making the radio call.

"One is naked." I announced, to which Joe Bro added, "Two is naked." Naked meant we were no longer being tracked. The SAMs had shut down almost instantaneously. We could then put our focus back on the helos. At least we knew that the Serbs were looking at us and, so far, they had not been able to see or track the helos at low altitude.

"Two, let's start heading west," I transmitted to Joe Bro; I wanted to get a little more distance between us and the SAMs.

"Sandy, Moccasin is two miles out."

"Vega, Sandy Five-Two, three." Joe Bro called for the signal. We waited in silence for Moccasin to call visual with Vega.

"Moccasin Six-Zero flight is overhead." Moccasin had made it to Vega's position but still couldn't see him.

"Five-One, Four-One, recommend you get Vega up if he sees the Moccasins." Meegs made a good suggestion: Since Moccasin couldn't see Vega, maybe Vega could see the helicopters and could help out.

"Vega, Sandy Five-Two. Confirm you see the helos."

"I believe so," Vega replied.

"Give them a vector if you can," Joe Bro added.

"It looks like they need to come a bit right . . . confirm they have a light on?" Vega questioned and then said to Moccasin, "Need to come south."

"Copy, call when we're overhead," Moccasin answered.

"Five-One, we've got to depart. We're westbound. Be advised CJs working, observed HARM shot." Meegs and Scrape had finally bingoed. They had stayed much longer than I had expected, so I knew they must have been riding on fumes.

"Sandy, Sandy, Vega Three-One, do they have my strobe?" Vega was rightly concerned that the pickup was taking way too long.

"At this time we're looking for his strobe, we've got two small lights on the ground, but no strobe."

"Yeah, for Vega Three-One, that was a car; I thought it was you guys." Vega misidentified the sound of a car nearby for that of the helicopters.

"Moccasin copies. Are you up strobe, sir?"

"That is affirmative," Vega replied.

"Hold it up in the air. Point it at the helicopter if you can."

"Roger, I'm not sure where you are now."

The tension was thick enough to cut with a knife. The helos had been circling around Vega's position for over five minutes now. Not only was this risky to the helos and Vega, but also we would have to call off the search due to low fuel if we didn't find him soon.

"Stand by for Vega Three-One, I think my strobe is inop."

"Copy, have we flown over you yet?" Moccasin asked.

"No, I think you are more north, northwest of me for a mile or two," Vega replied.

Meegs had continued to monitor the radio during his departure and suggested to me that Vega use his pen-gun flare. It shoots a signal flare up a couple of hundred feet. It was designed to penetrate the jungle canopy of Vietnam. However, it was also an overt signal that the Serbs would be able to see.

"OK, we need you to get out a pen-gun flare." Joe Bro passed on the suggestion.

"Vega, if we're this close, make an overt signal and we'll get you," Moccasin added in agreement.

"How about a regular flare?" Vega said, when he came across an alternative while searching through his survival kit for his pen gun.

"Moccasin Six-Zero, sounds good . . . and we're good vis on Vega Three-One," Moccasin said seeing the flare as soon as Vega set it off.

"Vega and Moccasin, if you are tally each other, kill the flare." Joe Bro wanted to make sure that the flare was put out as soon as possible.

"We are bingo, bingo, bingo. Kill the flare," Moccasin then transmitted. The meaning of that radio call puzzled us until we later found out that in the special operations community "bingo" means that the side gunner's machine gun has reached the aft stop. In our fixed-wing world, bingo means you are out of gas.

"Overhead, you visual me? For Vega Three-One, you got me?" Vega was concerned about the bingo call as well.

"And Vega give them a vector if you need to," Joe Bro suggested.

"Yeah, they got me right just about overhead."

The SAMs had been quiet for the last 10 minutes but suddenly came back up. Joe Bro called being tracked by one to the south. He put out chaff and beamed the threat.

"Sandy Five-One is Magnum that position." I made the Magnum radio call again, hoping the Serb SAMs were listening and thinking I was shooting a HARM at them.

"Sandy Five-Two is naked," Joe Bro called. It worked again—the SAMs shut down, expecting a HARM to be heading their way.

"Moccasin, say your status." While reacting to the SAMs, we had lost track of the pickup.

"We are outbound at this time . . . about 20 miles from good-guy land." That was the best radio call I had ever heard in my life. Vega was aboard the helos, and they were headed back to Bosnia.

"Sandy, you are being tracked with eyes by SAM," Moonbeam transmitted, relaying some intel to us as we turned west.

"Survivor authenticated, no injuries," Moccasin called, informing us of Vega's remarkably good physical condition.

"All stations SAM launch." This call from Magic jolted us back to reality. The Serbs, seeing us turn west, launched a SAM at Joe Bro and me. Fortunately, we were out of their range, and neither of us even saw the missile.

Joe Bro and I continued west to the border, and then our waiting began. Moccasin's flight to the border would take another 10 minutes, and it seemed forever before he called to let us know he had made it out.

I relayed this information on victor by transmitting the most rewarding call I have ever made: "Miller time!"

Joe Bro and I turned towards home. I calculated my gas and had just enough to make it back to Aviano. We landed at Aviano exhausted but extremely happy after our six-hour mission. I quickly shut down my A-10, got out to join the celebration on the ramp, and began hugging everyone I met. I had trained all my life for this moment, and I simply could not contain the joy that came from what we had just accomplished.

We eventually made it to the squadron and were trying to debrief when we heard that Vega had made it back to Aviano. We all piled into cars and drove onto the ramp where a C-130 had just parked. A large group clustered around Vega, hugging everyone in sight. I looked down at Vega's boots and saw that they were still covered in Serbian mud. I reached down and scraped off a bit for a souvenir. Vega was then taken to the hospital to have his slightly burned hand treated.

It was now morning, and most of us were starving. The bowling alley was the only place open for breakfast. Over pancakes and omelets, the six of us Sandys, along with Capt Rip Woodard and some of the F-16CJ pilots, reveled in our accomplishments. We couldn't celebrate too long; we were in need of crew rest before another night of strikes. *C'est la guerre.*

Photo courtesy of author

Vega 31's boots with caked-on Serbian mud

Photo courtesy of editors

Rip Woodard (on ABCCC), Buster Cherrey, Slobee O'Brien, Goldie Haun, Joe Bro Brosious, Meegs Meger, and Scrape Johnson (not pictured) were the Sandys involved in the Vega 31 rescue

Memorable Missions

Capt Mike "Hook" Shenk

I did not go with the 81st EFS in March of 1999 when it deployed to Aviano to participate in air operations over the former Yugoslavia. I was scheduled to separate from the active Air Force in April and by regulation could not be sent off station. I remained behind to help run what was left of the squadron at Spangdahlem and prepare for my upcoming separation. At that time I was a flight commander and had just completed my checkout as an AFAC.

I had mixed emotions about not going to Aviano and missing the action. I really wanted to be there, but since I was not a CSAR-qualified pilot, and that was our mission, I figured I would have little chance to participate. On the other hand, I was happy to finally have some time to spend with my wife, Christine, and our two children, Michael and Megan.

On Sunday, 28 March, Maj Greg "V Neck" Vanderneck called me at home from squadron ops. He told me I was to pack and leave ASAP on a short trip to Headquarters USAFE at Ramstein AB, Germany. He said he couldn't tell me much but that USAFE leadership wanted an 81st FS rep around to answer A-10 questions. I packed my A-3 bag for a three-day trip, an assumption I would soon regret; I then hit the road.

At Ramstein I met with Lt Col Greg "Snoopy" Schulze. Only a few months before, he had been the commander of the 81st FS. Snoopy filled me in on the plan to use our Hogs as AFACs and strikers against the Serb forces in Kosovo. He further explained that he was going to be briefing this plan to Maj Gen William T. Hobbins, USAFE's director of air and space operations, and Gen John Jumper, commander of USAFE and NATO's Allied Air Forces Central Europe (AIRCENT). I would be expected to answer questions about tactics and capabilities. Snoopy was current and qualified in the Hog and could have easily fielded these questions. However, they also planned to be in Brussels the next morning to brief Gen Wesley Clark, USA, NATO's SACEUR and commander of EUCOM. The USAFE leadership thought having a line pilot around would add credibility to the plan and their briefing. The trip to Brussels was subsequently scrubbed because of weather. I assumed that at some point the USAFE planners briefed General Clark over the phone.

I returned to Spangdahlem, and the next day I went to squadron operations, where V Neck had another tasker for me. He said I was to take our last flyable jet to Aviano; that was my first indication the plan had been approved. Aviano had been crammed with jets, so there had to be a good reason for them to allow us to park another A-10 on the ramp. V Neck added that if I left soon, I might be able to catch a scheduled C-130 back to Spangdahlem that evening but cautioned that it might be an overnight trip. Fortunately, I still had my A-3 bag in the trunk of my car from my trip to Ramstein; I was airborne en route to Aviano an hour and a half later.

It was a quick trip to Aviano. As soon as I arrived, I looked into the availability of transportation back to Spangdahlem and was told to expect a flight in two or three days. So I checked into the Hotel Antares and ran into Capt Buster Cherry, who was scheduled to command one of the packages that Snoopy had briefed me on earlier. I was surprised at how quickly the CAOC (affectionately and accurately tagged CHAOS by those who have worked there) had put the plan into action. I guessed that our squadron leadership and weapons gurus had been working on it for a while.

I ran into Maj Goldie Haun at the hotel bar. He was on his way back to his room but required little encouragement to stay and tell me what he could about the Vega 31 pickup. As he told me about the intensity and heroics of the rescue, I felt a great deal of pride to be a member of a squadron that had performed so well in the face of adversity.

Before we left the bar, Goldie asked me if I was interested in staying at Aviano; the squadron was shorthanded and in need of AFAC-qualified pilots and top-three squadron supervisors. He said that if I was interested, the squadron commander could probably arrange an extension on my separation date.

The next day I was plugged into the top-three spot on the schedule. There was no transportation to Spangdahlem, and the schedulers had already learned not to let anyone go home without being tasked. I decided to stay and talk to our commander, Lt Col Kimos Haave. He started work on getting my separation date extended, and I wished that I had packed for more than three days. What follows is my recollection of a few of the more memorable missions I flew during OAF.

On 7 April I was scheduled to fly an AFAC mission as number two in a two-ship using the call sign Bear 11. Buster would be my flight lead and the mission commander (MC) for the entire KEZ package. I was looking forward to going up with him in hopes of getting some pointers from one of the best in the business. Our brief was scheduled for 0200, and it looked like it could be a long, wicked day; our mission was scheduled for three 45-minute periods in the AOR and four air refuelings, for a total mission time of about seven hours. The initial trip to the tanker would take an hour and 40 minutes.

It sounded like a pretty simple mission: fly the airplane to the right country, find targets, and destroy them. In actuality it was much more demanding—particularly for the MC. Although I would expect Buster to say it was no big deal, I am quite sure that he was very busy for most of the mission.

As the campaign progressed, the missions became more routine and the MC job a little easier. However, those early missions required diligent oversight by a very capable MC to ensure that the packages were effective and to minimize the chance of an allied loss. The MC had to fly his own airplane, be a good flight lead, and do the target search and AFAC thing while also being responsible for a myriad of other duties. Those duties included, but were not limited to, coordinating SEAD, CAP, and jammer coverage; deconflicting the airspace used by dozens of aircraft; and adjusting the plan in real time for any contingency. Even with perfectly clear communication, that would be a challenge. Throw in comm jamming, accents from 28 different languages, and failure of half of the aircraft's Have Quick radios to work in the secure and antijam modes, and it starts to look like a very bad dream. Only MCs know the disappointment of locating a target in their binoculars and at the same time learning that the SEAD aircraft are bingo. They will be distracted for several valuable minutes to handle this problem—just one of many they will work during their vul period—while the target is escaping.

Kosovo had been split in half to help deconflict friendly aircraft. We were working in the eastern half of the country and had been alternating vuls with Meegs Meger and his wingman, Johnny "CBU" Hamilton. I covered Buster as he searched for targets during the first vul period without much luck. We headed south, got some gas over Macedonia and Albania and headed back over Kosovo to continue our search for Serb military assets. Our efforts to find valid targets continued to be stymied by disciplined Serb ground forces. They were aware of our presence and were careful not to move on the ground and draw attention to themselves. The fact that we had to remain above 10,000 feet AGL during our search made finding Serb forces that much harder.

During our second vul period, ABCCC personnel (using the call sign Bookshelf) passed the CAOC's direction to find and identify a Straight Flush radar. They said it was located in a valley west of Pec, in the far western part of the country. A Straight Flush is the short-range acquisition and fire-control radar associated with the SA-6 Gainful SAM system. Our vulnerability to this system prompted the establishment of a policy that prohibited us from entering a region without SEAD. We found it ironic that now we were being directed to virtually fly over a suspected SA-6 site. Buster called to confirm that they really wanted our A-10s to locate a Straight Flush. When the answer came back "yes," we spent some time searching over the mountainous region of western Kosovo, where tops were up to 8,700 feet above

Photo courtesy of FAS

SA-6 Gainful

mean sea level (MSL). We searched from an altitude of 19,000 feet MSL to maintain our minimum altitude of 10,000 feet AGL, which made it even more difficult to locate targets on the valley floor—often more than 2,000 feet below the peaks.

We searched for about 20 to 30 minutes and then told Bookshelf that we could not establish contact with the Straight Flush—we couldn't see it, and it didn't shoot at us. Since we had been briefed that the destruction of enemy air defenses was not our mission, I'm not sure that we would have been allowed to kill the SA-6 even if we had found it.

It was while we were looking for the Straight Flush that I realized how much trust flight leads place in their wingmen during combat. Target search was a tricky thing. We had great binoculars, but using them meant having to fly left-handed and having a field of view limited to only what can be seen through the binoculars. I found it disconcerting to know that, when I was using those binos, I would probably not see a threat until it was too late. AFACs could concentrate on target search and not worry (too much) about threats if their wingmen diligently cleared for threats to the formation. Buster showed a great deal of faith in my ability to compensate for his vulnerability when he searched for that SA-6 with his binoculars over the mountains of western Kosovo. Most of my remaining OAF missions were flown over Kosovo as a flight-lead AFAC, and I relied on my wingmen to cover me. They never let me down, and I owe them my life.

After nearly completing the last of our three planned vul periods in the KEZ, we got a call from Bookshelf on an "unsecure" radio announcing that the KEZ would be closing early for the day. We headed south for the tanker, curious about the reason for the early closure. As we rendezvoused with the tanker, the Bookshelf crew asked us to contact them on our secure radio. Buster went off frequency to talk to Bookshelf and left me to handle the tanker coordination. We had refueled, departed the tanker, and headed north by the time Buster filled me in on the plan.

Serbian ground forces had been very disciplined, curtailing their movements when they knew we were overhead. Our intelligence people had determined that, as soon as we departed the AOR, they would resume their rampage across the country. Someone convinced the CAOC to run an unannounced KEZ vul period with the hope of catching the Serbs off guard. Buster had been off frequency to coordinate the unscheduled vul and to ensure we had all the necessary support: SEAD, tankers, and counterair (whose details no one had yet planned).

We went back into the KEZ and found Meegs already working a target area with reports of medium AAA in the area. We offered to come in above them to provide some mutual support. But after another 20 minutes, I began to lose faith in this plan. I had been in the cockpit for about seven hours, my rear hurt, and I was out of water bottles and piddle packs. It was becoming a survival situation for me, and I hadn't even been shot at yet. It's a good thing we didn't throw in the towel because our luck changed in a hurry.

Buster's radio call, as Meegs reminded us later, was "I got a whole schmit-load of movers!" Before he could finish the sentence, I picked up the convoy he was talking about—eight or so vehicles southbound on a dirt road. I could tell they were really hauling because, even from 16,000 feet, I could see the vehicles moving in three dimensions as they pounded through the terrain. I remember seeing the front end of one APC coming up and then crashing back down—spewing up dirt and dust. Buster quickly rolled in, locked up a vehicle with a Maverick, and fired.

That one attack not only destroyed the vehicle it hit, but also furthered our efforts by splitting the convoy into north and south elements, providing a mark for other fighters. Splitting the convoy was important because it allowed us to attack three or four of the vehicles and to hand off the remaining ones to Meegs and his CBUs. Using a Maverick missile or a 500 lb Mk-82 bomb to mark a target was a technique we quickly embraced. These larger munitions had the potential to destroy a target element, their visual effects lasted longer, and they were easier to see from the extreme altitudes at which we worked. They had proven to be better marks than the more traditional, and much smaller, white-phosphorous rockets.

Buster attacked the northern target element again with two Mk-82s. Before we had a chance to evaluate his damage, he found another convoy about a mile northeast of the first and attacked it by dropping his last two Mk-82s and strafing with his 30 mm cannon. Meegs was still working fighters on the southern element of the first convoy. A flight of two F-16CGs arrived to strike for Buster but missed with their first LGB attack and then lost sight of the target. Buster told me to hit the target with my Mk-82s and directed the F-16s to watch the target area for my bombs. I rolled in—north to south—and strung four bombs along the convoy. It was a good pass, and the bombs were effective as more than just a mark. Buster's call as I came off target was, "Oh, that's beautiful. Hit my wingman's smoke." The F-16s then ran a successful LGB attack and destroyed the southern-

USAF Photo

APC destroyed by A-10

most vehicle before having to depart for fuel. We then attempted a couple of IIR Maverick passes but could not lock on to the targets because the many fires on the ground washed out the IR contrast. Even so, the convoy had been pretty well destroyed.

Buster and I worked south to look for more targets. Buster, again trusting my ability to cover him, looked through his binoculars and thought he saw some muzzle flashes on the ground. We were constantly getting jammed on at least one of our three radios—and occasionally on all of them. Other friendly aircraft were using one of our two partially clear radios, and Buster was transmitting on the remaining radio, trying to talk my eyes onto the target area, when I saw two groups of large, dark smoke clouds appear between our jets. I started to jink and called out the threat. As I finished my call, I could still hear Buster transmitting on the same frequency and realized that he had not heard my threat call. We had stepped on each other's transmissions. That meant Buster and I were simultaneously transmitting to each other, and since a radio's receiver is disabled during its transmissions, neither of us heard the other's call. I again tried to alert him, but my warning was either jammed or stepped on. I don't remember being too concerned about my own safety—probably because it looked as though they were shooting at him and not me. I do remember the incredible feeling of helplessness—watching my friend and flight lead getting shot at and not being able to communicate with him. I thought he was going to take a hit because the AAA airbursts looked huge compared to the size of his aircraft. I eventually got ahold of him and we beat feet out of the area.

After we regrouped and headed back into the target area, I started to think about them shooting at me. Although I definitely felt some fear, I was hoping that they would shoot at us again so we could see where it came from and retaliate. Again—as Buster searched for targets—I saw more airbursts. We had returned at a little higher altitude than the first time, so the clouds of flak were now below us. I called the threat to Buster, and he searched for their position on the ground. While these gunners were apparently having no trouble finding us, we were having no luck finding them. Fortunately our high altitude and constant maneuvering kept them from being able to hit us.

While we were in the area looking for the shooters, Buster found yet another convoy. We were too low on gas to set up an attack, so we headed for the tanker and passed that target off to another set of fighters. On the way out we heard Meegs call, "I think I took a hit." During a rocket pass he had noticed AAA muzzle flashes, and then his caution panel lit up as he pulled off target. He quickly realized his aircraft was losing hydraulic fluid, and, even though he was able to stop the leak, he eventually lost one of his two hydraulic systems. On the ground, his crew chief determined that he had not taken a hit but had just suffered from a noncombat-related hydraulic failure. What a coincidence!

On 14 May I was scheduled to fly a mission check ride with Capt Scrape Johnson. I would fly as an AFAC, work the eastern half of Kosovo, and use Snoopy 61 as our call sign. Scrape would evaluate me while flying my wing. I was pumped about the mission—the weather was great, and we had some good target information from our squadron intelligence. We were passed new target coordinates over the radio as we entered the AOR, and I commenced what I would now describe as a wild-goose chase. Such chases were not uncommon since targets passed in this fashion were considered high priority, and we were required to search for them. We learned from experience that these precise coordinates seldom resulted in actually finding a viable military target—I had much better luck just looking for targets in the main areas of interest. We, nevertheless, spent a good half hour plotting coordinates and searching those areas.

I found a large tunnel south of Urosevac with fresh tank tracks leading to its entrance. I could just make something out at the opening but was unable to identify it with the binoculars because of the shadows. I set up for a Maverick pass, thinking I might be able to use the IR seeker to confirm that the object was a valid target. If so, I planned to launch the Maverick, destroy the target, and seal off the tunnel and all its equipment.

Unfortunately, I was still unable to ID the object and began my slow climb back to altitude. While my Hog, with its grossly underpowered engines, strained to get me back to altitude, I rolled into an easy right turn and started using the binos to try to ID the object again. It was then that I heard Scrape's excited voice call, "BREAK!"

I had been flying with my knees; my left hand was on the throttles, and the binos were in my right. I was not in a good position to execute the break turn. I dropped the binos, rolled right, honked back on the stick, and put out a string of flares. As I checked six I saw the smoke trail of a SAM behind my aircraft. The smoke trail went all the way down to the ground and ended in a burned-out house on the north end of a small town. I felt as though I was looking down a 15,000-foot kite string. I was not at all happy with the guy flying the kite. I asked

USAF Photo by TSgt Blake Borsic

Capt David "Beau" Easterling straps in for another sortie over the KEZ

Scrape if he could tell exactly where the missile had come from, thinking that he was in a better position to attack, since he had more altitude and airspeed than I. He said, "No," so I replied, "One will be in with the gun; Two cover."

I checked my airspeed and altitude, and then cursed my engines for not having more thrust. I wanted to roll in right away and shoot, but I needed more altitude to minimize the chance of getting hit by another missile. I checked my gas and realized that this was going to be our only pass on this target before we had to head for the tanker. I set up for a 60-degree strafe pass and checked that the gun-ready light was on. As I rolled in, I thought about the gravity of this situation; I was looking death in the face. I put the pipper on the target and let fly with 150 rounds or so and started my recovery. I couldn't tell for sure whether the rounds had hit their mark—but I didn't receive any return fire.

We headed south for gas and passed to ABCCC the information about the SAM launch and our subsequent attack. We had just pulled up behind the tanker when a two-ship of Turkish TF-16s pulled up, declared emergency fuel, and jumped on the tanker in front of me during my scheduled air-refueling time. I was angry because I was really in a hurry to get back and look for whatever had shot at me. We refueled, and as we were about to go back in country, Scrape noticed that he had expended all of his chaff. We couldn't go in country without it, so we had to head home early. As I recalled this sortie and put the details down on paper, I realized that I had never said thanks for that "break" call—thanks, Scrape!

I was again flying as an AFAC on another unusual mission, but this time with Col Alan Thompson, the 40th EOG commander, on my wing. This is not the most exciting story, but for me it is representative of the entire conflict; it was always interesting, if seldom extraordinary.

On this day the weather was fairly poor. An F-14 was working the western half of the country, coordinating through-the-weather deliveries for strike aircraft with compatible capabilities. Most of the other strikers had been sent home, but ABCCC was kind enough to let us stay and look for holes in the weather. We were using call sign Cobra 41 and working the eastern half of the KEZ. We were operating above a low undercast and had spent a great deal of time just looking for holes. I set up an east-west, zigzag search pattern starting in the south and working north. We had little success; every hole I found would close up before I could get the binos up to look through it. We worked further north, and I found a larger hole over Serbia proper, about 15 miles north of the Kosovo border. It was nicely aligned and situated directly over our fixed target—an ammunition-storage facility. As I positioned our flight for an attack, I thought it would be great not to have to land with our Mk-82s, especially since I had dragged us so deep into bad-guy land.

I set up an attack from the west with the sun and wind at our back. I rolled in, pickled my bombs, pulled off, and started working south so I could monitor the boss's attack. He rolled in; as he dove down the chute, I saw what looked like flash-bulbs at the Super Bowl. The entire side of a large hill lit up with muzzle flashes for what seemed to be 30 to 40 seconds.

I called, "Cobra Four-Two, work south, jink! Triple-A north!"

I saw his aircraft roll and turn south as the muzzle flashes continued. Shortly after his bombs hit, the muzzle flashes stopped, but I had a great bead on their position. Once we were back together I rolled in with the Maverick. I planned on locking up any hot spot on the side of that hill and firing. When I found a hot spot, I cross-checked my HUD to confirm that the Maverick was looking at the hill and not the town just to the south. The Maverick symbology indicated that the hot spot was on the border of the hill and the town. I thought for a second and came off dry. In the time it took to reposition and take another look, the clouds had covered the target area, and we were low on fuel.

Like I said, this was not the most exciting story but one that best reflects my experiences during OAF. Most of my tactical decisions erred on the conservative side. Late at night I sometimes second-guess myself when I think about the conflict. I wonder if I should have been more aggressive, shot more rounds, or dropped more bombs. Then I remember three things: (1) We all made it home alive, (2) I did my best to avoid civilian losses, and (3)—well, I guess there were only two things. Nevertheless, those two were important because, as Stanley Kubrick wrote in *Full Metal Jacket*, "The dead know only one thing—that it is better to be alive."

Big Brother

Lt Col Mark "Coke" Koechle

I initially expected the air war over Kosovo to be similar to the one in Desert Storm, and that it would have similar results. As a veteran of 43 of the latter's *actual* combat sorties—which involved dropping bombs and getting shot at—I could see some similarities. However, it was much more difficult to find targets in Kosovo; often the ones we did find were given sanctuary by our restrictive ROEs. The political constraints were much more stringent in and around the villages of Kosovo than they had been in the Iraqi and Kuwaiti desert. The Serbs used the media at every opportunity to discredit the NATO coalition by claiming that our allied pilots committed war crimes. Such claims, if substantiated, could have easily turned world opinion against the coalition and forced NATO to halt its air campaign against fielded Serbian forces. That would have allowed the Serbs to continue their genocide and atrocities against the Kosovar Albanians. Strict ROEs, the (not-so) real-time target-approval process, and the denials for strikes on valid targets caused our pilots to become disgruntled with the whole command and control process—often causing us to wonder whose side the guy making those decisions was actually on. The 81st FS Panthers had adopted the tactic of having all AFACs fly with a wingman, which we dubbed a "tethered fighter." Capt Slobee O'Brien and I had been paired during that portion of the war and had flown several very successful missions together. None was more unusual than the sortie on 11 May, during which Slobee was the AFAC and flight lead of Uzi 11, and I was his tethered fighter and overall KEZ mission commander. The AFAC's job was to find valid targets and then control the fighters while they attacked those targets. The wingman's responsibilities were to provide visual lookout for the flight, communication backup, and firepower support, as well as assist the AFAC in any other way necessary. The tethered fighter could im-

USAF Photo by SrA Jeffery Allen

Lt Col Coke Koechle, 81st EFS/DO, getting ready for a combat mission at Aviano AB

mediately attack targets if the planned strikers were either not available or too far away.

We flew an uneventful 45-minute vul period over Kosovo and then headed southwest for the tanker orbiting in Albania. After topping off, Moonbeam (ABCCC) told us to head to a certain village north of Pristina to search for targets that had been reported earlier. Once in the area, Moonbeam gave us a talk-on to a specific L-shaped building that had a bus parked alongside it and directed us to strike the building. This was highly unusual, since most ROEs prohibited us from hitting permanent structures for fear of harming innocent people and causing collateral damage. The idea of a talk-on from Moonbeam was also unusual, but I didn't think much about it since other fighters could have passed on the target description earlier in the day. We surveyed the area with our binoculars and, while we saw no movement, we were convinced that this was the correct target. We each dropped three Mk-82 500 lb bombs on, or in the immediate vicinity of, the building and saw it and the bus begin to smolder. We reported the effects of our attack to Moonbeam and moved on to look for other valid targets in the area.

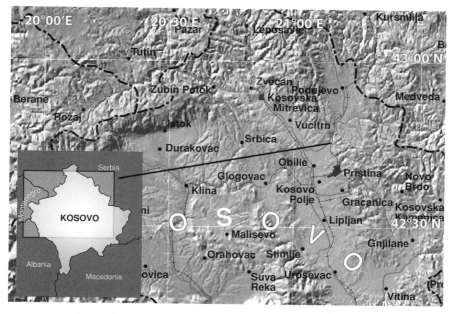

Location of L-shaped building north of Pristina

I had been near this area several days earlier and wanted to check some potential targets that I had seen, so we proceeded about 15 miles north of the smoking building. We found what looked like tracked vehicles in a tree line and mortar pits along a road, and were just about to employ our remaining ordnance when Moonbeam called again.

"Uzi One-One, do you still have contact with the L-shaped building?"

"No," Slobee replied, "We have another potential target and are just about to strike it."

"Well, we'd like you to go back to the L-shaped building. There are enemy soldiers walking around outside of it now, and we want you to strike it again."

After several seconds of silence, Slobee said "Uzi copies."

I don't know what was going through my flight lead's mind, but it was plainly obvious to me that *someone* had that building in sight and was providing real-time intelligence to the CAOC. I had an eerie feeling and pictured special forces on the ground near the target, or a Mr. Clark type from a Tom Clancy book. Then I thought that maybe it could be some KLA/UCK ground troops with a satellite-communications link to our forces. It really bothered me that, potentially, there were good guys down there and we didn't know where they were.

We flew back to the building, which was just barely burning, and each dropped our last Mk-82 and fired a Maverick missile into it. It quickly erupted into a raging inferno, and the bus was completely destroyed.

Moonbeam then said, "That looks like it'll do the trick. Now we want you to proceed northeast by about 10 miles to these coordinates [UTM coordinates provided], and there should be at least 20 pieces of armor in a field."

By this time we were sure there was someone on the ground directing our attacks, but for some reason we weren't talking directly to him. Incompatible radios? Fear of compromise? We didn't know.

We flew directly to the coordinates and spent 10 minutes looking for armor. All we could see were open fields with some barns located in and around them. We asked Moonbeam to repeat the coordinates, and when it did so, they confirmed that we were in the right place. Then Moonbeam said that there should be a large, U-shaped pole barn at the end of an east-west dirt road. We already had that in sight—since it was the largest reference in the area.

Moonbeam then said, "The tanks and APCs are inside that barn; you are cleared to strike it."

Well, thanks for telling us. We now had to rush the attack because gas was getting low and becoming a factor. We each shot our remaining Maverick into separate corners of the "U," made three high-angle strafe passes using two to three trigger pulls per pass. I shot about 700 rounds into the barn, and Slobee shot about 400. We did not see any large explosions as the barn began to burn, but I did see what appeared to be smaller secondary explosions from inside and yellow-green smoke rising from the burning barn. Moonbeam told us that we had direct hits and had destroyed many of the armored vehicles; we still couldn't figure out how he knew that. We then egressed the target area for the tanker air-refueling track about 100 NM to the south. All in all, it had been a very successful day—much more satisfying than others, since we had found and destroyed or damaged tasked targets. We cautiously discussed our information "source," vaguely speculating about who or what it could be and hoping that it wouldn't be compromised. We did not learn the real story until later that evening.

That day Col Alan Thompson, 40th EOG commander, and two of our fellow Panthers had been in CAOC's battle-staff room when our strikes occurred. The battle-staff room resembles a *Dr. Strangelove* movie set—a "room with the big boards." They said that a USAF Predator drone had been orbiting in our area and had picked out, fixed, and identified potential targets. The CAOC then passed coordinates, instructions, and attack clearance to us through Moonbeam.

Through Predator, and possibly other intelligence sources, the CAOC had identified the L-shaped building as a makeshift Serb army command post. Our first attack had seriously damaged the building, but the Predator operators had still seen activity in and around the building, so we were directed to strike it again. During the second strike, the Predator had been in position to allow its operator to witness the impacts and assess the damage. The operator passed the BDA to the CAOC, who in turn immediately passed it to us. The Predator operators had also determined that armored vehicles were stored in the U-shaped barn. So as soon as the CAOC was convinced the command post had been destroyed, we were directed to find and strike that barn. Our pilots at the CAOC watched real-time transmissions from the Predator as Slobee and I attacked the barn. They said the Maverick impacts were devastating but were really surprised to see CBU bomblets exploding on and very near the buildings. We were also confused by what they had seen—we not only had not dropped any CBUs, but we weren't even carrying CBUs. We finally figured out from the sequence of attacks that they had actually seen our high-explosive incendiary 30 mm cannon rounds exploding on impact. While we were strafing the building, they watched as one whole side of the barn was blown away, exposing many burning hulks.

The evolution of airpower has brought our tactics a long way—from the days of flying bailing-wire and fabric airplanes and hand-dropping 10 lb bombs into enemy trenches to using UAVs to provide air-strike coordination to a pair of fighters. While this concept had been discussed on many occasions, to the best of my knowledge this was the first time that it was actually attempted in combat. On this occasion it was unplanned "pickup CAS," which probably contributed to its success and made the results seem even more impressive. From that day forward, we tasked our squadron intel to brief when and where Predator would be flying. We were unable to repeat that real-time coordination but still tried to use its information to find fielded forces on future sorties. Unfortunately, information was usually hours old, and it often turned out that the targets had moved or had inaccurate coordinates. None of the Predator's efforts during the rest of our OAF missions were as successful as that first "trial mission." With some dedicated work, the concept of using UAVs for target search and talk-ons could become a viable tactic in future conflicts in which AFAC assets are too limited to cover all required areas. Even so, there is no substitute for putting a set of Mk-1 eyeballs on a potential target before unleashing lethal airpower against it.

Fear, Luck, and Divine Intervention

Capt Rip "Rubble" Woodard

The operation had entered its third week, but having to wake up in the middle of the night had not yet become routine. Today's operation would be our third in daylight, and everyone was optimistic because yesterday afternoon's forecast had projected good weather. Weather in the KEZ had frustrated our attempts during the first two days, preventing us from finding any targets. We hoped that today we would finally get to do our job.

At a 6,000-foot elevation in the mountains north of Aviano, we found that our hotel was covered with a wet snow that continued to fall as we stepped out the hotel door in the middle of the night. We looked at each other with a sinking feeling as our expectation for good weather evaporated. We had driven halfway down the mountain before the snow turned to rain and fog. During the past two months, determining the weather while driving down the road had evolved into a "fighter-pilot science." Noting the elevation on the mountain at which we could see Aviano AB gave us a better estimate of ceiling and visibility than the weatherman could. Today seemed to be the worst yet—since we didn't see the base until we drove through the gate.

We went through the standard preflight planning and briefings hoping that conditions would improve. I was scheduled to fly with Buster, a squadron flight commander and a no-nonsense pilot who had total concentration on the job at hand. He was especially focused this morning since the latest weather brief said the weather in Kosovo was breaking up. We were briefed and ready to go an hour before sunrise, but the weather still had not lifted. Low ceilings forced the whole package at Aviano to sit on the ground and remain on standby. The weather was the same down the whole length of the Italian coast—everyone was on standby.

About 30 minutes after our scheduled takeoff time, the weather finally improved to the required 500-foot ceiling and one-mile visibility; we then got approval to launch. Taking off in poor weather puts additional demands on Hog drivers. Most fighters use their air-to-air radar to maintain positive separation between members of their formation when taking off and flying into the weather. Since we did not have air-to-air radar, we had to fly with our instruments and perform a procedural trail departure to ensure that we had safe separation between our aircraft. We took off 20 seconds apart, flew set airspeeds, maintained the same ground track, and climbed at a specific power setting. We kept the variables constant and relied on the differences between our departure times to keep us safely separated during the climb out. As Two, I waited 20 seconds after Buster started his roll before I released my brakes. I watched Buster disappear into the weather, and 20 seconds later so did I. If the instrument departure were executed properly, I would break out on top of the clouds with Buster slightly above and about a mile and a half in front of me—the distance he would cover in 20 seconds at climb speed. That was the theory but not what happened. I did not realize it at the time, but the moment Buster entered the weather would be the last I would see of him until we were both back on the ground at Aviano—almost two hours later.

Our two-ship was the third A-10 flight to launch that morning. We monitored the common VHF radio frequency and could hear the members of other flights describe the weather they were experiencing. Those descriptions became the best forecast of what lay ahead of us. The weather had become a real problem. Passing 6,000 feet, I noticed that ice had formed on the nose of the Maverick missiles, the rocket pods, and the leading edge of the wings. I told Buster, and he acknowledged having the same problem. We continued to climb in an attempt to find an altitude where the icing would stop, but it only seemed to get worse until we passed 17,000 feet. The A-10 flights ahead of us had also reported icing, and all aircraft were still in the weather when they leveled off at 25,000 feet, our final altitude for the track down south. Fortunately, a flight of two F-16s, which had taken off behind us and had climbed steeper and flown above us on departure, had just broken out at 30,000 feet and said that the weather above was clear. We decided to continue our climb to find clear weather and help the ice sublime. Unfortunately, our Hogs were loaded for combat with four Mk-82 bombs, two Maverick missiles, two rocket pods, an ALQ-131 jamming pod, and two AIM-9 missiles. That load made us extremely heavy, increased our drag, and precluded a quick climb.

We remained in the weather during our climb and flight down the Adriatic. After about 45 minutes, we finally reached 30,000 feet and could see sunlight above us. Leveling off approximately two miles in trail behind Buster, I was still in the weather and unable to see him. While doing an ops check to see how much fuel was remaining, I saw the master caution light begin to flash and looked to investigate. The right-generator caution light was illuminated, and the number-two (right) engine tachometer was wildly fluctuating between 30 and 90 percent. At this point, I was flying the aircraft about five degrees nose high to maintain level flight at 170 knots indicated airspeed (KIAS).

I immediately radioed Buster to let him know I had a problem and pulled the throttle back on number two in an attempt to recover the engine. When I moved the throttle, the engine immediately spooled back and flamed out. The right engine nacelle now generated drag rather than thrust. That and the combination of high altitude, low airspeed, and a dirty configuration caused the aircraft to yaw right and begin a descent. I immediately pushed the nose five to 10 degrees nose low, attempting to gain airspeed. As the aircraft yawed to the right, a chopped tone came over the headset indicating a stalled condition, which was immediately followed by a loud pop and buzzing sound as the number-one (left) engine compressor stalled. Things were getting serious in a hurry. I tried to stay calm and inform Buster what was happening.

While making the radio call, I saw the main attitude direction indicator (ADI) freeze in the centered position, both steering bars came into view, and all my caution-warning lights illuminated—and the bottom dropped out of my stomach. Those indications told me that I had lost all alternating current (AC) electrical power and that the aircraft had just reverted to direct current (DC) battery power. Not wanting to believe what I saw, I looked at the number-one engine as it rolled back below 30 percent, approximately 12 percent below what was needed for the generators to provide the much-needed AC electrical power. With virtually no thrust, the aircraft began to descend rapidly into the weather, and I soon lost what little sunlight I had been able to see through the clouds. I knew that the only way to clear a compressor stall was to completely shut down the engine, but the idea was still not one I wanted to entertain.

I then checked the DC-powered standby ADI, which showed the aircraft 15 degrees nose high and 20 degrees of right bank—the same attitude it indicated when I had leveled off. My confidence in this old piece of equipment was shot. With the main attitude indicator frozen, the standby attitude indicator unreliable, and no visual references due to the weather, I was forced to use the "needle and ball" of the turn-and-slip indicator to keep the aircraft in coordinated flight. My voice jumped about 10 octaves as I tried to tell Buster that I had just experienced a "double-engine flameout."

This situation calls for a "boldface emergency procedure." I had long ago been required to commit to memory the steps I now needed to take—but I had never dreamed of actually using them. My initial A-10 training instructor had even made jokes about this emergency, swearing it could never happen in the A-10 because the engines were too reliable. Some guys in the squadron even joked in our monthly emergency-procedures training that if it ever happened they would just jump out using the ejection procedure. With that in mind, I had to decide and act in a hurry.

The five boldface steps that I had long before committed to memory:

1. **THROTTLES – OFF**

2. **APU** [auxiliary power unit] **– START**

3. **FLIGHT CONTROLS – MAN** [manual] **REVERSION**

4. **LEFT ENGINE – MOTOR**

5. **LEFT ENGINE – START**

Thinking that I still had a little time before needing to make an ejection decision, I started to rapidly repeat these steps in my mind. We had decided to fly without antiexposure suits because they would have made our eight-hour missions miserable. However, now the thought of ejecting at high altitude, in the weather, over the Adriatic, and without an antiexposure suit was not very appealing either. I knew that I had to attempt the restart—I did not know that the procedure, which had not yet been successfully used, was intended for use in good weather and at lower altitudes.

Passing 29,000 feet, I executed the first step, pulling the throttles back, forcing them over the hump, and into the cut-off position. I knew that I was now committed, and it was not a heart-warming feeling. As soon as the throttles were in the off position, the cockpit rapidly depressurized, and frost began forming on the inside of the canopy. Unfortunately, I was still far above the normal operating envelope for starting APU. I remembered that the aircraft flight manual (Dash-1) guaranteed that the APU would start only at or below 15,000 feet, but it might start as high as 20,000 feet. I waited for the aircraft to descend at least 9,000 more feet.

With both engines shut down, there was no hydraulic pressure to power the normal operation of the flight controls. The control stick locked, so I had no ability to roll or turn the aircraft. I bypassed the next boldface step and selected flight controls manual reversion.

The manual system is designed to give the A-10 a limited flight-control capability to improve its combat survivability in the event the aircraft is shot up and loses hydraulic pressure. It uses a cable-and-pulley system to move small electrical trim tabs which act as flight controls. The amount of control that these tabs can provide is a function of airspeed. Since the control surfaces are only a few inches wide, greater airspeed allows the tabs to provide more control. The Dash-1 gives numerous warnings when using this system. It warns against low power settings and directs that airspeed be maintained between 200 and 300 KIAS so that the trim tabs will develop enough control authority to control large pitch changes. It now dawned on me that it was impossible to keep the power above idle during a double-engine flameout. I also realized that the aircraft was already slower than recommended, due to its having no thrust, high altitude, and a heavy combat load. Nevertheless, I had no choice other than putting the aircraft into manual reversion to regain even limited control.

As I executed manual reversion, I experienced the meaning of the words contained in the fine print of another Dash-1 warning, which said that when transitioning to manual reversion, the aircraft may pitch up or down with excessive positive or negative G forces. As I flipped the switch, the aircraft pitched violently down, threw me up, and pinned me on the canopy—"Mr. Toad's wild ride" had begun. The standby ADI now indicated a banked, nose-low attitude, and the vertical velocity indicator (VVI) was pegged at 6,000 feet-per-minute down. I pulled myself back into the seat with the stick and then continued to pull back on it for all I was worth in an attempt to break the dive. Unable to stop the descent, I slid to the front of the ejection seat and hooked my feet on the brake pedals to get better leverage. Pulling with both arms and trimming the elevator tab to its limit failed to break the dive—I began to panic.

The altimeter was now unwinding extremely fast, and panic crept into my voice as I let Buster know what was happening. He responded with an irritatingly relaxed voice, telling me to just calm down and go through the boldface. He declared an emergency with Magic, the NAEW, and let them know I was looking for a place to make an emergency landing. For the time being, all I could do was try to gain and maintain aircraft control, and avoid entering an unusual attitude. I attempted to keep my wings level by staring at the turn-and-slip indicator. I tried to keep the DC-powered turn needle and the slip indicator's ball centered. That ball—suspended in a curved, liquid-filled tube below the turn-needle—measures aerodynamic slip and is very reliable because it's powered only by physics. I flew the aircraft with reference only to the turn-and-slip, airspeed, and VVIs—and waited until I reached an altitude where I would be able to start the APU.

I do not know how long the descent really took, but I seemed to pass through 20,000 feet in the blink of an eye. Hoping to improve my chances, I waited until I passed 17,000 feet before I attempted to start the APU. When I flipped the switch, the start initially looked good. However, the APU's operating temperature then appeared to drop rapidly. I stared at the indications for some time with the sickening thought that the APU had failed. I finally realized that the APU really had started, was operating normally, and indicated cooler-than-normal operating temperature only because of the altitude and ambient conditions. I continued to modify the boldface procedure. Instead of completing the next step to start engines, I turned on the APU generator to get AC electrical power and warm up the main attitude indicator.

Passing 15,000 feet I motored the number-one engine until its temperature dropped to below 100 degrees and then brought the throttle over the hump to idle. By the time I had reached 12,500 feet, the engine had stabilized in idle, and I immediately shoved it to max. With it running at full power, I was finally able to slow my descent rate to about 4,000 feet per minute on the VVI. Now—for the first time since my engines' compressors stalled—I realized that I might be able to fly out of this situation. The boldface ends at this point, and it would normally be time to pull out the checklist and go through the cleanup items. However, I was still in a descent and not really ready to take my hands off the controls to get out a checklist. I thought that if I could start the number-two engine I would have enough power to break the descent completely. So passing 8,000 feet I motored down the temperature and attempted a start. The second engine started and stabilized. With both engines operating normally, I bottomed out at about 6,500 feet—and, finally, the plane felt controllable.

I did not realize how pumped up I had been on adrenaline. The aircraft appeared to be flying normally now that I had both engines and could control the pitch. I failed to remember the 23–30 pounds of pressure I had to exert to move the control stick when I had tested the manual reversion system on functional check flights. After this experience, and while still using the reversion system, the stick felt light as a feather.

With the aircraft level at 6,500 feet, I told Buster I had the plane under control. He had been descending and getting emergency vectors from NAEW in an attempt to stay near and in radio contact with me. Since I was still concentrating on flying, Buster started going through the checklist to help me clean up the unfinished items. He reminded me to put the flight controls back to normal. That step reconnects the hydraulic actuators to the flight-control system. The Dash-1 gives the same warning about rapid pitch changes when returning to the normal flight-control system. As I switched the flight controls back to normal, the aircraft violently pitched up—this time forcing me heavily into the seat. I grabbed the stick and started fighting for control. I was wildly going from stop to stop on the controls, trying to find neutral. The controls were so light, it initially felt like the stick had broken off in my hand.

After thinking for a few seconds that I was going to depart controlled flight, I let go of the stick to see if the aircraft would settle down. It did. I gently took hold of the stick and focused all my attention on maintaining level flight. I was experiencing the "leans"—a condition in which my brain and my instruments disagreed on the attitude for level flight. Since I was still in the weather, there were no outside visual references to confirm which was correct. Normally the right way to fight this condition is to believe the instruments. However, knowing that they had experienced a power interruption and had been brought back on-line in other than straight and level, unaccelerated flight, I knew that their gyros might have precessed. I had less-than-full confidence that they were correct. Buster started telling me to head to steer-point alpha, a point along the Italian coast from where we could reach a divert base. Unfortunately, when the aircraft lost AC power, the INS had dumped and was useless. I had no idea where I was, or even if the aircraft-heading system was usable.

Buster started asking Magic for directions to get the two of us together and headed towards Cervia AB, our divert base located on the east coast of Italy. Magic was unable to help us; its personnel did not have me on radar, but they were able to tell us that Cervia currently had a 300-foot ceiling and one-mile visibility. I told Buster I didn't like that option because it meant that I would have to take my eyes off the instruments to study the instrument-approach plates for a bunch of strange fields. I had the approach and radio frequencies around Aviano memorized and really wanted to go there. Magic again stated that it did not have me on radar but said Primo might.

Primo was the call sign for the 606th Expeditionary Air Control Squadron out of Spangdahlem. I had not known that the squadron was in place because it had not been operational during the first few days of the war. The Primo controller came over guard frequency loud and clear, telling Buster and me to reset our transponders so he could find us. Within seconds, he had us both identified and had started giving me vectors back towards Aviano. He did an awesome job of giving me snap headings to all the closest bases and letting me know the weather at each so I could make the decision. He also started giving vectors to Buster to get our flight, now about 20 miles apart, back together. Primo also coordinated with all the agencies along the coast so that I had to talk with him only. He got me all the way to Aviano before handing me off to the approach controller.

While flying home, I noticed that the number-two engine was running hotter than number one. I still did not know what had caused the original problem, so I set the right throttle at 85 percent and planned on flying a simulated, single-engine approach. I still had doubts about the instruments' accuracy, and since there was a mountain range just north of the base, Aviano approach gave me no-gyro vectors to landing. During the approach, the controller said, "Turn right" or "Turn left," when needed. I then rolled into a half-standard rate turn; he timed my turn, monitored my position on radar, and then said, "Stop turn" to control my heading and eliminate any chance that a heading error in my navigation system would cause an accident. I followed his instructions and finally broke out of the weather 500 feet above and two miles from the approach end of the runway. We had been flying for one hour and 45 minutes, and this was the first time (without depending on the instruments) that I had a reference by which I could determine my attitude.

The crash vehicles were waiting to meet me as I landed and rolled out on the runway. I taxied clear of the active and waited to shut down. The rescue crews looked at me with some confusion, not knowing what needed to be done. I was exhausted and still sweating like a pig although it was cold and rainy outside. I told them I needed to shut down and have the plane impounded. But first, I wanted a minute to talk to the squadron and get my thoughts together.

Capt Rip Woodard and aircraft 956

Sitting there on the taxiway—getting my stuff together—I listened as the FM radio came to life. It was Buster saying that the weather was clearing in Kosovo and we needed to hurry and get down there. He had already contacted squadron ops, located a spare aircraft for me on spot 18, and arranged for ops to warm it up. He had also coordinated for his aircraft to be hot-refueled while I moved to the spare. Still dazed and confused, I acknowledged, shut down, and got a ride to the spare.

After briefing maintenance on what had happened to aircraft 956, I moved to the spare and started getting it ready to go. Running through the after-start checklist, I saw the squadron commander pull up. He jumped out of his car and got on the maintainer's headset to talk with me. After asking me what had happened, he told me, "Good job" and "Go ahead and shut down." I was relieved; there was no way we could make the tanker times, and I did not feel the need to push my luck twice in one day. Fortunately for me, nobody had been able to attack any targets that morning. I only had to take grief from Buster for about 24 hours for ruining his day.

About eight months later, I was attending a safety ceremony at the Pentagon. Maj Gen Francis C. Gideon Jr., chief of Air Force Safety, was one of the generals in attendance. Coincidentally, he was the test pilot who had ejected from an A-10 after both engines flamed out while test-firing the gun. We sat and talked for a few minutes about what had happened and then discussed a few shortcomings in the boldface procedures. He asked what had helped me work through the emergency. I thought the things that contributed most to my getting through that experience were fear, luck, and divine intervention.

My Turn in the Barrel

Introduction

Lt Col Chris "Kimos" Haave

My first time in combat was one of my significant life experiences, as it has been for most military professionals. Our OAF stories show just how strange some of those combat experiences were. We had a close view of OAF combat, a closer one than some of our support teammates and fellow strikers who employed precision-guided munitions from relatively high altitudes. Their combat duties often kept them focused on interpreting their sensors and radarscopes, but we Hog drivers (and other FACs) watched with revulsion as Serbian atrocities unfolded before us. We spent most of our time putting eyeballs and ordnance directly on enemy troops whose identity we confirmed firsthand with our gyrostabilized binos.

The war was very real for our maintainers, who worked in shifts and hustled 24 hours a day to launch, recover, and reload our jets—and to repair the two combat-damaged Hogs. Some of our noncombat experiences, on the other hand, seemed unreal. Even when we were flying over the KEZ and working 12-hour days, we still slept in nice hotels, ate in restaurants, and sunbathed at the hotel pool.

Most of our pilots and maintainers had no previous combat experience. That included both colonels and both squadron commanders at Gioia del Colle, who received their baptism of fire over Kosovo. I will never forget Dirt Fluhr's radio call on 7 April: "Hey, they're shooting at us!" as we checked out a convoy of civilian and military vehicles northwest of Prizren. Our reaction that day was similar to many battlefield responses recorded in history—a warrior's training takes over, and he acts aggressively and dispassionately to eliminate the threat immediately.

259

Many of our first combat experiences included shouldering the mission's heavy responsibility and acquiring the "I'd better not blow this!" syndrome. Maintainers understood and internalized the importance of preparing the aircraft, building up and loading the weapons, installing and setting the self-protection countermeasures pod, and loading and setting the chaff and flares—all of these systems had to work. Pilots experienced similar character-building pressures when they led young wingmen in combat, squeezed the trigger near a civilian village, and decided what got shot and what didn't in a highly politicized conflict.

AFACs knew that the responsibility to find and accurately identify enemy forces was all theirs. They also knew that incoming fighters trusted them implicitly; they expected to be talked-on to only valid targets. Likewise, the fighters knew that their obligation was to hit valid targets only. Due to the unpredictable nature of locating and identifying the enemy, strikers would normally have to wait at their contact point until the AFAC could find a target. The strikers would often consume most of their available fuel and become anxious to unload their ordnance by the time the AFAC was ready to direct their attack on a target. Attacking quickly required that the strikers have complete trust in the AFAC. Not once did any striker question the validity of any target during the dozens of attacks I directed.

Okay, Two, Big Eyes Out!

1st Lt Allen "JAKS" Duckworth

"Okay, Two, big eyes out!" came the flight lead's simple yet meaningful order. I was flying on Capt Jim "Meegs" Meger's wing, and we were about five seconds from crossing the Kosovo-Albania border. This would be my first-ever combat mission. I had been flying the A-10 for only 10 months; not only was this my first combat mission, but it was also my first flight without a grade sheet. Less than two weeks earlier, I finished my mission-qualification training, kissed my wife good-bye, and boarded a plane with Lt Glib Gibson, another new wingman. We were excited because we would finally join the rest of the squadron in

Italy. We had heard many stories of the great time to be had in Aviano and expected to experience unbounded fun between flying peacekeeping missions over Bosnia-Herzegovina. Instead, as we quickly learned, we were going to war.

At first the A-10 was tasked for nothing more than covering CSAR alert and a little CAS alert. Since I was not a qualified Sandy, I was told that I would probably not be needed. Capt Buster Cherrey had pulled me aside prior to the first bombs falling and had given me the choice of staying in Aviano or going back to Germany, where I could get some flying, at least. I initially thought that I should go home, fly, and spend more time with Cheryl, my wife of only seven months. However, I finally decided to stay and help if I could. By the time I got back to Buster to tell him my decision, he had already decided to keep me there. Since the A-10 did fight, I was very happy with that decision.

So there I was—flying into Kosovo to find and kill a real enemy who was, most likely, trying to find and kill us. I remember thinking to myself, "What am I doing here so soon?" That thought quickly gave way to the realization that I really needed to have "big eyes." I spent nearly all of my time scanning the ground for AAA and SAMs while we were on the other side of the *fence*, a term we used to describe the boundary between friendly and enemy territory. Although we did not find anything to destroy, I was excited to join the brotherhood of combat pilots, and I knew there would be more missions.

More missions came. Except for often being tired, I found myself quickly getting used to the combat-ops tempo. I flew mostly early morning sorties; I went to bed at about 1930 hours and got as much sleep as I could before my 0200 wake up. Each time I flew, I felt—and rightly so—that it was my responsibility to keep my flight lead and myself alive. However, as fatigue built up and challenged my discipline, I was tempted to stop clearing and slip into the more exciting task of looking for targets. I often had to remind myself that it was my job to be looking for threats and that the AFAC would find the targets.

On several occasions the AFAC did find targets. I was flying with Maj Lester Less on an AFAC mission and instead of looking in Kosovo, we began our search in Serbian proper—in the Kumanovo Valley. As we approached the town of Vranje from the south, Lester found an area he wanted to search more thoroughly. A few moments later he keyed the radio and excitedly half-yelled, "Okay! Okay! We've got military vehicles down there!" We both felt an immediate surge of adrenalin. Neither of us had ever fired weapons in combat, and Lester decided to use a Maverick missile to kill one vehicle and have it serve as a mark for me. His missile was a direct hit, allowing me to verify that the vehicles I saw were the same ones he meant for us to attack. He told me to drop two bombs on a row of four trucks in the same area. As I positioned myself to roll in for my Mk-82 delivery, I thought about how much I did not want to miss those targets. This was for real. I wanted to know that I could do it right, but even more importantly, I wanted to contribute to the effort. After completing my diving delivery and safe-escape maneuver, I looked back at the target area to see where my bombs had hit. About 15 seconds later, I got my answer as all four trucks disappeared under two huge fireballs. My first time to employ weapons in combat had been a success.

Not all of my missions were on an AFAC's wing. In fact, my most successful mission occurred when I was flying on Capt

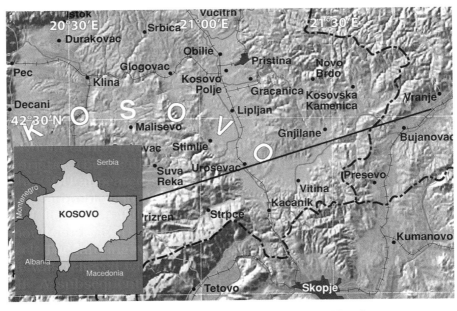

Location of military vehicles south of Vranje

Nate "Foghorn" Brauner's wing in a two-ship of strikers. Our primary job was to kill the targets that our AFAC might find and assign to us in western Kosovo. However, if a striker flight lead was AFAC qualified, as Foghorn was, he was often allowed to search for targets while waiting. If he found any enemy forces, he would call the designated AFAC to take a look. On this day as we waited, Foghorn searched the area of Dakovica. He saw something and talked my eyes onto a small area on the southern edge of town, asking what I saw there. By this time in the air campaign, the Serbs had learned to hide nearly every piece of equipment they had. I could not believe it; here were two-dozen trucks and APCs parked in an open area! I told Foghorn what I saw, and he quickly responded, "Yeah, that's what I see, too." The AFAC, Capt JD McDonough, also had trouble believing our target description—it seemed too good to be true. He took a look and cleared us to kill it. We each dropped four Mk-82s, launched one Maverick, and fired hundreds of rounds of 30 mm—my first time to use the gun in combat. By the time we departed, nearly every vehicle was burning. On later missions, I would steal a quick glance when I flew in that area to see if the vehicles' hulks were still there. We must have destroyed or damaged them all beyond repair because they remained there even after the air campaign ended. Although many fellow pilots teased Foghorn about inflating his BDA, I knew he was right on at least this occasion—we had British imagery to prove it.

I had flown a total of 30 combat missions by the end of the conflict. Not all of them were successful because on various days we had bad weather, could not find targets, or experienced aircraft malfunctions that forced an early RTB. And on some days we became the targets of Serb SAMs and AAA. Even though the Serbs did not often shoot at me, I retained a healthy degree of unease each time I flew. On every sor-

Photo courtesy of author

Lt JAKS Duckworth following a combat mission

263

tie it was important to me to be a good wingman; I wanted my flight leads to be confident that they could count on me to add to, rather than diminish, our flights' combat capability. After all, Glib and I had been brand-new wingmen when the air war started, and we had to prove ourselves. My biggest fear, therefore, was not being shot down—but failing my flight lead.

First Time Out Front

Capt Nate "Foghorn" Brauner

I felt a surge of excitement as I departed our squadron's makeshift ops center for the jet parked on Gioia's ramp. I hadn't flown in three days and was stepping for my sixth combat sortie. However, I felt excited today because I would lead a flight into combat for the first time. I climbed into the aircrew minivan, got comfortable, and began to reflect on the series of events that had occurred during the past six months—the events that began with my arrival at Spangdahlem and brought me here, sitting in the crew van en route to a combat-loaded aircraft.

USAF Photo by TSgt Blake Borsic

Panther taxiing at Gioia del Colle AB, Italy

I hadn't been flying much. I had arrived at Spangdahlem as a new pilot in early March, just three weeks before the campaign started and while the squadron was still engaged in "split ops." For the past six months the Panthers had maintained a near-constant presence at Aviano with half the squadron, keeping the other half at home in Germany. It was a tough situation for everyone in the 81st. The delicate peace negotiations seemed to drag on for years; however, they now seemed close to breaking down, as they had on several occasions. The Panthers had been sent to Aviano in anticipation of the need for air strikes should the negotiations fail. They had been sent to provide CSAR support in case one of our planes got shot down, not to conduct air strikes.

When I arrived at Spangdahlem, the squadron showed the long-term effects of its split ops. Several bachelors even considered Aviano more "home" than they did Spangdahlem. The deployed Panthers had been staying at a mountain chalet just north of Aviano—affectionately known as "Mr. C's." Its owner was a former pilot and an aviation enthusiast—to say he was hospitable to his American guests would have been a gross understatement. The Panthers were comfortable there despite the married pilots' families being several hundred miles away. They were quite happy to enjoy the Italian food and wine, and receive the American per diem to pay for it all. The women were striking, the scenery was equally luscious, and the flying was good. It was as close to a fighter pilot's dream as was possible in post–Cold War Europe. The constant deployment was seemingly never going to end, and the squadron had established a well-defined routine. When I met Kimos, the Panther squadron commander, he assured me that I would get well acquainted with life in northern Italy and that I would also be a candidate to go with the squadron when it deployed to the Air Warrior CAS exercise at Nellis AFB in early April. He said, "It is going to be a very busy spring, so don't get too comfortable relaxing in Germany." He couldn't have been more correct. I would be on the road quite a bit, but the real reason was one that even our most experienced pilots did not foresee at the time.

The deployments were an exciting prospect, but I still had several hurdles to jump before I could participate. I hadn't flown the A-10 since mid-December, thanks to a mountain-bike accident while I was at home on leave. A clavicle fracture and resulting surgery had kept me out of the cockpit, and it would be the end of March before I could fly again. It was a bad position to be in; I hoped that I would be healed enough to start flying and make our April deployment to Nellis. I wanted to be on that trip—and all others like it.

My heart sank on 15 March when all of our planes and combat-ready pilots were directed to deploy immediately to Aviano. I had been out of flying for three months, and when our squadron's time came, I wasn't qualified to go. It grated on me like nothing I had ever known. I have been entranced by listening to war stories ever since I was a doolie at the academy. I wondered how I would I react when it was my turn. Would I carry away the same perceptions and learn the same lessons that others had? I had no doubt about my training. And now—when the call came—I had to carry water while the rest of the team took to the field. It wasn't a good feeling. I was convinced that there must be some way to join the fight, but how to do so eluded me.

As I continued to heal and wait for my opportunity to join the effort, I prepared for my recurrency flights by studying "the threat" in the classified tactics manuals we kept in our squadron vault. I also listened to the first reports that came back from Aviano—invariably through the wives' network—of Panthers sitting CSAR alert as the first interdiction strikes were launched. On 27 March, I was home eating a late dinner and enjoying my recently installed satellite TV, when CNN broke in with the news of the first allied plane to be shot down. I was riveted by the news accounts of the crash and didn't sleep more than an hour or two that whole night. The task to rescue the pilot would fall to our 81st pilots. Because of the locations of the targets the F-117s were tasked to attack, I knew the wreckage must be deep inside Serb territory, which would make the rescue difficult. Nevertheless, it was all over six hours later. Once again, the pilots of the A-10s had risen to the occasion and performed their duty in an exceptional manner. Unlike a previous F-16 shoot down several years earlier, there were no press conferences, no smiling for the cameras, and no million-dollar book deals. The pilots involved were serious about this conflict and did not want any attention or publicity to distract them from their primary job—flying combat missions. I felt a surge of pride at being counted as one of them, and that only served to strengthen my resolve to join them as soon as possible.

The two flights I needed to regain all of my currencies happened in rapid succession the following week. My instructor was Lt Col Snoopy Schulze, the Panthers' previous commander. Snoopy was an old hat at flying in Germany and quickly got me up to speed after months of inactivity. I was now ready and chomping at the bit to go.

Finally my call came—not to join the squadron at Aviano but to be the squadron's rep at the CAOC in Vicenza, Italy. Going to the CAOC was kind of like paying my dues. It was imperative that we had an A-10 rep there—an experienced flyer who understood our mission and could help with planning the details of the air war. It was a thankless but important job that most units pawned off on their lieutenants. The rep often felt like a small cat that had been dropped into a pen of hungry dogs. We looked at it as a sanity check on the whole process, and most of our captains had already served there for at least a week. It was time for me to pay my dues, and I was ecstatic just to get a chance to play a role—any role. I could contribute to the cause from my new position and, with some luck, join the squadron in about a week.

The CAOC was a loose collection of prefab metal buildings. The arrangement of the successive additions appeared haphazard, and their orientation suggested an accelerated growth to satisfy the CAOC's expanding missions. New areas had been added in any space available—immediate needs clearly outweighed any desire for aesthetic beauty. I arrived on 10 April—still early in the war. Inside, officers frantically worked to align the scarce in-theater resources to support an increased air presence in the skies over the Balkans. It was obvious that our initial in-theater assets were not sufficient after President Milosevic refused to concede his position following the first few nights of allied raids. One of my first tasks was to help define the new and expanded role A-10s could play in the KEZ. More often than not, I was merely a conduit—passing information and ideas between the squadron leadership at

Aviano (and later at Gioia) and the appropriate people at the CAOC. I had become the voice of the squadron.

Being the squadron voice could be a good thing or a very bad thing, depending on the day's events and who was sitting in the big chair. The man running the air war was Lt Gen Mike Short, whom we called Senior. He had flown the A-10 in the 81st during a previous assignment and had a son, whom we called Junior, in our squadron. Although it wasn't obvious, he had a special affinity for Hog drivers and paid close attention to any news of our operations. Senior was tough as nails, much like a high school football coach who was busy directing the game of his life. No one in the CAOC ever took Senior lightly. His questions (or orders) were always direct and spot-on. He knew the game better than anyone else in the room and was familiar with most, if not all, of the details. He had subordinate experts tackle the details that he didn't personally have time to address. None of us ever lost sight of the fact that Senior knew his stuff and would call us on the carpet if we failed him. He was always deadly serious. We took our breaks and killed time in the unit rep's room by cracking jokes, surfing the net, or trading stories; but we knew when we came up front and Senior was in the big chair, there would be no latitude for levity. I couldn't imagine anyone pulling the wool over Senior's eyes. It seemed that he generally knew the answer before he asked the question and just wanted to keep people on their toes.

I remember on one occasion being called into the CAOC's main room to answer to Senior. It seemed that someone had told him that A-10s were going to bomb through the weather— release our bombs on coordinates without being able to visually identify the target. There is no way that we would have done that. Our navigational systems were not accurate enough, and even if they were, we had not trained that way. I couldn't imagine any Hog driver who would have been willing to drop his weapons blindly without knowing what he might hit. It just wasn't in our thought process. Senior sent for me; when I arrived he gave me a hard look and said, "What's this I hear about A-10s wanting to bomb through the weather on coordinates?" I must have looked fairly shocked and assured him that with all the civilians on the ground, we had no desire or inclination to start fighting this war that way. With a short grunt and a terse, "That's the right answer," Senior turned back to work. He had known the answer all along—he just wanted to make sure I knew it.

Senior's aptitude and extensive knowledge was shared by most, but not all, of the senior officers in the CAOC. Men like Lt Col Paul C. "Sticky" Strickland, Maj James "Dibbs" Dibble, and Lt Col Walrus Heise, to name a few, kept the place functioning. They dealt with daily issues as trivial as how to get gas to the rental cars and as critical as reorganizing the war's SEAD support. They kept the big picture and sidelined those who didn't.

There were a few others whose priorities, war-planning abilities, or aptitude for leading men was disappointing. We had one officer in the CAOC who focused his efforts on ensuring that people didn't pop microwave popcorn anywhere in the building, because he didn't want to smell burnt popcorn. We had a war on and he's worrying about people popping popcorn. On one occasion he called me to the floor after some of our jets had been shot at and returned fire. "Why are your guys getting shot at? . . . Don't they know that they aren't supposed to be looking for targets in these areas?" He blurted this out as he waved at a wide area hashed out on a 1:500-scale map.

His wave depicted an area, inside Kosovo along the Macedonian border, where we were prohibited from actively looking for targets. The restriction had been put into place for several reasons, including a desire to keep NATO ground troops inside Macedonia, but close to the Macedonia-Yugoslav border, from being drawn into the conflict. The Serbs had discovered our self-imposed no-attack zone and were using our ROEs against us. The restriction had an unintended consequence of turning the entire area into a "safe haven" for the Serbs. They roamed freely through that zone, and often we were powerless to stop them.

I explained to him that the A-10s had to transit the restricted zone using the ingress routes planned by his CAOC airspace experts to get into their assigned areas. It was during their transit that, while they weren't searching for targets, they had noticed the AAA. "Well, I don't want them hanging out in there. Tell them not to fly over there any more. That's too close to Macedonia!" He was excited, and his gestures only served to amplify his emotional outburst. A German colonel, who was standing behind him, smiled knowingly. He had observed this exchange and had probably overheard 10 more diatribes that night on as many subjects—par for the course when this particular officer was in charge. So I gave him the best "Yes, sir" I could manage and was dismissed from the main room.

Most nights were uneventful. Our pilots flew the scheduled missions, reported their BDA, and the war went on. I will never forget, however, the contrast in leadership I witnessed in the main room of the CAOC. There were times when it seemed that the war was being run by people who had been there before, had the big picture, and were doing their best to make this operation run the way it should. At other times other people were in charge who did just the opposite. Many of us felt much aggravation and irritation when these types were in charge. I learned later that my frustration, from having to personally answer their questions in the CAOC, paled compared to that felt by the people flying operational missions over Kosovo when an officer of this type was in charge.

I had been lost in my thoughts for some time when TSgt Damien Fortunato stepped lightly on the brakes—forcing me back to the present—and brought the aircrew minivan to a stop near my aircraft. Damien was one of our life-support NCOs. We had served together in the same squadron at Pope, and he was now part of the 74th FS contingent that had come over to supplement us at Gioia. It was nice to have some familiar faces in both squadrons. "Here you go, sir," Damien said. It was time to start thinking about the mission at hand. I thanked him, stepped out of the van, and walked towards tail number 80-984.

The weapons troops were busy putting the finishing touches on the CBU-87s slung underneath the aircraft. One of the ammo troops had written some personalized messages to the Serbs on the CBU canisters. I was sure that if I got the opportunity to drop them, the soldiers on the ground would have no question as to their meaning. We were all focused on the task at hand, and it was evident that everyone on the flight line took great pride in his or her work. This was the first shooting war for many of us. Morale was high, and so was our efficiency. The jets rarely broke, but when they did, they were fixed in a fraction of the time that we had come to expect back home. That accomplishment was due, in great part, to the great enthusiasm we had for our jobs and to the fact that we rarely, if ever, wanted for necessary parts. It was a great feeling to be part of that team.

USAF Photo

Crew chief performing an early morning preflight

Amn Joe Ulshafer was busy annotating the aircraft forms to document the maintenance work that had been done on the jet since it had returned from the first go that morning. Joe was a young first-term airman on his first assignment with the 81st FS. In recent times, shooting wars have been scarce (thankfully), so I couldn't help thinking that the experience he was gaining from this war would serve him well for the rest of his time in the Air Force. He looked up as I came around the jet.

Joe flashed me a sharp salute and a smile. Salutes out here were a lot sharper than back home—probably a reflection of the excitement. He asked if I was ready to give the Serbs a dose of their own medicine. "They don't stand a chance," I replied. Continuing, I asked, "How did the jet come down?"

We settled into some friendly banter about the jet. I always thought it was good to know how the jet, which I was getting

271

ready to strap on, had been flying recently so I would know what to look for. I didn't expect any problems. We were both part of the same team, and it was important to let the crew chiefs know what we were doing. I showed Joe on my map where we were going to start off—north of Pristina near Podujevo—and that we'd be looking for some tanks and APCs at the location where they had been located by imagery. They knew they were part of the team and liked seeing us take off with bombs and come home clean; he now had an idea of what we were going after, and that made a big difference.

The mission that I briefed to Joe wasn't going to be as easy as it appears in Hollywood movies. Imagery was suspect; our needs were not high on the CAOC's targeting and intelligence-support priority list. Satellite reconnaissance was well suited to support interdiction strikes against fixed targets, but most of our targets were mobile forces. Those forces would be photographed at 1400 on the day prior, and the information was accurate at the time it was taken. However, unlike fixed targets, they had 18 hours to move before we would be in the predicted area. Out of necessity, Lt Stephen "Al" Smith, our intelligence officer, and his enlisted troops did their best to get us the most current pictures from all sources. Al and the others spent all night sifting through image databases, which were sorted only by basic encyclopedia (BE) numbers that had no correlation to the target type, date of the imagery, or its location. It was a laborious and dull task, repeated every night to find the right combination of target type, location, and date of image. Without the hard work of Al and his team, we would have had far less success at finding targets. Their pictures told us where the enemy forces had been and when they had been there; they also provided us with a starting point for our searches. Although our confidence in the target's current location was not as good as we would have liked, it was far better than nothing. With people like Al and Joe on our team, we were optimistic.

Ground ops were pretty standard. It had been a beautiful day so far and a stark contrast to the previous foggy mornings. The light from a brilliant sun, filtered by high cirrus clouds, fell onto red poppy fields dancing in a gentle, wind-driven rhythm just outside the base perimeter. Looking at that beauty, I found it surreal to imagine that we would launch in 40 minutes—take off to wage war and wreak havoc and destruction on the Serb army.

As I led Capt Rip Woodard airborne, I felt another surge of excitement. This was it! I was in the lead of Taco flight, making the decisions. I was the one who would do the target search, ID the target, and dictate the tactics. I had been excited on my first six sorties, but this was different. This time I was responsible for the flight, which was both exhilarating and sobering. It reminded me of the first time, after I had received my driver's license, that my parents had let me take the car out by myself on the interstate. I had approached that with a nervous excitement—excited about the new opportunity and praying, "Please God, don't let me screw this up." This was no different.

Rip joined on me and we flew east over the Adriatic, performed our systems checks, and looked over each other's jets. We continued east across Albania and into southern Macedonia, where we rendezvoused with our tanker—a KC-135 that would refuel most of the A-10s going into the KEZ during our vul period. The actual air refueling was a relatively simple task. Because of the distances, almost every aircraft required aerial refueling to complete its mission. That demand made the management of aircraft schedules, flow patterns, and gas offloads critical. I had witnessed firsthand the CAOC's complex planning process which ensured that it all flowed smoothly during execution. Their planners developed tanker, SEAD, and ABCCC schedules, put together airspace-control plans, and integrated the resources and the requirements of the 700-plus aircraft armada. Even the A-10, which consumed relatively little fuel, still required refueling if it was to stay airborne in the target area from three to six hours at a time. Tankers seemed to be everywhere, but unless they were well managed, there would never be enough gas when and where it was needed. So while *hitting the tanker* (our term for the actual refueling) was a relatively simple task, it required a great deal of coordination and effort to make it work.

We flowed on and off the tanker during our planned refueling time and headed for the eastern side of Kosovo. The AFAC today was one of the augmenting Pope pilots—Capt Larry Card, a young 74th FS weapons officer. I was glad to be working with Larry, whom I had known since we were in the same squadron at the academy. He had been a sharp, introspective cadet then, and he had since become an excellent fighter pilot. I checked in with him just prior to crossing the Kosovo border. He was busy FACing a pair of British Harriers and sent us north to check on sites near Podujevo. I put Rip in a wedge formation position—about 45 degrees back on the left side—where he could comfortably maneuver and clear for threats as we flew north.

Over the radio we could hear Larry working the flight of Harriers on his target. It sounded like they were missing short. The Harriers were normally great to work because they had actually been trained for CAS, which meant they were proficient at looking outside the cockpit to visually acquire targets. Even though we weren't flying CAS missions in Kosovo, what we were doing required many of the same strengths and skills. We saw a big difference between pilots who trained to acquire targets visually and those who trained to bomb coordinates. It was much easier to talk the first group onto targets. The Harrier pilots could be expected to find the target visually, but their BLU-755s hit short almost every time because of a software glitch in their aiming and delivery system. I couldn't help thinking how frustrating that was for both the Harrier pilots and the AFAC as I continued leading my flight north.

In the midst of the communication between Larry and his Harriers, we heard a standard call from NAEW: "Aircraft, Derringer 060/80, say call sign." Most of these calls reflected the dynamic environment and the difficulty NAEW had in keeping track of many maneuvering aircraft. NAEW would occasionally lose track of someone, locate a return, and then query him or her to make sure the controller had the correct call signs. "Derringer" was a geographical point from which to describe a radial direction and distance in nautical miles. Derringer was colocated with Slatina, the Pristina airport. The NAEW had asked the aircraft located on the 060 radial (east, northeast) from Slatina at a distance of 80 NM to identify itself. We were about 10 minutes north of the border when I heard an NAEW transmission on strike frequency that I had not yet heard during OAF: "Outlaw, spades, Derringer 070 for 75, southwest bound!"

What did those brevity terms mean? It had been a little while since I had reviewed all the terms in our manuals. Nevertheless, I knew "outlaw" meant that an aircraft met the bad-guy point-of-origin criteria, and "spades" said that it wasn't squawking the right IFF transponder codes—that wasn't good. Usually I would hear those calls right before an unknown aircraft was declared a bandit (enemy aircraft), and that wasn't good either. I quickly pulled out my 1:250 chart to plot the position. The plot came out right near the Bulgarian border, inside Serbia. And it was heading this way.

Another, older voice came over the radio: "Aircraft, Derringer 070 for 75, tracking 230, this is Magic on Guard; identify yourself immediately!" This wasn't supposed to happen. The F-16CJs, who had been in an orbit overhead providing SEAD support for us, called NAEW and departed their orbit to intercept the intruder. I could hear their fangs sticking through the floorboards over the radio. Blood was in the air, and they could smell it.

Looking back at my map, I tried to get a rough estimate of the distance between us and the contact the NAEW had identified. It was about 45 miles. Time for us to pull back a bit. We both still had all of our ordnance on board. I had two cans of CBU-87 and Rip had four Mk-82s, along with our Mavericks. I didn't feel like getting into an air-to-air engagement with all of that on board, but I sure didn't want to get rid of it and give the outlaw a mission kill. "Taco, let's hook left. Line reference steer-point five." I had given Rip a copy of my lineup card when we briefed the sortie; today, steer-point five was Skopje, Macedonia—nominally friendly airspace.

Rip maneuvered into a good defensive line-abreast position, about a mile and a half off my right side. NAEW transmitted on Guard again, directing the unknown aircraft at Derringer 080 for 65 to identify itself. There was no response. I looked down at my map—30 miles to Skopje. He was obviously going a lot faster than we were. Thirty seconds passed as I increased my scan outside the cockpit, looking across the formation and behind us. I knew that Rip was doing the same thing in his cockpit.

"Mink Three-One, Bandit, Derringer 080 for 60, southwest bound, hot!" NAEW called out to the F-16CGs. "All aircraft in NBA, this is Magic. Chariot directs retrograde." NBA was the code word that we were using for eastern Kosovo.

Great. NAEW was now declaring the contact of a bandit—an enemy aircraft heading towards friendly aircraft. Time to make sure that both of us had our switches ready for an air-to-air fight. "Taco, check AIM-9 in Select, master arm to arm, gun rate high. Let's push it over. No lower than 160," I said as I traded altitude for airspeed, but still stayed above 16,000 feet.

"Two," came Rip's immediate response to indicate he understood and would comply with my instructions. I expected that he would have had his switches set, but I had to be sure. In the background, almost drowned out by the excitement of the moment, I could hear the low growl of the AIM-9 seeker head looking for a target.

"Bandit, Derringer, 090 for 56, southwest bound, descending, hot!" I checked the distance—about 25 miles. Suddenly, despite all the coalition aircraft out there, I felt very alone. Time to get some information from NAEW.

"Magic, Taco One, say BRAA to Bandit," I transmitted as I asked the NAEW for the bandit's bearing, range, altitude, and aspect.

Pause. "Taco, Magic, unable, stand by," came the reply.

Stand by??!!! You can't be serious! NAEW controllers had never shown stellar performance getting us information when we had trained together in the past, but at least they had given us some close control when we were at medium altitude. Now, when it really mattered—and we weren't at Red Flag over the Nellis ranges—all they could do is say "stand by." I wanted to reach out and wring their necks. They probably didn't even know what my position was—let alone how close the bandit was to any of us. I increased the amount of time that I was checking six—the airspace behind our aircraft.

"Bandit, Derringer, 090 for 52, heading 240, hot!"

I looked down and checked my chaff and flare settings. We were quickly approaching the point where I was going to have to turn the formation to be ready to fight. Two green ready lights stared up at me from the panel. Everything was set. I hacked the clock and started mentally calculating the range.

"Magic, Mink Three-One. Contact target, closing for VID (visual identification)," a charged but steady voice came over the radio. It was the same voice that I had heard earlier when the F-16s had departed their holding point to intercept the Bandit. There was a very pregnant pause. I checked six again. The next call sent a shiver down my spine.

"Magic, Mink Three-One. Target is an EA-6. Turning south now."

I was relieved, upset, and mad—most of all I couldn't believe my ears. We had almost shot one of our own aircraft—an EA-6B—because he wasn't in his planned orbit, and the NAEW didn't know who or what he was. I could have been taking part in an impromptu CSAR had it not been for the professionalism of Mink 31 and his ability to visually identify an EA-6B. I had a flashback to when that had not happened—when two friendly Black Hawk helicopters had been misidentified and shot down by friendly fighters, taking the lives of Lt Laura Piper and 25 other people flying low over northern Iraq. I was also mad because we had lost about 10 minutes of our available time over Kosovo; it was time to get back to our mission.

We deselected our AIM-9s and turned north. Rip floated back to a good wedge position, and I could see him pick up the gentle rhythm of checking our six and providing cover against AAA and SAM threats. Irregularly, his jet would move—slight changes in heading and pitch angles—just enough to give him a better view of the ground beneath us and to remain unpredictable. In front, I was doing the same thing. I picked out visual landmarks that would help orient and guide me into the target area. It gave us something to do while the adrenaline worked its way out of our system.

We arrived near Podujevo after taking an easterly and slightly circuitous 20-minute route, about the same time the adrenaline wore off. Podujevo lay in the middle of a long valley that pointed south towards Pristina and terminated in the north at the Serbian border. Like most of Kosovo, this was an agricultural area, and the fields were full of the spring crops.

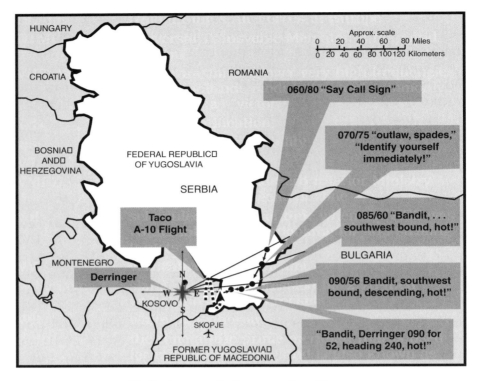

Call sign . . . Outlaw . . . Bandit . . .

We didn't see many farmers operating heavy farm equipment these days. With the oil embargo in full effect, there probably wasn't any gas to spare, and most of the work was likely being done by hand. We rarely saw any traffic on the roads. The Serbs either had learned their lesson or had figured out our ROEs. They knew that civilian vehicles were safe (at least from A-10s); therefore, civilian vehicles were the only type we would see on the roads.

Today there was little movement on the ground, and the few vehicles I did see on city streets were definitely civilian. I checked along the tree lines and in other areas that our imagery from the past two days had indicated as likely locations for Serb equipment. There was nothing. If the Serb army was in the vicinity of Podujevo, it was well hidden.

In the background, I could overhear the communication between other fighters and AFACs. I called Larry and told him that there wasn't anything to be found around Podujevo, and asked, "Do you have anything else for us?" "Taco, check with Stew Two-One. He's working over near G-Town," Larry said. We sometimes referred to the major cities in Kosovo by their first initial. It kept the chatter down and gave the Serbs who were listening something else to figure out. He quickly passed me coordinates and pushed me to the backup frequency. I sent Rip to the assigned frequency for the eastern half of Kosovo, checked him in, and was almost immediately contacted by Stew 21.

"Taco, Stew Two-One, good voice; say ordnance and playtime." I recognized the voice of Maj Bumpy Feldhausen, one of the boys from Pope. I replied, "Stew, Taco, One's got two by CBU-87, Maverick, and the gun. Number Two has four by Mk-82s. We've got another 20 minutes of playtime." "Roger," Bumpy said, "we've got some arty positions in the tree line in our target area. We're halfway between G-Town and Vranje. Confirm you have the coordinates."

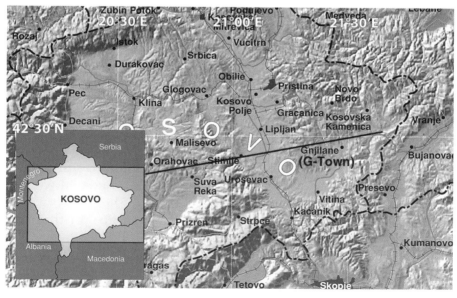

Artillery positions between G-Town and Vranje

279

I looked at the INS. "Another five minutes away," I told him.

"Copy all. I want you guys in at 200 and below. We'll hold over you, 210 and above, and we can provide your cover. When you get into the target area, I'll give you a talk-on."

"Taco Zero-One," I replied. Switching frequencies, I compared fuels with Rip. We'd have enough for about 15 minutes in the target area. I plotted the position of the target on one of my 1:50 maps. It was within a kilometer of the corner of the map, halfway up the side of a hill on the eastern side of a fairly nondescript small valley. It wasn't going to be easy finding it—especially without being able to reference the map features to the immediate south and west of the target. To see all of that, I would have to juggle two other 1:50 maps in the cockpit along with the one I already had out and the 1:250 that I was using for navigation. It wasn't an easy thing to do.

We were almost there—only three miles away. I looked out and saw Stew 21 circling over the valley to the south, slightly higher than us and about four miles away. "Stew, Taco's visual, ready for the talk-on," I announced.

"Right beneath you, there's a fairly long town in the middle of the valley, oriented north-south. Call contact."

I looked down into the valley. There were a lot of towns. I came back inside, checked my map, checked the compass, back outside. Yep, there was the town that he was talking about, and it was pretty much north-south. "Contact," I replied and then added, "Confirm that there is a hardball road leading through the length of the town."

"Affirmative," came the answer. "Let's call the length of that town one unit. Now look on the eastern side of that town. There's a dirtball road leading southeast up into the hills. Call contact."

I looked down. There were a lot of dirtball roads, some more prominent than others. "I see a lot of dirtball roads," I said.

"Right, this one is the most prominent one. It leads out in a straight line to the southeast and hits a tree line in the hills about two to three units away from the town."

I looked down. None of the roads that led out the town to the southeast ran into a tree line. I checked my orientation. OK, I was looking to the southeast of the town. No trees. My frustration started to build.

"Stew, Taco's not contact with that tree line," I admitted.

"It's right underneath me now. I'll put down a mark to show you."

I looked up to watch him. He wasn't over the town. Where was he? I looked off to the south. Searching, searching . . . I had lost him while I was looking for the target. One potato, two . . . wait a minute—there he was—only he was a lot further south than he should be. How was he going to mark this target area from so far away? Then it dawned on me—I was looking at the wrong hillside. I swore to myself. How could I be so stupid? I had been looking at the wrong area. My INS pointed to the area that I was looking in, but it must have drifted. I looked about three miles south, underneath the area where Bumpy was circling. There was another elongated town in the valley, with a hardball road leading through it. "Stupid idiot!" I cursed at myself for a novice mistake!

I called Rip on FM to say that we had been orbiting too far to the north and were shifting south. Rip acknowledged, and we started south just in time to watch Bumpy roll in and put down two Willy Pete rockets on the side of the hills. One landed near but on the north side of a dirtball road; the other Willy Pete landed about 200 meters north of that.

"Stew, Taco's contact with your smokes. We were looking in the wrong area," I admitted, somewhat sheepishly. I still felt stupid.

"Roger that," he replied. "There are four revetments in the field just on the south side of the road, south of my southern mark. I'd like you to lay down your CBUs right on the tree line—I think that they may have some of their stuff hidden in the trees. The two closest revetments to the tree line have something in them."

"Copy all," I replied. Then to Rip, "Shooter-cover, bombs, gun. Winds are out of the west at 60 knots." That meant that I would be coming in with a tailwind to make this work. Even though each one of these bombs weighed about 1,000 lbs 60 knots of wind would definitely affect it as it fell for about 12,000 feet. Rip acknowledged my plan and shifted his orbit to the west, so he could look through me to the target area.

I checked all of my switches. All the lights were green, and I was at the right altitude—everything was ready. "Taco One can be 'in' in 10 seconds," I said.

"Continue."

"One's in hot!" I rolled to the left, slicing down out of the sky. Down, steeper and steeper, my nose pointed at the earth—green and brown earth replaced the blue sky in my windscreen. In the background, I heard Bumpy's clearance. I rolled out, straightened my wings, and waited a few moments for the low altitude safety and target enhancement (LASTE) bombing solution to stabilize and indicate that I had lined up just right of the target. I had misjudged the winds slightly and had to compensate by adding about five degrees of bank. I clicked forward on the trim to reduce stick forces and attempted to relax—I tried not to jerk the stick or make any sudden inputs that might throw the LASTE solution and the CBU-87 canisters off target. Slowly, in seconds that were like minutes, the pipper approached the target. As it got closer, it seemed to accelerate. I resisted the urge to push forward on the stick to slow the pipper's movement and make the weapons-release point easier to judge. If I had done that, I would have "bunted" the aircraft, fooled the computer, and caused the canisters to impact long of the target. Temporal distortion is normal during a diving delivery—it just seemed much more intense now that I was doing the job for real. I waited until the pipper was superimposed on the target, pressed the pickle button, and felt the two clunks as the two canisters left the jet and started their ballistic fall.

I pulled back on the stick, felt the Gs build up as I brought the nose up to 35 degrees of pitch, and then rolled into a slight bank to the right. I looked down and could see some of the flares I had expended trailing behind my jet; my left index finger persisted in hammering away at the flare button. I continued my right-hand climbing turn towards the sun while looking back at the target area. It seemed to take an eternity, and then I saw two small puffs when the canisters opened. Half a second later, the whole area along the tree line erupted in a beautiful shower of silver and white sparkles as the bomblets detonated. It reminded me of one of my chemistry labs when we had set fire to magnesium shavings. Only this was on a much larger scale. I looked away and scanned the ground for threats.

"Good hits, Taco," came Bumpy. "Have your wingman drop his Mk-82s north of your hits. We're going to clear you off on this target and look for some more targets."

"Copy all," I said. "Two, I want you in out of the west in one minute. One's climbing for energy," I directed on FM. I continued my climb, slowly ascending out of danger, and reached the relative safety of altitude. About a minute later, I was happy with my position. "One's cover," I announced.

"Roger, Two will be 'in' in 10," Rip replied.

"Continue." I replied and offset myself to the southwest, where I would be in a good position to monitor his attack.

"Two's in hot," Rip called, as he rolled in towards the target.

I scanned the area beneath him. He was clear, and his nose was pointing at the area that was still smoking from my attack. "Cleared hot, Two."

Four seconds later, Rip was pulling back skyward, arching away from the ground. "Two's off, switch error," he said. "I was in singles."

Great—neither one of us was at our peak today. It was a simple error, but because of it, Rip had released only one of his four bombs. He was going to have to make another pass. I looked down. His lone bomb impacted on the northern revetment, throwing dust high into the air. Neither one of us had gotten secondaries, although there was some black smoke coming from the southern revetment, which had fallen under my CBU pattern. Something was burning in there.

I checked the fuel. We would have enough for another pass and still have about 10 minutes to spare; no problem.

I looked at Rip, who was climbing, and then I saw something really neat. There were little white clouds underneath him that I hadn't noticed before. They were small, like little cumulus bits of popcorn. Something wasn't right—time slowed way down. Some of the clouds looked like they had little silver centers; then they'd disappear. Now more clouds were around him. Hairs stood up on the back of my neck—they were shooting at Rip! Instantly, it seemed time was speeding up again—just like the pipper was approaching the target. Only this was much more real, and yet—surreal. What do I say? I urgently fumbled for words as I pressed the mike switch.

"Taco Two, keep the jet moving. Climb! Triple-A beneath you." I could now see that it was all bursting beneath him by a good 4,000–5,000 feet, so I was less worried. Rip started moving his jet a little more. The little clouds started to disappear.

"Say location." Rip's voice sounded controlled but worried.

"It's stopped now. Let's egress north. Keep climbing." I responded.

The AAA had appeared beneath Rip when he was about a mile or two southwest of the target. As we moved away, I looked back over my shoulder and tried to get a good look at the area, but couldn't acquire any AAA pits or military positions.

"Taco, Stew, say location of triple-A. Do you need assistance?" Bumpy asked over the common frequency.

"Stew, stand by." I needed a second. Get away from the threat. Pull out the 1:50. Find it on the map. Plot the position. My attempt to determine the AAA coordinates was frustrated by its location just off the southwest corner of the target map.

We circled north of the target and climbed a bit higher. If the airbursts were limited to the places where I had seen them, we should be safe. They had used only medium-caliber AAA, but if they had MANPADS it would be more of a threat. I told Bumpy and Rip what I had seen and that my plan was to climb up above 200, look down with my stabilized binoculars, and see what I could make out while Rip maintained cover.

"Roger. Let me know if you need us down there." This was an important target for us. People had shot at us, and now we were going to finish our attack. Bumpy had every right to be interested, but, for now, it was my game.

We circled around to the south, and I scanned the area with my eyes. A road snaked away to the southwest through a pass and then continued south towards Gnjilane. On the southwest side of the road, the terrain climbed into the hills, which were dotted with trees. On the northwest side, there was a small hill with a plateau on top, and beyond that the terrain climbed into another range of hills. The hill with the plateau must have something on it—if I were a Serb, I would want to hold that ground.

Calling, "One is 'heads down,'" I raised the binoculars and looked at the hill. It appeared no different than the surrounding landscape, which consisted of three fields of a yellow crop that was probably wheat, two solitary large trees, and what appeared to be a farmhouse in the northern corner. No tracks, no unusual shadows, no revetments. Nothing.

I scanned the fields around the hill. Still nothing. I widened my scan, moving up towards the hills in the west and a reservoir that was tucked neatly away. Nothing. After about three to four minutes of this, I passed the lead to Rip to let him take a look. He found nothing.

I checked our fuel—we had another seven or eight minutes, tops. I made up my mind. "Two, let's go back to the original target and drop the rest of your Mk-82s there. I'll stay in a high cover to the south and watch for any more triple-A. I want to take out the rest of those revetments, but if anymore triple-A comes up, we still have the gun and Stew flight."

Rip agreed. We moved our orbit back to the original target, and I called cover. Within 30 seconds, Rip rolled in from the west, dropping a string of three bombs across the middle of the remaining revetments. He pulled off to the south, puking out flares and turning towards me.

About 10 seconds into his climb out, the AAA started again, and I was ready for it. I called for Rip to keep his jet moving and quickly scanned the ground. Where was it coming from? Out the corner of my eye, I could see Rip's jet maneuvering and remaining unpredictable. But there was nothing on the ground. The AAA stopped about five seconds after it appeared. Short, controlled bursts, I thought. These guys are regular army, not just a bunch of thugs who got their hands on some military hardware. They're disciplined, and they're smart.

We moved north while Rip climbed back to altitude. Once he regained his energy, we moved back in to look for the AAA. I told Rip to stay high in cover, and I descended to take a better look. I dropped down to about 15,000 feet and started taking a closer look at the area around the hill and the rising terrain to the west. Nothing.

"One, come hard right and climb; they're shooting again." Rip's voice broke through my concentration. I had already been moving the jet, but now I pulled back on the stick and started a climb. My left index finger quickly started hitting the flare button. I saw some of the small popcorn clouds with the silver centers about 3,000–4,000 feet underneath me. Then they were gone. I scanned the ground, but they weren't firing anymore. Nothing to see. I looked at our gas. Three minutes, tops. Time to call Bumpy. "Stew, Taco."

"Go ahead," Bumpy replied.

I said, "We just got shot at again by some of the triple-A. We're looking for it, but no luck. We have to bingo out in about three minutes. Any chance I can give you a handoff?"

It was like asking a child if he wanted ice cream. Bumpy was on his way over before I could finish the request. I described what I had seen and when it had happened. All the time, I was looking out, trying to find some last-minute clues that would alert me to the AAA position. The three minutes came and passed with no new revelations, so I passed the target to Bumpy and left.

During the flight home we made the normal in-flight reports to ABCCC and looked each other over as we accomplished our battle-damage checks for any unexpected problems. I felt like I had come off an emotional roller coaster. It had been my first time to lead a formation in combat, and everything had happened. We had to defend against a possible air threat; we searched for, found, and attacked targets; and we had been shot at by AAA. What a mission! However, the people who had shot at us were still alive back there, and that really angered me. I still had some nagging questions: What else did I miss? How lucky did I get? I later found that these questions persisted—no matter how successful the sortie was.

Bumpy joined us after he landed and debriefed. We met at the Truck Stop—a favorite eating place on the road back to the hotel. He had not been able to find the source of the AAA either, and we had a good laugh about it over a glass of wine. That had been my first combat flight lead mission, and I couldn't wait to do it again.

My First Combat Sortie

1st Lt Scott "Hummer" Cerone

I couldn't sleep during the night before my first sortie. In spite of the air conditioner, my room was stagnant. It was too hot to wear anything. I could taste the lemons in the orchard outside my second-floor window. The warm Italian breeze also carried in mosquitoes that buzzed in my ears throughout the night. I turned the television on and off repeatedly. My mind was racing. I was still awake when the alarm clock went off at three A.M. on 11 May 1999.

I showered and headed out, driving to the base with Lt Col Surgeon Dahl, my flight lead. Today would be his fini-flight with the 81st FS from Spangdahlem. He flew with the Flying Tigers during the Gulf War and, after today's mission, would head back to Pope to become their operations officer. So today, I was getting to fly my first combat sortie with my soon-to-be ops officer.

In the squadron building we were briefed by intel, and then Surgeon briefed me on our sortie. We walked to life support and put on our gear—no wallets, no patches, no rings. We carried dog tags and a 9 mm Berretta. I chambered the first round before holstering it in my vest.

I experienced a special feeling walking to my jet at sunrise. My harness, G suit, and survival vest (with all its buckles, straps, and zippers) were as comfortable as Hugh Hefner's smoking robe and silk pajamas. The sun began to trim the clouds with pink as the gray sky gave way to Mediterranean blue. I wanted to be airborne.

My jet was lightly loaded. I was carrying two cans of CBU-87 cluster bombs, which weighed 1,000 lbs each; two AGM-65D Maverick missiles; two AIM-9 Sidewinder missiles; an ECM pod; and 1,000 rounds of 30 mm depleted-uranium bullets. I strapped into the jet and started the engines. Before I taxied, a maintenance van pulled up in front of my jet. SSgt "Chunk" Barth, a maintenance specialist in my squadron, ran over and climbed up the side of my jet to wish me luck on my first sortie. He shook my hand and yelled, "Go get 'em, sir."

I finished my preflight checks and started to taxi. I returned my crew chief's salute as I pulled out of the chocks. He then jumped up to pat his jet one last time for good luck. The guys in the maintenance van were pumping their fists in the air. These young airmen and NCOs are the heart and soul of the military—they are the heroes.

After takeoff, Surgeon and I refueled over the Adriatic Sea, and then flew south of Montenegro into Albania. The rugged terrain reminded me of the Rocky Mountains in early spring, when the peaks are still dusted with snow. Looking down onto Albania and Macedonia, I could see the orange terra-cotta tiles that cover the roofs of the local houses and other buildings. As we flew closer, Surgeon pointed out the numerous refugee camps scattered along the border of Macedonia and Kosovo. After seeing these camps from the air, I realized that no one can get an accurate feeling of how many people fled Kosovo by watching CNN—even on a 32-inch Zenith.

"Fence-in," Surgeon called to me. I set my switches to arm my weapons and self-protection systems.

"Gunhog One-One, SA-6 at Derringer is active." That call was made by the NAEW controller as we moved into Kosovo to warn us of the active SAM site.

Surgeon replied that he copied the information about the SA-6 site near the city of Pristina being active and pointed out artillery sites that had already been bombed. The scorched craters looked like black stars painted on the ground. The countryside was breathtaking in its beauty and ruin. I could not find one house with an intact roof.

We started searching for targets in an area that intel had said the Serbs were using as a vehicle-refueling point. Surgeon put me in a high-cover position as he scanned the area for the refueling point. My job was to keep an eye out for AAA or SAMs fired at our formation. I continually rolled up to check beneath our jets and change my heading. While I was in a right-hand turn looking out the right side of my cockpit, I saw something flash on the ground. I was in the perfect location to catch the morning sun's reflected glint off the windshields of two west-facing parked trucks.

I called Surgeon on our FM radio and told him what I saw. He asked that I give him a talk-on, so I described the area around the trucks. He could not break out the vehicles and wanted to make sure we were both looking at the same place before we dropped our CBUs. He told me that he was going to roll in with the gun, and I realized that this game was real.

Surgeon squeezed off a healthy burst of 30 mm bullets that hit just to the west of the trucks. As he pulled off target I focused on the ground, ready to call break to Surgeon should the Serbs start firing. Surgeon pumped out four self-protection flares when he pulled off, and the bright red flares contrasted with the muted greens and browns of the background.

I told Surgeon where his bullets hit compared to where I had seen the trucks. He told me that he was going to roll in with his CBU. He entered a 45-degree dive-bomb pass, pickled, and pulled off; his bomblets also hit just west of the trucks. He climbed back to altitude and told me to set up for a rip-2 pass with my CBU-87.

I checked and rechecked my switches. My fuzing was set, and I had green ready lights. I checked my bomb-pass parameters one more time and then committed myself to the attack. "Two's in," I called and then started my roll in, accelerating towards the ground.

"Two, come off dry to the south," Surgeon called me off. I broke off my pass, pulled out of my dive, started my climb to the south, and began punching out flares. My heart was racing. What did I do wrong?

Surgeon told me that he wanted me to roll in from the southwest to avoid the SA-6 that was active to our northwest. When I reached altitude, I checked my switches one last time. Now I was nervous. This would be the fourth pass on the same target. Everything that I'd read and heard from experienced guys said to never hang around a target too long. How long was too long?

I cracked my wings and rolled down the chute. I was completely focused on those two trucks. The lime green pipper slowly tracked up my HUD; I pickled and felt the thumps of the munitions leaving my jet. G forces pushed me heavily into my seat as I pulled hard on the stick during my safe-escape maneuver. I climbed, pumped out flares, and changed my heading so that I could look back over my shoulder to watch for my impacts. The bomblets covered an area as big as a football field, and in the middle of all the sparkles I saw a large, orange flash.

"Did you see that Two?"

"Affirm."

"Those are secondaries."

"Two copies."

Surgeon set up for another attack while I held in a high-cover position. He rolled in and dropped his second CBU on the target. A thick, black column of smoke started to form. We moved on to western Kosovo.

Surgeon called the FAC covering the west side of the KEZ to see if he had any targets for us. Surgeon stressed that we had four Maverick missiles left. He really wanted to shoot a Maverick on his last combat sortie here. But the FAC didn't have any targets and we were low on gas, so we headed home.

As we left Kosovo, Surgeon told me to look back at the target area we had worked. I rolled my wings and pulled the nose of my jet around to get a better view. From 20 miles away I could see the dark column of smoke reaching up to the sky. No one could have survived all that.

That was the first of my 18 sorties in Kosovo and typical of what it took to find and kill two fuel trucks. I became a flight lead a few rides later and flew most of my sorties as an AFAC. As such, I had to follow the ROEs closely, a requirement that continued to frustrate us throughout the campaign. We had to call Italy for CAOC approval to attack targets if they were within so many miles of the border of Albania or Macedonia. The ROEs put most vehicles off limits, and only those painted army green were considered valid targets. When those two ROEs were established, ABCCC repeatedly broadcast the detailed restrictions in the clear over an unsecure radio. Afterwards, we saw hundreds of white and yellow vehicles driving throughout Kosovo every day. The Serbs had to have been laughing at us while they shook those cans of spray paint.

We routinely located valid military targets, and called the CAOC for permission to hit them, only to be denied by a director sitting in Italy. I still do not understand why we had to get that clearance to drop on a target in Kosovo. A brigadier general and former CAOC director during OAF tried to explain it to me once in the Officers' Club bar at Nellis. He had served as a colonel during OAF and been promoted six months after the conflict.

I had asked him, "Sir, did you guys plot the target coordinates we passed on 1:50 or 1:250 maps?" I used this question to try to understand how he, in Italy, developed his judgment on those targets. The 1:50 scale maps that AFACs carried in Kosovo were extremely detailed. Plus, I had a beautiful view of the target from my cockpit. He said that they had used 1:250s, maps that I knew showed much less detail.

I continued, "So, sir, why did you guys deny us clearance to hit some of those targets?"

He responded, "Well you need to understand the politics of the war. Do you really think striking that one target would have mattered in the overall campaign?" Then the recently promoted general added, "It really would not have mattered."

I stared into my drink in astonishment. So he knew it didn't matter. Great, I thought, soon he'll get promoted again and will be one of the leaders for the next war.

"Sir, the next time we send our boys into combat to get shot at, we better make sure that it matters." I refused to stand there and listen to his doublespeak. I walked away and ordered another drink.

From Wingman to Flight Lead

1st Lt Stu "Co" Martin

I began Operation Allied Force as an experienced wingman—I finished it as an inexperienced two-ship flight lead. I had developed a complete and utter confidence in the capabilities of the A-10 during the one and one-half years I had flown the Hog. However, I often thought that we were not very realistic with our expectations for the airframe during peacetime training. My OAF experience opened my eyes and provided insights that increased my love for, and confidence in, the Hog.

The OAF conflict was not what I expected. I had previously flown medium-altitude sorties over war-torn Bosnia, so it came as no surprise when we employed under many of the same constraints. Those constraints, such as having to AFAC and employ weapons from medium altitude, led to the predictable difficulty in identifying and destroying tactical-sized targets. What I did not expect was that the ROEs would change on a daily basis and that tactical decision making would be taken out of the cockpit and given to someone in the CAOC—hundreds of miles from the AOR. The cumulative effect was that these constraints frustrated our ability to kill enemy targets that we badly wanted to destroy. In retrospect, our operations seemed to reflect more political than military considerations. That was frustrating for everyone involved— because we were capable of so much more.

For me, the war began in earnest after our departure from Aviano AB. In the beginning, our flying was constrained by the A-10's limited mission taskings and bad weather. My last mission at Aviano was typical of our frustration. I flew over 10 hours, tanked four or five times, and brought home all my bombs because of bad weather in the AOR. After the decision was made to move our A-10s to Gioia del Colle in southern Italy, a quick look at the map made me smile. It would take only half an hour to fly from Gioia, across the Adriatic, and into the AOR. Finally, we could spend the lion's share of our time finding targets and not droning back and forth to Aviano.

I arrived in advance of the main party, only to find a bare base with an old dormitory that would serve as our operations section. All we were able to accomplish during the 24 hours prior to the arrival of the squadron was to break down all the bunk beds to make room for furniture and equipment—items that weren't there and that we didn't own. In spite of that, the 81st was flying combat sorties within 48 hours of deploying to southern Italy. Our experiences were often surreal. We would fly, attack targets, and get shot at. Then only hours later, we would be at the Truck Stop, drinking vino and eating pasta. On "English night" we would even watch a movie at the local theater. Every once and awhile, you'd stop and think about the weird and incongruous aspects of our lives.

Mission Check

A war was being fought. Nevertheless, the peacetime administrative routine continued—much to my surprise. I flew my mission-qual check ride over Kosovo with Lt Col Kimos Haave, our squadron commander. I flew as his wingman and remembered going into the brief thinking, "Cool, don't get shot down, Stu, and you should pass this ride." I realized that Kimos was going to apply peacetime check ride criteria about halfway through the brief. Therefore he would need to see me drop bombs or shoot something—and I might have to hit the target using CBU-87s for the first time. In retrospect, I think it made sense. I also realized that I might not complete the check because on more than one occasion I had returned with all my ordnance due to a lack of viable targets or bad weather. Finding targets in the AOR seemed to be either feast or famine. On some days, we'd drop all our bombs, shoot the gun, and, if the right target came along, launch a Maverick. Other times, we'd fly back with all our ordnance since A-10s rarely ever hit "dump" targets. I felt better bringing back my ordnance knowing that, on a later date, I could drop it on the skull of some town-burning Serb.

I signed out at the ops desk and learned that I'd be flying aircraft 992; that jet had my name painted on the nose, and I was immensely proud of her. I thought she was the best in the fleet—a status due mostly to the efforts of her crew chief, SSgt Donny Trostle. Don wasn't there when I arrived at the jet, but no matter; she had been code-one for the past 15 sorties. I knew that she could safely carry me through harm's way. Preflight, taxi, and takeoff were normal, but I remember thinking how sluggish the controls seemed as we lumbered into the warm morning air. The two CBUs were roughly the same weight as four Mk-82s, a load I was familiar with; however, the CBUs had the aerodynamics of two barn doors, produced considerable drag, and significantly degraded the aircraft's flying characteristics.

Once we entered the KEZ, the search for targets began. Kimos was given a target area that included a factory complex constructed of red brick in southeastern Serbia between Presevo and Vranje. Using his binos, he spotted three tanks lined up in the factory's parking lot and rolled in for a medium-altitude Maverick attack. Unlike a real tank, this target disintegrated when the Maverick hit it. Kimos concluded that the tank was a decoy and that the factory complex was likely producing decoys. He then directed me to set up for a CBU attack on the western end of the factory complex, which also contained mortar positions and lighter vehicles. I knew from studying CBU ballistics that I could get a HUD solution only if I bombed with a tailwind. The winds were strong out of the west, so I set up and rolled down the chute from west-northwest. I say "rolled down the chute," but at our gross weights and altitudes we did not have the thrust or aerodynamic authority to do much more than smoothly coax the jet to fall to the correct dive angle. With my pipper on the target and at the desired combination of altitude, dive angle, and airspeed, I hammered down on the pickle button and felt the familiar clunk of ordnance being released. However, something wasn't right—I felt only one clunk. Sure enough, only one can of CBU came off, and my other station was still showing a "green ready." Since my thumb was still on the pickle button, I knew it had to be an aircraft malfunction. I initiated my safe-escape maneuver and began the climb back to altitude. Much to my chagrin, the CBU hit well short of the target. I discussed the problem with Kimos, and we decided that I should check all of my switches and try to deliver it one more time. I rolled down the chute and pickled on the target, but nothing came off the jet. With the end of our vul time approaching, Kimos decided to attack the target with his CBUs. Those, unfortunately, also hit extremely short of the target. We then departed the KEZ for home.

I had a "hung" CBU, and, depending on the circumstances, I would either land with it or attempt to jettison it over the Adriatic. The weather for the approach and landing was good. The CBU appeared secure on an inboard station and did not pose a problem for landing. We decided that I would land with it. I flew a straight-in approach with Kimos flying chase to monitor the CBU and warn me of any problems he might detect. The landing was uneventful, but Kimos later told me that he was relieved when I touched down and the CBU didn't fall off. A subsequent inspection reveled that the ejection carts had correctly fired when I had attempted to release the CBUs. However, during much recent use, some cart-generated car-

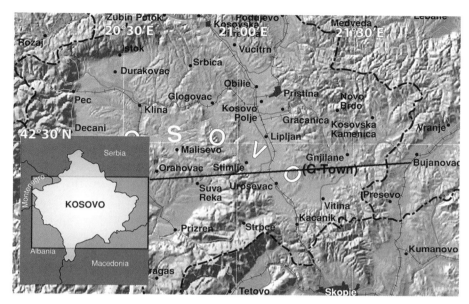

Location of tank decoys between Presevo and Vranje

bon had been deposited on the mechanical linkage and ejector orifices. Those carts' hot gas would normally be used to overcome the forces required to open the two mechanical suspension hooks and release the CBUs. When I had hammered down on the pickle button, a firing pulse had been generated; the ejection carts had fired, but the generated gas pressure had been insufficient to open the hooks and release the CBU. Nonetheless, Don Trostle never forgave me for "breaking" our jet and ruining 992's streak of flawless performances.

During the debrief Kimos voiced his disappointment with our bombing. However, he admitted he couldn't very well downgrade me on my bombing accuracy when both of our CBUs had hit short. We reviewed the tape, and everything appeared normal with both of us pickling on the target. I discussed the problem with Maj Goldie Haun, our weapons officer. He stated that anomalies in our bombing computer's algorithms often cause CBUs to hit short when bombing with a strong tailwind—we had 70 knots at altitude.

295

4 June 1999

Capt Scott R. "Hummer" Cerone, a member of the 74th FS out of Pope AFB, and I were paired up for a mission. Hummer and I had gone through our initial introduction to fighter fundamentals and the A-10 replacement training unit courses together. In addition, we both recently had pinned on captain rank and passed our flight-lead check rides on the same day, 31 May 1999. Hummer was an AFAC, so according to the rules, he was the only one in our flight qualified to pick out and direct strikes on targets. We decided that I would be the flight lead for the sortie. I would give him the tactical lead in the KEZ so that he could find targets and comply with the ATO. We were young flight leads and flew that day with our "fangs out"—happy to be flying on our own and not with some older, more staid member of the squadron.

Hummer and I got a handoff from an excited Foghorn who had apparently located 12 APCs in a field. Foghorn talked louder than ever over the radios and was hair-on-fire as he departed for gas. When Hummer and I arrived, we looked for something other than bales of hay. We used binos and our Mavericks but finally asked an F-14 AFAC to recce the area with his pod—all with no luck. Hummer and I gave up on those targets and proceeded to an area north of D-Town. We dropped our Mk-82s on some small revets before I spotted a large revet, which I was convinced contained an arty piece. I talked Hummer's eyes onto it and got clearance from him to launch one of my Mavericks. I hammered down, and the Maverick hit the target less than 30 seconds later. Hummer, unfortunately, lost the missile at burnout, from his viewing angle he thought the Maverick had "gone stupid" and had flown towards the west. I guess he was trying to see if it hit northern Pristina, probably thinking, "How are we gonna explain this one!" I got his eyes back into the target area, but for a few minutes I was unsure whether he had actually cleared me to hit that target. We talked about a possible miscommunication during our debrief but, with some map study, became convinced that we had been looking at the same target. Later that year, after I had been reassigned to the 74th FS, I ran into

Hummer at Pope. He kiddingly said, "We both had hit 'bags of dirty diapers' that day."

6 June 1999

Hummer and I were paired again. After checking in with all the appropriate agencies, we entered the KEZ and proceeded to an area north of D-Town. We got a handoff from an F-14 AFAC who was trying to talk a flight of Hogs (Corvette 71) onto several APCs that he had located with his targeting pod. We called contact on the targets, and the F-14 departed. Hummer told me he was going to use his binoculars to visually ID these targets. With Corvette 71 flight orbiting to the north, Hummer took a couple of laps around the field. After a minute of silence, he came over the radio and told me he'd cover me while I got a visual: "Tell me what you see down there."

In a less than a minute it became obvious to me that the APCs were actually a red car and a white pickup truck. I told Hummer what I saw, and he agreed. Hummer then did a lower pass, confirmed that the targets were invalid, and sent the other Hogs home.

During the rest of the sortie, JSTARS personnel had us on a wild-goose chase, trying to talk us onto a convoy they believed to be in a creek bed south of Pec. For 20 minutes, we unsuccessfully tried to find the vehicles corresponding to the radar contacts that an increasingly frustrated controller so clearly saw on his scope. As we exited the AOR, I pointed out to Hummer that Pec was burning. We learned later from the news that the peace talks had stalled and that the Serbs were buying time as they withdrew. A few of this mission's remarkable events have now become some of my most enduring memories.

Epilogue

Lt Col Chris "Kimos" Haave

The personal stories in this book are reflective of the challenges, frustrations, and triumphs experienced by dedicated warriors—combatants who exhibited human emotions as they did their best in the crucible of combat. We wrote this book with the humble understanding that our success in OAF was built on the contributions and sacrifices of aviation giants. Those giants—pilots, maintainers, and support personnel— faced greater personal discomfort and family sacrifice during their service in Korea, Vietnam, and the Persian Gulf than we did during OAF. The heroes that today's A-10 community holds high include the Raven, Misty, and Nail FACs, as well as the Sandy CSAR warriors of previous wars.

Our objective in this book was to help document the A-10's contributions to achieving US, NATO, and UN objectives in Kosovo. The primary application of force in the KEZ flowed through the AFAC's direct control of all NATO's attack missions, which helped terminate Serb ethnic cleansing and defeat the Serbian Third Army in the field—one of Slobodan Milosevic's main centers of gravity. In OAF's charged international environment, combat operations were complicated by many diverse political concerns, which led to our units' being constrained by numerous and ever-changing operational limitations. In spite of that, skilled and experienced A-10 pilots— with hundreds of hours spent looking at the ground—demonstrated their ability to discern what was actually going on in the hills, trees, and villages of Kosovo. We are convinced that the A-10 made a significant contribution to defeating the Serbs on the ground in Kosovo.

The level of tactical information available to the operational and strategic decision makers reached an all-time high in OAF. This book recounted a few of the countless times the CAOC actively participated in the decision to attack individual targets. On some of those occasions, AFACs found and positively identified groups of moving targets and requested CAOC approval to attack. All too often, by the time the approval came, the targets had found sanctuary in the forests or villages. The increasing use of data links and unmanned air and space reconnaissance vehicles (such as Predator) has made much real-time information available to command-level staffs and has fueled the temptation to direct even individual attacks. One last OAF story follows as an example.

The operator of a Predator on station over Kosovo located a tank and simultaneously transmitted its video image to the CAOC at Vicenza, Italy, and to SHAPE headquarters in Mons, Belgium. Both Lt Gen Mike Short and Gen Wesley Clark were able to watch this tank in real time while personnel in the CAOC attempted to help the AFAC visually acquire the tank by relaying directions through the ABCCC.

General Short's son, Capt Chris "Junior" Short, was an 81st FS flight commander and the AFAC on duty at that location. The Predator's optics provided a highly magnified image of the tank, but one with a very narrow field of view—similar to what one would see through a soda straw. Unfortunately, Junior had a very wide field of view from his ROE altitude. The officer in the CAOC had difficulty relating the Predator image to what Junior could see. Junior could not find the tank. General Clark called the CAOC to make sure they understood that he wanted the tank killed. The CAOC called ABCCC to ensure that Junior understood that the CAOC wanted the tank dead. Junior still couldn't find it. Finally, to put more pressure on Junior, ABCCC transmitted, "[General Short's call sign] really wants you to find and kill that tank." Junior replied, "Tell Dad I can't find the [expletive deleted] tank!"

The ability to prevail and achieve a favorable political outcome in future warfare is critical. In a highly integrated joint and coalition environment, success in asymmetric warfare will likely depend on the ability of flexible and capable offensive airpower to control the ground situation from the air. One of the command and control difficulties in that environment will be the development and application of appropriate ROEs in the rapidly changing tactical, strategic, and political environment. While many of these factors contributed to the complexity of the air campaign over Kosovo, OAF was not the most problematic of possible scenarios. Its complexity would have been greatly exacerbated had friendly troops been mixed with civilians in contact with the Serb Third Army and in need of air support. In future conflicts, these and other considerations could combine with real-time battlefield reconnaissance and lead to an increased desire by higher echelons of command to inappropriately control fluid tactical situations. Our hope is that future air and space leaders will resist that temptation and choose to provide clear, centralized guidance that will enable the tactical war fighters to achieve our political leaders' objectives through decentralized execution.

Hog folks remain a humble breed of fighter jocks and wrench-turners in a high-tech Air Force where standoff munitions, computer-released weapons, laser- and GPS-guided munitions, advanced medium range air-to-air missiles (AMRAAM), drones, and sophisticated electronic warfare are the norm. They don't mind hearing the thousandth joke about the lack of speed and sophistication of the A-10; they just quietly go out and make a difference in the air and on the ground. We believe that the A-10 Warthog and its highly trained professionals offer the nation a robust ground-attack capability that can rapidly adapt to the challenges, threats, and objectives in a joint and coalition combat environment. We hope that Air Force leaders remain committed to such a capability and support regular and appropriate weapon-system upgrades for this aircraft. The nation needs warriors—like those who fly the A-10—warriors who are able to search the battlefield with the Mk-1 eyeball, locate the aggressor and the victims, go toe-to-toe with the enemy, look him squarely in the eye, and shoot with malice.

Appendix

History of Attacking Fielded Forces:
Post-Vietnam to Kosovo

Lt Col Phil "Goldie" Haun

From World War I, through our Vietnam experience, and up to our recent past, the idea of interdiction has remained fairly consistent and is reflected in the latest version of Air Force Doctrine Document (AFDD) 1, *Air Force Basic Doctrine*, 1 September 1997, which defines interdiction as "operations to divert, disrupt, delay, or destroy the enemy's surface military potential before it can be used effectively against friendly forces."[1] An amended definition of air interdiction has evolved in the USAF as an outcome of the combat experience of Operation Allied Force over Kosovo in 1999; that evolution is reflected in AFDD 2-1.3, *Counterland*, 27 August 1999, which expands the scope to include both lethal and nonlethal systems, stating that "air interdiction . . . is employed to destroy, disrupt, divert, or delay the enemy's surface military potential before it can effectively engage friendly forces, *or otherwise achieve its objectives* [emphasis added]."[2] The phrase "or otherwise achieve its objectives" acknowledges that airpower, as demonstrated over Kosovo, can be used in the "direct attack" of an army without the presence or foreseeable presence of friendly ground forces. The attack of fielded enemy ground forces by airpower is an old concept, but the idea that airpower can achieve military objectives in lieu of ground action is a new and highly controversial idea.

This appendix will first review the USAF's post-Vietnam experience in the direct attack of enemy fielded forces as envisioned in the AirLand Battle doctrine developed during the 1980s, and as experienced by the USAF in attacking the Iraqi Republican Guard in the Gulf War. It will then examine the events leading to the use of A-10 AFACs over Kosovo in directly attacking the Serbian Third Army. Finally, this appendix will give a brief history of A-10 operations in Operation Allied

Force, which the reader can use along with the chronology, at the front, to provide context to this book's various stories.

As with the Korean War, many of the lessons learned about air interdiction in Vietnam were lost, including the evolution of the Misty FAC's Fast-FAC mission. The focus of the US military turned once again towards Europe and the continuing threat of invasion by the Soviet Union. From the late '70s and through the '80s, the US Army and Air Force worked to develop systems such as the Apache, air tactical missile systems (ATACMS), A-10, and JSTARS in preparation to defeat the Red Army. Air-Land Battle doctrine provided the joint vision for integrating air and land operations. Air interdiction was an essential element of AirLand Battle and a NATO term, *battlefield air interdiction* (BAI), was adopted to emphasize the interdiction of second-echelon ground forces moving towards, but not yet engaged with, friendly ground forces.[3] The high-threat environment of Central Europe and the plethora of targets that would arise from a massive land battle limited the potential effectiveness of Fast FACs. The detection of rear-echelon forces would be the responsibility of such systems as JSTARS—not a difficult task, considering the wave of Soviet armor anticipated to thunder down the Fulda Gap. NATO aircrews studied X-ray, Yankee, and Zulu folders containing imagery and maps of the routes the Red Army would need to use.[4] They likewise flew missions over West Germany, up to the inter-German border, to become familiar with the terrain over which they would have to fight.

The fall of the Berlin Wall in November of 1989 and the end of the Cold War left the United States victorious but lacking a Soviet threat on which to base its military force structure and Air-Land Battle doctrine. As the United States began to dismantle its forces in Europe, the focus shifted abruptly to Southwest Asia and the Iraqi invasion of Kuwait on 2 August 1990.

Attacking the Republican Guard

On 17 January 1991, the United States and coalition forces launched the Gulf War air offensive. Waves of aircraft flooded into Kuwait and Iraq, attacking key integrated air defense system nodes; airfields; command and control systems; nuclear, biological, and chemical (NBC) sites; and electric plants.[5] Daybreak of the first day witnessed the commencement of attacks against Iraqi ground forces in Kuwait. Among the centers of gravity identified by Gen H. Norman Schwarzkopf, the US joint forces commander, were the seven elite Republican Guard divisions held in reserve along the Iraq-Kuwait border.[6] While aerial attack continued against key strategic targets in Iraq, 75 percent of strike missions focused on the Iraqi ground forces in Kuwait.[7]

US casualties in a ground invasion were predicted to be as high as 15,000.[8] Concern over this possibility prompted Secretary of Defense Richard B. "Dick" Cheney, Gen Colin L. Powell, and Gen H. Norman Schwarzkopf to develop a strategy emphasizing the use of airpower before a ground battle to significantly reduce the size of the Iraqi army, its capability to maneuver, and its will to fight. This air-first strategy proved highly successful, with friendly casualty rates below even the most optimistic estimates and friendly ground forces achieving objectives ahead of schedule and against only limited Iraqi resistance. However, this aerial achievement was not accomplished without major modifications to existing tactics.

The Gulf War air offensive consisted of three phases, conducted nearly simultaneously. Phases one and two were directed against strategic and air-superiority target sets including leadership, command and control facilities, NBC facilities, airfields, aircraft, and the IADS. Phase three targeted Iraqi fielded forces, calling for 50 percent attrition of Iraq's 5,000 pieces of dug-in armor and artillery prior to any ground offensive.[9] In this phase, Schwarzkopf was most concerned with the three heavy divisions of the seven Republican Guard divisions along the Kuwait-Iraq border.[10] These units were widely dispersed and well dug in with thousands of earthen berms protecting their T-72 tanks.[11] Their defenses included AAA, infrared SA-13 SAMs, and radar-guided SA-6 SAMs.

Phase three required the unprecedented success of airpower against a fielded army.[12] A briefing by Brig Gen Buster C. Glosson, air-planning chief, to Schwarzkopf in December 1990 estimated that the Republican Guard would suffer 50 percent attrition in only five days, assuming 600 sorties a day.[13] Air planners divided Kuwait and Iraq into a grid pattern of 30 by 30 NM squares known as "kill boxes." Strike aircraft were assigned individual kill boxes to perform armed reconnaissance in locating and destroying Iraqi forces.[14] The task of attacking the elite Republican Guard fell to F-16s and B-52s, while A-10s were employed against the regular Iraqi divisions dug in along the Kuwait-Saudi border.[15]

By the fifth day of phase three, coalition air attacks against the Republican Guard were still far short of the 50 percent destruction expected by Schwarzkopf.[16] Postwar analysis indicated that the Republican Guard's heavy-division armor actually suffered only 24–34 percent attrition during the entire 38 days of the air campaign.[17] Glosson's five-day estimate proved overly optimistic for two reasons. First, the number of sorties flown against the Republican Guard fell well short of 600 per day. A combination of initial overemphasis on phase one strategic operations, a reluctance to employ A-10s deep into the battlespace, and unanticipated Scud-hunting missions reduced the number of sorties available to attack the Republican Guard. For the first five days, total strikes against Republican Guard units were constant at around 100 missions per day. By the end of the 10th day, a cumulative sortie count against the Republican Guard totaled 728 missions.[18] Second, air attacks were not as effective as war-gaming analysis had predicted.[19] The aircrews of US aircraft used medium-altitude tactics to reduce the threat from Iraqi air defenses. While this greatly improved survivability, US pilots had trained with low-altitude tactics appropriate to a war in central Europe and were relatively unfamiliar with medium-altitude tactics. Unforeseen difficulties with target identification, poor weather, and inaccuracies in delivering ballistic weapons from medium altitude all reduced effectiveness.

Increasing the number of sorties against the Republican Guard solved the first issue. However, the tactical problem of how to best destroy a dug in army remained. In response, the joint air operations center (JAOC) incorporated three changes to improve the efficiency of the operational air forces. The first tactic involved directing the unique firepower of the A-10 against exposed and vulnerable Republican Guard forces. On 27 February, Glosson instructed A-10 commanders to prepare an attack on the Republican Guard Tawakalna armored division.[20] Facing such a heavily defended force, A-10s flew 48 aircraft in six waves of eight-ship formations, instead of their usual two-ship tactics. Three days of such wing-sized attacks were mounted against the division. The Iraqis responded by stepping up their deception efforts and by digging their forces even deeper into the desert sand. Although the US Army was unable to assess the effectiveness of allied attacks, the Tawakalna division's degraded air defenses and increased use of decoys were considered positive indicators.[21]

The second innovation was the F-111F's introduction of "tank plinking." Targets could be located and attacked from medium altitude with infrared targeting pods and laser-guided bombs.[22] The pods could clearly distinguish the infrared image of the warm Iraqi armor against the cold desert background.[23] This method provided the additional advantage of using targeting-pod video to verify successful attacks and boost BDA estimates.

The final tactical innovation reintroduced the Fast FAC mission. F-16CG (Block 40s) from Hill AFB, Utah, began flying as "Killer Scouts."[24] This innovation mirrored the Misty FAC hunter-killer tactics during Vietnam but was renamed to avoid confusion with hunter-killer SEAD tactics currently used by F-4G Wild Weasels and F-16s. Killer Scouts took off early and reconnoitered their assigned kill boxes. They were allocated sufficient air-refueling tankers to remain on station for long periods to become familiar with the territory and increase their situational awareness. Like the Misty FACs, the Killer Scouts carried a minimum munitions load to reduce drag and increase endurance. When they identified Iraqi positions, they usually brought in F-16 strikers for the attack. Along with identifying viable target areas for attack, they also assisted in the collection of BDA. To do that, the Killer Scouts relied primarily on their own eyes, aided somewhat by binoculars. Unfortunately, operating at medium altitude made it difficult to accurately determine the number of targets destroyed. The Killer Scout role had its limitations, but this innovation led to the more efficient use of F-16s against Iraqi fielded forces.

Following the Gulf War, the USAF remained deployed in Southwest Asia, maintained two no-fly zones over Iraq, and responded to sporadic infringements by Saddam Hussein's remaining forces. Elsewhere, the dissolution of Yugoslavia and the Bosnian Serbs' ethnic cleansing of Muslims in April of 1992 led to the US military's involvement with the UN peacekeeping force in Bosnia. Meanwhile famine in war-torn Somalia brought a US military presence to Mogadishu from December 1992 until its hasty withdrawal in May of 1994. In September of 1995, US airpower was again needed. This time Operation Deliberate Force, an 11-day campaign, helped force Serbia to accept the Dayton Peace Accords.[25] By the late '90s, NATO was convinced that airpower was an effective tool to coerce Slobodan Milosevic, the Serbian president, and that it might be needed to solve the growing unrest in Kosovo.

Kosovo: Direct Attack of the Serbian Third Army

Tensions between Belgrade and Kosovo increased during the late 1980s. Slobodan Milosevic used protests by minority Serbs residing in the ethnically Albanian-dominated province as the foundation for his Serbian nationalist platform and his subsequent rise to the Serbian presidency in 1987.[26] By 1989, Belgrade had revoked Kosovo's status as an autonomous region and placed restrictions on land ownership and government jobs for Kosovo Albanians.[27] During the 1990s, Kosovar dissension spawned a series of both violent and nonviolent protest.[28] Opposition became violent in 1997 with the formation of a small group of lightly armed guerrilla fighters known as the KLA. In response to KLA ambushes of Serbian police in early 1998, Serbian forces conducted brutal retaliatory attacks against suspected KLA positions.[29] KLA support swelled within Kosovo and led to an escalation of KLA activity. In July of 1998, Serbian forces conducted a village-by-village search for KLA members, displacing over 200,000 Kosovars in the process.[30] The magnitude of the humanitarian crisis captured the attention of the international community.

In response to the KLA and Serbian exchanges, the UN Security Council passed Resolution 1160 in March 1998 and Resolution 1199 in September 1998. The resolutions condemned Serbia's excessive use of force, established an arms embargo, and called for an immediate cease-fire and the introduction of international monitors.[31] The latter demand was met in the cease-fire negotiated between US envoys and Belgrade in October 1998.[32]

However, the massacre of 45 Kosovar Albanians at Racak on 19 January 1999 quickly brought the cease-fire to an end.[33] Under threat of NATO air strikes, Serbian and Kosovar representatives were summoned to Rambouillet, France, to negotiate a peace agreement.[34] The compromise included the key items of a NATO-led implementation force; the recognition of the international borders of the Former Republic of Yugoslavia, made up of Serbia, Montenegro, and Kosovo; and an interim three-year agreement, after which a final settlement of Kosovo could be arranged.[35] The Kosovar delegation initially refused to agree unless reference was made to a future referendum to decide the fate of Kosovo. Under the threat of the withdrawal of international support, including financial and military aid to the KLA, the Kosovar delegates reluctantly signed on 18 March 1999.[36] The Serbs, unwilling to accept a NATO-led military force within Kosovo, remained recalcitrant. In the face of diplomatic impasse, NATO air strikes were ordered to commence on 24 March.

Initial planning for NATO air strikes against Serbia began as early as June of 1998.[37] Targeting for the strikes focused on fixed command and control and military facilities in Kosovo, Montenegro, and Serbia. These targets were selected for a variety of reasons, one being the low risk of collateral damage.[38] The strikes were intended as the punishment portion of NATO's coercive carrot-and-stick strategy. The air plan in no way resembled a decisive air campaign, with the initial target list including only 100 targets.[39] Of these, only 50 were eventually approved, sufficient for only two or three nights of strikes.[40] Additionally, the desire to maintain consensus among the 19 NATO countries was reflected in the constrained nature of the strikes.

In February 1999, in the midst of the Rambouillet talks, Gen Wesley Clark, SACEUR, became concerned over the prospect of increased ethnic-cleansing operations by the Serbian army within Kosovo once NATO air operations commenced. Two of NATO's stated military objectives involved dealing directly with the Serbian fielded forces: to deter further

Serbian action against the Kosovars and to reduce the ability of the Serbian military to continue offensive operations against them.[41] Gen Wesley Clark ordered Lt Gen Mike Short, his CFACC, to increase the scope of air planning to include direct attacks on the Serbian fielded forces in Kosovo.

Concealed within the verdant, cloud-covered valley of Kosovo were 40,000 soldiers of the Serbian Third Army equipped with hundreds of tanks, APCs, and artillery pieces interspersed among over a million Kosovars. In addition, a wall of mobile, radar-guided SAMs, MANPADS, and AAA (as well as a squadron of MiG-21 fighters) protected the Third Army against NATO air forces.[42]

In developing air plans against the Serbian Third Army, US planners assumed air superiority and relied on SEAD and electronic jamming assets to confuse and degrade the Serbian IADS. Assuming strike aircraft could safely enter Kosovo, two tactical problems still remained: how to locate and identify the targets and how to attack them successfully while limiting collateral damage. A-10 AFACs trained in visual reconnaissance and ASC were selected for the task.[43] A-10 AFACs would search out targets identified by either JSTARS (in real-time) or by intelligence, surveillance, and reconnaissance (ISR) assets during pre-mission planning. Once targets were identified, the A-10 AFACs would control strikes using available NATO aircraft.

Beginning at 1900 Zulu on 24 March 1999, NATO air forces struck Serbian targets.[44] These attacks focused on the Serbian IADS, military command and control nodes, and airfields and aircraft.[45] NATO commenced the war with 214 dedicated combat aircraft, 112 of which were from the United States.[46] Initial NATO strikes were met with minimal resistance from Serbian SAMs and fighters. Rather, the primary response took place within Kosovo and was directed at the Kosovar population.

With the breakdown of the Rambouillet peace talks and subsequent withdrawal of international observers on 19 March 1999, Serb ground forces commenced the systematic expulsion of Kosovo's ethnic Albanians, code-named Operation Horseshoe.[47] Ethnic-cleansing operations were stepped up once NATO bombing began, leaving several hundred thousand

310

displaced refugees seeking safety in Albania and Macedonia or fleeing to the foothills within Kosovo.

Responding to the rapidly deteriorating situation within Kosovo, General Clark ordered General Short to commence attacks on Serbian fielded forces on 30 March. Poor weather delayed the first successful A-10 strikes until 6 April.[48] During OAF, A-10 AFACs flew over 1,000 missions and controlled many other strikers in the attacks on Serb forces in the KEZ. Their attacks ended on 9 June 1999, when a peace agreement was reached.

History of A-10s in Kosovo

A-10s first flew over the Balkans in 1993 when NATO aircraft began conducting air operations over Bosnia. Except for occasional relief provided by other Air Force, Reserve, and Guard A-10 units, the 81st FS maintained a continual presence at Aviano until 1997. The A-10s were the only NVG fighter aircraft capable of providing both day and night CAS and AFAC coverage for UN and NATO ground forces. F-16CG squadrons of the 31st Fighter Wing at Aviano were eventually trained to use NVGs and assumed most of the AFAC duties over Bosnia. With the continual presence of A-10s in the Balkans no longer required, the 81st needed only to conduct yearly deployments to Aviano to remain familiar with Balkan operations and provide AFAC coverage when the 31st FW was deployed elsewhere.

In January 1999, the 81st deployed six A-10s to replace an Aviano F-16CG squadron that had departed on a stateside deployment. The number of A-10s committed to Balkan operations continued to increase throughout OAF. With tensions rising in Kosovo following the Racak massacre, A-10s were ordered to remain at Aviano, and the squadron increased the number of aircraft to 15 by the commencement of NATO air strikes on 24 March. As the 81st deployed to Gioia del Colle AB in southern Italy, it reached 23 aircraft and leveled at that number. On 21 May, an additional 18 Air Force Reserve aircraft became operational at Trapani, Sicily, to bring the total to 41 A-10s supporting OAF.

A-10s were initially tasked with providing CSAR for NATO aircrews; A-10 pilots from the 81st FS, using Sandy call signs, were the mission commanders for the dramatic rescue of an F-117 pilot shot down near Belgrade on the fourth night of strikes. A-10s provided on-scene command, tracked the survivor's location, coordinated the rescue effort, and provided cover for rescue helicopters during the ingress, survivor pickup, and egress of enemy territory.

Sandy was the call sign for A-1E Skyraiders that performed on-scene command of CSARs during Vietnam. A-10s have continued to use the Sandy call sign to signify the type of mission being conducted. A-10 Sandys provided CSAR coverage for all NATO aircraft flying over Kosovo and Serbia, both day and night, throughout OAF.

On 26 March, the CAOC notified the 81st to commence AFAC missions on 30 March. Although all NATO air strikes to this point had taken place at night, a shortage of EA-6B jammers and F-16CJ SEAD aircraft prevented adding any AFAC day missions since all conventional fighter and bomber aircraft operating in Serbia or Kosovo were required to have jamming and SEAD support. NATO's limiting factor was EA-6B and F-16CJ airframes—not aircrews; the solution was to double-turn SEAD aircraft to support AFAC missions during the day and strike missions at night. Launching from Aviano, A-10s flew sorties of six to seven hours down the Adriatic, across Albania and up into Kosovo. Low-level clouds over Kosovo prevented aerial attacks until 6 April, when A-10 AFACs located and struck a Serbian truck park; that strike was followed by two more successful days of attacking convoys of Serbian tanks and APCs.

The excessive en route time from Aviano to Kosovo reduced the A-10's time on station and prevented an air frame from flying two daylight missions per day. Fifteen days into the war, the CAOC ordered the 81st FS to redeploy to Gioia. On 11 April 1999, the jets from Aviano were joined in the move by an additional three aircraft from Spangdahlem. At Gioia, the sortie-duration times were reduced, on-station times were increased, and the jets could fly two daylight missions per day. A detachment from the 74th FS at Pope arrived in late April with five aircraft, nine pilots, and 65 maintenance personnel to augment 81st FS operations. A British GR-7 Harrier squadron, an Italian Tornado squadron, and an Italian F-104 Starfighter squadron were also located at Gioia. The Harriers flew as strike aircraft for A-10 AFACs on a daily basis, and the proximity of operations made for a close working relationship.

A-10 AFAC operations at Gioia commenced within 24 hours of arrival. With the growing success of strikes against their Third Army, the Serbs increased their active air defenses. A-10 AFACs began reporting barrage-fired AAA and SAM launches. On 2 May, an A-10 AFAC was struck by an SA-14 infrared-guided SAM and was forced to recover at Skopje AB, Macedonia. On 11 May, another A-10 AFAC was struck beneath the cockpit by a mobile SAM; fortunately, that missile failed to detonate, and the jet was able to recover to Gioia.

AFAC operations over Kosovo grew to cover most of the day and half of the night. A-10s covered two four-hour daylight windows, all the while maintaining four aircraft on CSAR alert during night operations. F-16CG AFACs provided some day coverage and also flew during a two- to three-hour night window. The US Navy provided day AFAC coverage as well with F-14s flying off the USS *Theodore Roosevelt*. Even more AFACs were needed to provide full coverage—24 hours a day, seven days a week—over Kosovo. The Air National Guard then stepped in to create the 104th EOG, a rainbowed group of 18 aircraft from units in Michigan, Massachusetts, and Idaho. By 19 May, the 104th had deployed to Trapani AB in western Sicily. The lengthy trip from Trapani to the KEZ precluded the 104th from being able to double-turn for day missions, but it was able to cover a midday AFAC window and then turn for late-night missions. Additionally, the 104th deployed three of its aircraft to Taszar, Hungary, in May to perform CSAR alert, thus improving the CSAR response time in the event of a shootdown over northern Serbia. The final aircraft to join the AFAC mission was the US Marine F/A-18D. A full squadron joined the 104th CSAR detachment at Taszar, and these aircraft were flying over Kosovo by late May.

Late May proved the most successful period for air attacks against Serb ground forces. Several factors influenced that

313

success and combined to provide a greater opportunity for NATO air attacks. Those factors included an increased force structure, improved weather conditions, and a KLA offensive in western Kosovo that forced the Serbian Third Army out of its hiding places. NATO increased the number of AFACs and strikers for near-continuous daylight operations until combat operations ceased on 10 June 1999. A-10s continued to provide airborne and ground CAS alert until the end of June as NATO occupation ground forces entered Kosovo.

Notes

1. Air Force Doctrine Document (AFDD) 1, *Air Force Basic Doctrine*, 1 September 1997, 50.

2. AFDD 2-1.3, *Counterland*, 27 August 1999, 31.

3. Lt Gen Tony McPeak, "TACAIR Missions and the Fire Support Coordination Line," *Air University Review*, September–October 1985, 70.

4. X-ray, Yankee, and Zulu are the military pronunciations for the letters X, Y, and Z, respectively.

5. Thomas A. Keaney and Eliot A. Cohen, *Gulf War Air Power Survey, Summary Report* (Washington, D.C.: Office of the Secretary of the Air Force, 1993), 12.

6. H. Norman Schwarzkopf and Peter Petre, *It Doesn't Take a Hero: General H. Norman Schwarzkopf, the Autobiography* (New York: Bantam, 1992), 371.

7. Keaney and Cohen, 65.

8. Gen Colin L. Powell with Joseph E. Persico, *My American Journey* (New York: Random House, 1995), 498.

9. Keaney and Cohen, 48–51.

10. Lt Col William F. Andrews, *Airpower against an Army: Challenge and Response in CENTAF's Duel with the Republican Army* (Maxwell Air Force Base [AFB], Ala.: Air University Press, 1998), 14.

11. National Training Center Handbook 100-91, *The Iraqi Army: Organization and Tactics*, 1991, 25–31.

12. Keaney and Cohen, 51.

13. Ibid., 49.

14. Keaney and Cohen, vol. 5, A Statistical Compendium and Chronology, pt. 1, 463–539.

15. Andrews, 29. Air Force assets were not the only air assets attacking fielded forces. Carrier-based strikers, including F/A-18s, also attacked fielded forces; however, they did not begin to attack the Republican Guard in earnest until a week after the air war had started.

16. Lt Col Christopher P. Weggeman, F-16 pilot with 388th TFW flying the Killer Scout mission against the Republican Guard, E-mail interview with author, 28 November 2000. The Army was concerned not only with armor but also support assets such as artillery, mechanized infantry vehicles, support vehicles, ammunition supplies, and POL storage.

17. Keaney and Cohen, 106.

18. Keaney and Cohen, A Statistical Compendium, pt. 1, 463–539. The majority of these missions, 569, were delivered by F-16s employing non-precision, free-falling general-purpose bombs as well as older-generation cluster bomb units (Mk-20 Rockeye, CBU-52, and CBU-58). Battlefield effectiveness was below expectations, which led to concern over the high consumption rates of the more modern, armor-piercing CBU-87 during the first two weeks. "CENTAF TACC/NCO Log, January-February 1991" (U), 30 January 1991, 21. (Secret) Information extracted is unclassified.

19. Weggeman interview.

20. William L. Smallwood, *Warthog: Flying the A-10 in the Gulf War* (Washington, D.C.: Brassey's, 1993), 123–24.

21. Andrews, 44.

22. Keaney and Cohen, *Summary Report,* 21; Andrews, 54; and Fred L. Frostic, *Air Campaign against the Iraqi Army in the Kuwaiti Theater of Operations,* Rand Report MR-357-AF (Santa Monica, Calif.: RAND, 1994). F-111Fs developed the tank-plinking tactic using their Pave Tack laser designator. Lessons learned during a Desert Shield exercise had shown the potential for identifying and targeting armor from medium altitude. On 5 February, two F-111Fs successfully dropped two GBU-12s on revetted positions. Within three days, 50 sorties a night were devoted to tank plinking. Navy A-6Es began dropping a limited number of LGBs, as did F-15E crews. The F-15Es were limited by the number of LANTIRN pods and quickly developed buddy lasing techniques.

23. Andrews, 56.

24. AFDD 2-1.3, 102. Counterland doctrine now incorporates the Killer Scout mission.

25. Col Robert C. Owen, ed., *Deliberate Force: A Case Study in Effective Air Campaigning* (Maxwell AFB, Ala.: Air University Press, 2000), xvii.

26. Noel Malcolm, *Kosovo: A Short History* (New York: New York University Press, 1998), 341.

27. Tim Judah, *Kosovo: War and Revenge* (New Haven, Conn.: Yale University Press, 2000), 62.

28. For purposes of this discussion, the term *Kosovars* refers to Kosovar Albanians.

29. William Buckley, ed., *Kosovo: Contending Voices on Balkan Interventions* (Grand Rapids, Mich.: William B. Eerdmans Pub. Co., 2000), 100. For purposes of this discussion, the terms *Serbia* and *Serbian* will be used to refer to those forces from the Federal Republic of Yugoslav. Likewise *Macedonia* will be used to refer to the Former Yugoslav Republic of Macedonia.

30. Judah, 171.

31. United Nations Security Council Resolution (UNSCR) 1160, 1998, n.p., on-line, Internet, 15 November 2001, available from http:/www.un.org/Docs/scres/1998/sres1160.htm; UNSCR 1199, 1998, n.p., on-line, Internet, 15 November 2001, available from http:/ www.un.org/Docs/scres/1998/sres1199.htm.

32. Dick Leurdijk and Dick Zandee, *Kosovo: From Crisis to Crisis* (Burlington, Vt.: Ashgate Pub. Co., 2001), 34; and US Department of State, *Erasing History: Ethnic Cleansing in Kosovo* (Washington, D.C.: US Department of State, May 1999), 6, on-line, Internet, 10 December 2002, available from http://www.state.gov/www/regions/eur/rpt_9905_ethnic_ksvo_toc.html. Though 2,000 observers of the Organization for Security and Cooper-

ation in Europe (OSCE) had agreed to participate, OSCE was never able to get that many into country before their withdrawal in March 1999.

33. Albert Schnabel and Ramesh Thakur, eds., *Kosovo and the Challenge of Humanitarian Intervention: Selective Indignation, Collective Action, and International Citizenship* (New York: United Nations University Press, 2000), 35.

34. Judah, 195. The Serbs were threatened by the air strikes if they did not come to an agreement, and the Kosovars were threatened that NATO would leave them to the mercy of the Serbs if they did not sign.

35. Ibid., 206.

36. Ministry of Defence (MOD), *Kosovo: Lessons from the Crisis* (London: Her Majesty's Stationery Office, 2000), 9.

37. Paul Strickland, "USAF Aerospace-Power Doctrine: Decisive or Coercive?" *Aerospace Power Journal* 14, no. 3 (fall 2000): 16.

38. MOD, *Kosovo: Lessons from the Crisis*, 34.

39. Wesley Clark, *Waging Modern War* (New York: Public Affairs, 2001), 176.

40. Strickland, 21.

41. HQ/USAFE Initial Report, *The Air War over Serbia: Aerospace Power in Operation Allied Force* (Ramstein AB, Germany: USAFE Studies and Analysis, 25 April 2000), 9.

42. R. Jeffrey Smith and William Drozdiak, "Anatomy of a Purge," *Washington Post*, 11 April 1999, A1.

43. Unpublished war diary of Maj Phil M. Haun. F-16CG (Block 40) AFACs with LANTIRN targeting pods were also used primarily as night AFACs. AFAC duties eventually expanded to include US Navy F-14s and Marine F/A-18D Hornets.

44. HQ/USAFE Initial Report, 15.

45. MOD, *Kosovo: Lessons from the Crisis*, 34.

46. HQ/USAFE Initial Report, 16. By the end of the war the number of USAF aircraft alone would rise to over 500.

47. US State Department, *Erasing History: Ethnic Cleansing in Kosovo*, 6.

48. Steven Lee Myers, "Serb Forces under Attack as Weather Clears," *New York Times*, 6 April 1999. By this time over 400,000 Kosovar Albanians had crossed the border into Albania and Macedonia.

Glossary

AAA	antiaircraft artillery
AB	air base
ABCCC	airborne battlefield command and control center (EC-130E)
AC	alternating current (electrical power with alternating polarity)
ACC	Air Combat Command
ADI	attitude direction indicator
ADVON	advanced echelon
AEF	Air Expeditionary Force
AEW	Air Expeditionary Wing
AFAC	airborne forward air controller, aka FAC(A)
AFSOUTH	Allied Forces Southern Europe; NATO's regional headquarters at Naples, Italy
AGL	above ground level
AGM	air-to-ground missile
AIM	air intercept missile
AI	air interdiction
AIRCENT	Allied Air Forces Central Europe (NATO)
AIRSOUTH	Allied Air Forces Southern Europe (NATO)
AMRAAM	advanced medium range air-to-air missile
AO	area of operations
AOR	area of responsibility
APC	armored personnel carrier
APU	auxiliary power unit
arty	artillery pieces
ASC	air strike control
ATACMS	air tactical missile systems
ATO	air tasking order
AWACS	airborne warning and control system (E-3)
BAI	battlefield air interdiction
bandit	an enemy aircraft
BDA	battle damage assessment

BE	basic encyclopedia number used to catalog targets
bingo	(1) brevity term used by tactical air forces to indicate a fuel level that requires termination of the mission and recovery to a tanker or home station; (2) brevity term used by special operations SAR helicopter forces to indicate that the door gunner is abeam the survivor
bino	gyro-stabilized binoculars; 12 power and 15 power
bomblet	a CBU submunition
bootleg	unscheduled (e.g., a bootlegged tanker is an unscheduled air-to-air refueling)
BRAA	tactical control format providing target bearing, range, altitude, and aspect, relative to a friendly aircraft
break	an aggressive, abrupt maneuver to defeat SAM, AAA, or air-to-air threats
BSD	battle staff directives
C3CM	command, control, and communications countermeasures
CAIFF	combined air interdiction of fielded forces
CANN	temporarily removing parts from an aircraft (cannibalization) so others can fly
CAP	combat air patrol
CAS	close air support
CAVOK	ceiling and visibility OK
CBU	cluster bomb unit
CEM	combined effects munition (CBU-87)
CFACC	combined forces air component commander
COAC	combined air operations center
Compass Call	an aircraft configured to perform tactical C3CM (EC-130H)
CP	control point
CSAR	combat search and rescue

DC	direct current (electrical power with constant polarity)
DCA	defensive counterair
DEAD	destruction of enemy air defenses
dirtball	dirt road
doolie	first year cadet at the AF Academy
EABS	expeditionary air base squadron
ECM	electronic countermeasures
EFS	expeditionary fighter squadron
ELS	expeditionary logistic squadron
EO	electro-optical
EOG	expeditionary operations group
ESS	expeditionary support squadron
EUCOM	US European Command
EW	electronic warfare
FAC	forward air controller
fence	the demarcation line between friendly and enemy territory
FG	fighter group
FL	flight level; thousands of feet when using a standard altimeter setting of 29.92 (FL 300 is 30,000 MSL with 29.92 set)
FLEX	force level execution targeting cell (located within the CAOC)
FM	type of radio that uses frequency modulation; used by A-10 pilots primarily for inter-formation communication
FOV	field of view
fox mike	military phonetic alphabet expression for FM and commonly used to refer to the FM radio
frag	(1) the "fragmented order" which tasked unit aircraft, weapons, targets, and TOTs; (2) a lethal piece of warhead case that is explosively projected from the point of detonation to its impact point
FS	fighter squadron
FW	fighter wing

GAU-8	A-10's internal 30 mm cannon (Avenger)
GPS	Global Positioning System
Guard	a common emergency frequency that all pilots monitor
hard deck	the lowest altitude for operations allowed by the ROE
hardball	paved road
HARM	high-speed antiradiation missile (AGM-88)
heads-down	when the pilot concentrates on things inside the aircraft or looking outside through the binoculars, and is unable to clear the airspace for threats or other aircraft
hitting the tanker	aircrew jargon for rejoining on, connecting to, and taking fuel from a tanker
Hog	one of several A-10 nicknames; also Warthog and Hawg
HUD	head-up-display
IADS	integrated air defense system
ICAOC	interim combined air operations center (ICAOC-5 was located at Vicenza, Italy, and often referred to as the CAOC)
ID	to identify
IFF	identification, friend or foe; a system that uses a transponder response to an interrogating radar that indicates the host aircraft to be a friend (if code is set correctly) or foe (if not set correctly)
IIR	imaging infrared
INS	inertial navigation system
IP	initial point
IR	infrared
ISOPREP	isolated personnel report, which documents unique information on an aircrew to allow for positive ID during a SAR
ISR	intelligence, surveillance, and reconnaissance
JAOC	joint air operations center

JSTARS	joint surveillance, target attack radar system (E-8)
KEZ	Kosovo engagement zone, which included Kosovo and southeast Serbia
KLA	Kosovo Liberation Army (English) or Ushtria Clirimtare e Kosoves ([UCK] Albanian)
LANTRIN	low-altitude navigation and targeting infrared for night
LASTE	low altitude safety and target enhancement system used in the A-10
lead	the term for leader, as in two-ship flight lead
LGB	laser-guided bomb
LOC	lines of communication
MANPADS	man portable air defense systems, which include heat-seeking, shoulder-fired missiles
Maverick	AGM-65D is a large antiarmor imaging-infrared (IIR) guided missile with a 125 lb shaped charge warhead
MC	mission commander
MET	mission essential task list, which is a commander's list of priority tasks, which help define their war-fighting requirements
MPC	mission planning cell
MR	mission ready, capable of flying assigned combat missions
MRE	meals ready to eat
MSL	altitude above mean sea level
MUP	Serb Interior Ministry police
NAEW	NATO airborne early warning aircraft, which used the call sign "Magic"
NATO	North Atlantic Treaty Organization
NBA	brevity term for the half of Kosovo east of 22 degrees east longitude
NCA	national command authorities, generally the president or secretary of defense
NFL	brevity term for the half of Kosovo west of 22 degrees east longitude

NM	nautical miles
NVG	night vision goggles
OAF	Operation Allied Force
OPCON	operational control
ORI	operational readiness inspection
OSC	on-scene commander for SAR operations
outlaw	brevity term for an aircraft that meets the enemy point of origin criteria
Pave Penny	a laser-spot recognition system that displays in the A-10 cockpit where a laser, from an external source, is designating
PERSCO	Personnel Accountability Team
pipper	center point of a gun/bomb sight
PLS	Personnel Locator System is the standard combat search-and-rescue system for the US military and NATO
POL	petroleum, oil, and lubricants
POW	prisoner of war
RAF	Royal Air Force
revets	brevity term for revetments
ROE	rule(s) of engagement
RTB	return to base
RTU	replacement training unit
RWR	radar warning receiver
SACEUR	supreme allied commander Europe
SAM	surface-to-air missile
SAN	naval SAM system
Sandy	call sign for fighters that control and support SAR operations
SAR	search and rescue
SEAD	suppression of enemy air defenses
secondary	additional explosion(s) caused by an initial explosion
shack	direct hit on a target
SHAPE	Supreme Headquarters Allied Powers Europe

sky hooked	conserve fuel by optimizing speed and altitude for maximum range
SOS	Special Operations Squadron
spades	brevity term indicates an aircraft is not squawking the right IFF transponder code
SPINS	special instructions
splash	weapons impact and explosion
Stan/Eval	standardization and evaluation
steer-point	preplanned geographical reference points (e.g., steer-point alpha)
stepped	to depart the squadron for the aircraft at the prebriefed "step time," a critical milestone in the sequence of getting a flight airborne on time
stepped-on	a simultaneous transmissions between two people, with neither hearing the other's transmission
strikers	attack aircraft who employ weapons under the control of an AFAC
talk-on	a FAC's description of the target and target area to assist an attacking aircraft to positively identify the target
taskings	missions fragged on the ATO
top three	designated senior squadron leadership, which includes the commander, ops officer, and another experienced person
triple-A	antiaircraft artillery
UAV	unmanned aerial vehicle (e.g., Predator, Laser Predator, and Hunter)
UCK	Ushtria Clirimtare E Kosoves (Albanian) and Kosovo Liberation Army ([KLA] English)
UHF	radio transmitting on ultra high frequencies and commonly referred to as "uniform"
UK	United Kingdom
UN	United Nations
undercast	a deck of clouds whose tops are below an aircraft's altitude
unsecure	nonencrypted radio

USAFE	United States Air Forces in Europe
UTM	Universal Transverse Mercator, a map grid system
VHF-AM	radio transmitting over very high frequencies using amplitude modulation and commonly referred to as "victor"
VID	visual identification
vis	brevity term for visibility
VJ	Serb army
VMEZ	Serb army (VJ) and Serb Interior Ministry police (MUP) engagement zone
vul	scheduled periods of time when the KEZ was vulnerable to AFACs looking for and striking targets
VVI	vertical velocity indicator
Willy Pete	slang phonetic expression for 2.75-inch white-phosphorous rockets
WP	white phosphorous
Zulu	the time at the prime meridian that is used for military planning and is also known as Coordinated Universal Time (UTC) and Greenwich mean time (GMT)

Index